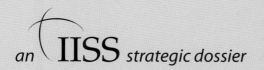
an **IISS** *strategic dossier*

ASIA-PACIFIC REGIONAL SECURITY ASSESSMENT 2023

Key developments and trends

published by

The International Institute for Strategic Studies

ARUNDEL HOUSE | 6 TEMPLE PLACE | LONDON | WC2R 2PG | UK

an IISS *strategic dossier*

ASIA-PACIFIC REGIONAL SECURITY ASSESSMENT 2023
Key developments and trends

The International Institute for Strategic Studies

ARUNDEL HOUSE | 6 TEMPLE PLACE | LONDON | WC2R 2PG | UK

DIRECTOR-GENERAL AND CHIEF EXECUTIVE **Dr John Chipman**
EDITORS **Dr Tim Huxley, Dr Lynn Kuok**
ASSOCIATE EDITOR **Jack May**
RESEARCH SUPPORT **Henry Boyd, Bryan Chang, Nick Childs, James Hackett, Haena Jo, Ithrana Lawrence, Matthieu Lebreton, Fenella McGerty, Shinsuke Nakano, Meia Nouwens, Brody Smith, Tom Waldwyn**
EDITORIAL **Nick Fargher, Jill Lally, Alasdair McKay, Adam Walters, Charlie Zawadzki**
GRAPHICS COORDINATOR **Nick Fargher**
DESIGN AND PRODUCTION **Alessandra Beluffi, Ravi Gopar, Jade Panganiban, James Parker, Kelly Verity**

This publication has been prepared by the Director-General and Chief Executive of the Institute and his staff. It incorporates commissioned contributions from recognised subject experts, which were reviewed by a range of experts in the field. The IISS would like to thank the various individuals who contributed their expertise to the compilation of this dossier. The responsibility for the contents is ours alone. The views expressed herein do not, and indeed cannot, represent a consensus of views among the worldwide membership of the Institute as a whole.

First published June 2023 by the International Institute for Strategic Studies.

COVER IMAGES: (top l) an Indian Air Force Mi-17 helicopter carries a G20 flag during the inauguration ceremony of the Aero India 2023 aviation exhibition in Bengaluru, India, 13 February 2023 (Prakash Singh/Bloomberg via Getty Images); (top m) the Hong Kong–Zhuhai–Macao Bridge (LIU KAIYOU/Getty Images); (top r) 3D rendering robotic arms with silicon wafers for semiconductor manufacturing (Phonlamai Photo/iStock/Getty Images); (bottom l) Australian Prime Minister Anthony Albanese, US President Joe Biden, Indian Prime Minister Narendra Modi and Japanese Prime Minister Kishida Fumio meet in Tokyo, 24 May 2022 (SAUL LOEB/AFP via Getty Images); (bottom r) an international fleet review takes place in waters off Japan, 6 November 2022 (Kyodo News via Getty Images).

Printed and bound in Singapore by KHL Printing Co Pte Ltd.

British Library Cataloguing in Publication Data
A catalogue record for this book is available from the British Library

Library of Congress Cataloging in Publication Data
A catalog record for this book has been requested

ISBN 978-1-03-259444-6 (pbk)
ISBN 978-1-00-345472-4 (ebk)

About The International Institute for Strategic Studies

The International Institute for Strategic Studies is an independent centre for research, information and debate on the problems of conflict, however caused, that have, or potentially have, an important military content. The Council and Staff of the Institute are international and its membership is drawn from over 100 countries. The Institute is independent and it alone decides what activities to conduct. It owes no allegiance to any government, any group of governments or any political or other organisation. The IISS stresses rigorous research with a forward-looking policy orientation that can improve wider public understanding of international security problems and influence the development of sounder public policy.

CONTENTS

COMMON ABBREVIATIONS

AI	artificial intelligence
ASBM	anti-ship ballistic missile
ASEAN	Association of Southeast Asian Nations
ASW	anti-submarine warfare
BMD	ballistic missile defence
BRI	Belt and Road Initiative
CCG	China Coast Guard
CCP	Chinese Communist Party
CFIUS	Committee on Foreign Investment in the US
CPEC	China–Pakistan Economic Corridor
DBP	Defense Buildup Program (Japan)
DSR	Digital Silk Road
EEZ	exclusive economic zone
FONOP	freedom-of-navigation operation
ICBM	intercontinental ballistic missile
INDOPACOM	US Indo-Pacific Command

IRBM	intermediate-range ballistic missile
JSDF	Japan Self-Defense Forces
MBT	main battle tank
NUG	National Unity Government (Myanmar)
PAFMM	People's Armed Forces Maritime Militia
PDF	People's Defence Force (Myanmar)
PLA	(Chinese) People's Liberation Army
PLAAF	PLA Air Force
PLAN	PLA Navy
Quad	Quadrilateral Security Dialogue
RAA	reciprocal access agreement
SAC	State Administration Council (Myanmar)
THAAD	Terminal High-Altitude Area Defense
UAV	uninhabited aerial vehicle
USV	uninhabited surface vehicle
UUV	uninhabited underwater vehicle

INTRODUCTION

The war in Ukraine has provided a bleak backdrop for discussions about international security ever since the Russian invasion in February 2022. While the conflict has affected many aspects of security and defence in the Asia-Pacific, the region has its own dynamics, and important security-related developments have occurred there since the invasion. As the Asia-Pacific recovers from the impacts of the coronavirus pandemic, China's economic and military power continues to grow. In response to the Chinese leadership's increasingly determined rhetoric emphasising the inevitability of Taiwan's 'reintegration' with the mainland, concerns have mounted over the threat posed to the island's security. With the support of some European states, the United States and its close regional allies – Australia and Japan – have intensified their efforts to balance China by increasing and coordinating their military power and diplomatic efforts throughout what they call the Indo-Pacific. Many Asian states have, to a greater or lesser degree, remained 'on the fence' as relations have become increasingly strained between China on one side and the US and some of its allies on the other. Such ambivalence is evident in the strategic postures of India (despite its membership of the 'Quad' alongside Australia, Japan and the US), most Southeast Asian states and even South Korea, a major US ally. The latter has remained acutely focused on the threat from North Korea, which stepped up significantly its missile testing in 2022. In Southeast Asia, the Association of Southeast Asian Nations (ASEAN) member states have maintained the grouping's consensus-based approach to regional political and security challenges. However, continuing conflict across Myanmar – provoked by the February 2021 military coup – has brought growing intramural strains.

THE WAR IN UKRAINE AND THE THREAT TO TAIWAN

This tenth edition of the annual *Asia-Pacific Regional Security Assessment* includes detailed discussion and analysis of major regional security themes by IISS experts. In their opening chapter, James Crabtree and Euan Graham argue that the war in Ukraine will likely have

long-term global ramifications, not least in the Asia-Pacific. They stress that 'lessons must be drawn with caution' – as much will hinge on the conflict's outcome, and because the Ukraine war is primarily land-based, contrasting with the maritime nature of many potential Asia-Pacific flashpoints. Nevertheless, the war has provided a reminder that 'unprovoked aggression and territorial conquest' by major powers remains a risk; for this reason, the conflict has deepened perceptions of military threat in the region. This development, they write, may accelerate existing trends in the Asia-Pacific towards higher military spending (see Figure 0.1), faster military modernisation and efforts to develop national defence capabilities. Moreover, the failure of Ukraine and the West to deter Russia's invasion may lead the US and its international partners to rethink how they deter China, particularly with regard to its potential use of force against Taiwan. At the same time, Crabtree and Graham suggest that Russia's apparently successful use of nuclear threats to deter direct Western military intervention in support of Ukraine may have 'compounded existing doubts' over the effectiveness of US extended nuclear deterrence in the Asia-Pacific. Crucially, they argue that the war has strengthened an already widespread conviction in the West that European security and Asia-Pacific security are linked. However, 'fiscal constraints and the overwhelming need to focus on Ukraine' mean that it is unlikely that European states or the European Union will be more ambitious in their approaches to the region 'in the short to medium term'.

While the war in Ukraine has been a focal point of global attention and concern, China's ever-growing power and increasingly assertive posture remain the leading long-term challenges to the existing international order, particularly in the Asia-Pacific. As Nigel Inkster emphasises in his chapter, US–China relations have become ever more strained as a result of 'trade and technology wars', major frictions over Beijing's stated determination to 'reunify' Taiwan with the Chinese mainland and related US efforts to strengthen ties with Taipei. However, he argues that China's goal of achieving 'reunification' with Taiwan in time for the centenary of the People's Republic of China in 2049 'can only be an aspiration'. In Inkster's view, claims by US military leaders that China may use military force against Taiwan within the next several years seem to be based not on 'firm intelligence' but rather on an assessment of when China will possess the necessary military capabilities for such an operation. He argues that Chinese decision-making on the matter will be shaped not just by an assessment of military capability but also by a consideration of likely US and allied non-military reactions – notably in terms of the potential impact of economic and financial sanctions on China. As Inkster states, 'military defeat or a pyrrhic victory could prove terminal' for the Chinese Communist Party's (CCP's) hold on power. Since the Russian invasion of Ukraine, there has been much international speculation over how the war might affect the likelihood and potential course of a conflict over Taiwan. Inkster makes the case that, despite Chinese military thinkers' analyses of the implications of Western support for Ukraine and the reasons for Russia's poor military performance, there is no evidence that the invasion and ensuing conflict have changed Chinese thinking about 'the timescale or methodology for attacking Taiwan'.

According to Inkster, Beijing's view of Taiwan as an internal challenge has shaped its assessment that a Chinese use of force to regain the island would be utterly dissimilar to the Ukraine war. He notes that such an operation could take various forms, 'ranging from a contested amphibious assault to concerted missile attacks and bombardments or a naval blockade'. While Inkster's view is that it is 'impossible' to say whether Beijing will decide to use force against Taiwan, he also emphasises that such a decision has 'become a function of the dynamic that has evolved between Beijing and Washington'. This point may help explain why the US has not abandoned its established policy of 'strategic ambiguity' regarding whether it would intervene to defend Taiwan: Washington fears that a clear and public US commitment to come to Taiwan's aid could precipitate the very Chinese action it seeks to deter. While US President Joe Biden stated three times between August 2021 and May 2022 that the US was willing to defend Taiwan militarily, on each occasion, White House officials quickly denied that US policy towards its 'One China' policy had changed. Nevertheless,

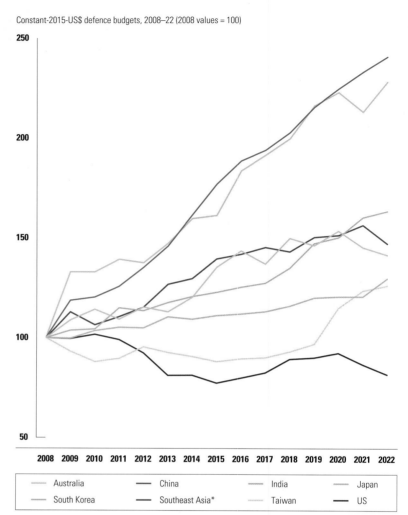

Figure 0.1: **Changes in selected Asia-Pacific defence budgets, 2008–22**

Constant-2015-US$ defence budgets, 2008–22 (2008 values = 100)

Australia · China · India · Japan · South Korea · Southeast Asia* · Taiwan · US

*Brunei, Cambodia, Indonesia, Malaysia, Myanmar, Philippines, Singapore, Thailand and Vietnam. No data available for Laos (or for Myanmar in 2008). Timor-Leste is excluded.

Source: IISS, Military Balance+, milbalplus.iiss.org

with the intention of boosting Taiwan's ability to defend itself, the Biden administration agreed to a series of major defence-equipment sales to the island, while official US contacts with Taiwan intensified after the administration issued new guidelines on the matter in April 2021. A visit to Taipei in August 2022 by Nancy Pelosi, then speaker of the US House of Representatives, accompanied by five Democratic Party members of the House, triggered a storm of protest from China that was accompanied by a set of People's Liberation Army (PLA) naval and air exercises around Taiwan, artillery live-firing into the Taiwan Strait, and missile test-firings into waters east of the island. However, Chinese attempts to

intimidate Taiwan have become a normal feature of cross-strait relations. Notably, incursions by Chinese military aircraft into Taiwan's Air Defence Identification Zone – which are widely interpreted as 'grey zone' tactics partly intended to erode the operational readiness of the island's air defences – are increasingly frequent and large-scale: during 2022, there were more than 1,700 incursions by Chinese aircraft, an increase of approximately 80% compared to the previous year.[1]

THE WIDER STRATEGIC CHALLENGE FROM CHINA

China's challenge to the existing Asia-Pacific order is, of course, much broader than its stated determination to 'reunify' with Taiwan. Its growing military power has been particularly manifest in the naval sphere, as it deploys ships throughout the Asia-Pacific and even further afield. This activity is a focus of the chapter by Nick Childs. The author assesses that despite the Euro-Atlantic 'storm' caused by the war in Ukraine, it is 'China's rise that will in the long term continue to make the strategic weather'. Notably, the October 2022 US National Defense Strategy focuses on China as the 'pacing challenge' for the US military establishment. Childs notes the June 2022 launch of China's third aircraft carrier, which he refers to as 'a major step in the transformation of the PLAN's [PLA Navy's] overall capabilities and aspirations'. In parallel with China's relentless production of new surface ships and submarines has been its development of important anti-ship weapons, notably the DF-21D and DF-26B anti-ship ballistic missiles, sometimes referred to as 'carrier killers', and the YJ-18 cruise missile. Moreover, in April 2022, China was reported to have tested a hypersonic missile. These new Chinese weapons pose an increasingly significant threat to the United States' and its allies' naval operations in Asia-Pacific waters. Moreover, they are supported by 'increasingly comprehensive' intelligence, surveillance and reconnaissance networks, including space-based and underwater systems (a development generally seen across the Asia-Pacific but particularly in China), which provide a formidable targeting capability that is likely to be further enhanced by artificial intelligence.

What makes Childs's chapter particularly important is the new light he casts on the region's shifting naval balance. He identifies three phases of twenty-first-century naval competition in the Asia-Pacific. The first phase saw a striking rise in naval investment and capability development, particularly by China. In the second phase, beginning around 2014–15, the PLAN's dramatic capability developments began to mature; ambitious naval plans on the part of the US and some of its regional allies, as well as India, also began to deliver results. In the third phase, dating approximately from the start of the present decade, the defence strategies of Australia, Japan and the US have seen

Chinese Ambassador to Cambodia Wang Wentian with Cambodian Minister for National Defence Tea Banh at a ground-breaking ceremony at Ream Naval Base near Sihanoukville, 8 June 2022

(Pann Bony/AFP via Getty Images)

a change in tone. While the Chinese fleet has expanded and moved towards true 'blue-water' capabilities, the US and its most important regional allies have increased their naval funding and readiness; importantly, these efforts are 'coalescing in ways that could facilitate a shift in the naval balance in their favour'. Childs also highlights an intensification of European naval efforts in the region, particularly by the United Kingdom and France, which 'could make a significant contribution in concert with the greater commitment of other regional players'. In sum, while China's maritime power 'has never been greater', 'the US and its allies and partners may be clawing back some significant advantages'.

Not all forecasts of China's growing strength and capabilities turn out to be accurate. The Belt and Road Initiative (BRI), which was launched in 2013, initially seemed poised to pose a major challenge to the established international order, particularly in the Asia-Pacific, due to its potential to improve China's access to 'dual-use' (civilian–military) strategic infrastructure and simultaneously enmesh Beijing's economically weaker client states in alleged 'debt traps'. However, it has failed to live up to its anticipated potential as an important instrument of China's international power. As Meia Nouwens writes in her chapter, far from being an impressive example of Chinese statecraft characterised by 'strategic, coordinated, plan-driven and target-oriented action in pursuit of clear, long-term goals using the tools of the state and operated by a unitary actor through directed steps', the reality of the BRI's implementation over the last decade has been less than impressive. Nouwens agrees with the authors of a review essay on China's BRI, who argue that it and its related initiative, the Digital Silk Road (DSR), might be seen more accurately as instruments of the CCP's 'partycraft', intended to promote a 'campaign-style mobilization' that is able to 'create bursts of energy and overcome bureaucratic inertia'.[2] Implementation of the BRI has proven uncoordinated, while 'debt-trap' diplomacy is, according to Nouwens, a myth unsupported by empirical evidence. China's 99-year lease on the port of Hambantota in Sri Lanka did not result from Colombo defaulting on a Chinese loan but rather from long-standing national economic problems. Indeed, she suggests that Beijing itself may have 'been caught in a debt trap of its own making': nearly 60% of China's overseas loans are currently held by countries considered to be in financial distress. Consequently, Nouwens maintains that China is likely to reduce significantly – or even halt – BRI-related lending. Although the PLAN has used Hambantota and the BRI-linked port of Gwadar in Pakistan – and despite the fact that China is reportedly building a naval facility at Ream Naval Base in Cambodia – there is no sign that Beijing has used the BRI to develop the region-wide network of dual-use naval logistics facilities that some observers had anticipated.

Moreover, Beijing has shifted its emphasis away from the heavy-infrastructure projects initially emphasised in the BRI towards what Nouwens refers to as 'global digital investment' through the DSR. China has also launched several new initiatives – including the Global Initiative on Data Security – which Nouwens argues is directed at what she refers to as the 'Global South'. These new initiatives appear to be intended to build on BRI and DSR investment by promoting 'Chinese narratives and norms'. Meanwhile, the US, European Union, Japan and other actors have launched their own strategic infrastructure initiatives – aimed particularly at the Asia-Pacific – with the intention of providing alternatives to Chinese investment. Although the funding for these initiatives does not match that provided by China during the BRI's early heyday, their fortuitous timing may provide their sponsors with 'a soft-power opportunity'.

JAPAN'S DETERIORATING SECURITY ENVIRONMENT: CHINA, RUSSIA AND NORTH KOREA

Despite both the trajectory of the Asia-Pacific naval balance and developments in the sphere of infrastructure investment suggesting that the strategic tide may not be turning altogether in Beijing's favour, the strategic challenges posed by China to the existing order in the region are tangible and seem likely to persist as long as the CCP remains in power and the country's economic expansion continues. As Robert Ward and Yuka Koshino argue in their chapter on Japan's security and defence policy under Prime Minister Kishida Fumio, Japan takes the Chinese challenge seriously. They identify three important triggers for Tokyo's growing concern: President Xi Jinping's strengthening rhetoric about China's intention to 'reintegrate' Taiwan; China's 'territorial needling' around the Senkaku/ Diaoyu islands, which Japan controls and China claims; and China's fast-growing military spending. Ward and Koshino stress that Taiwan's security has been a particularly important concern for Tokyo since the previous administration of Suga Yoshihide (2020–21), noting that Kishida's assertion at the 2022 IISS Shangri-La Dialogue that 'Ukraine today may be East Asia tomorrow' underlined this concern. They also emphasise that China's response to Pelosi's visit to Taipei in August 2022 – which included the firing of ballistic missiles into waters within Tokyo's exclusive economic zone – highlighted the close linkage between the security of Taiwan and that of Japan, as well as the vulnerability of the Senkaku/Diaoyu islands and the strategic importance of the Nansei Islands to the west of Taiwan.

China, though, is not the only challenge to Japan's security. As Ward and Koshino make clear, relations with Russia have worsened since early 2022 because of Tokyo's immediate alignment with the other members of the G7 in condemning and imposing sanctions in response to Russia's invasion of Ukraine. Bilateral talks over the Russian-occupied 'Northern Territories' (comprising four islands claimed by Japan) have stalled, leading to a hardening of Tokyo's position. The strengthening of China–Russia strategic relations (seen, for example, in the joint patrols by the Chinese and Russian air forces close to Japan in November 2022) has also concerned Tokyo. More worrying for Japan, though, was North Korea's intensified missile-testing programme during 2022: as Ward and Koshino note, Pyongyang launched 'around 90 cruise and ballistic missiles' – the record for a single year. However, while in March 2022 North Korea ended its self-imposed moratorium on testing nuclear devices, a year later it had failed to conduct its much-anticipated seventh nuclear test.

ASIAN AMBIVALENCE AMID STRATEGIC RIVALRY

A significant cross-cutting feature of the Asia-Pacific strategic environment remained evident during 2022 and the first half of 2023: the preference of many regional states to try to avoid taking sides in the growing confrontation between the US (supported by its Western allies) on one side and China (and, less importantly, Russia and North Korea) on the other – the latter group comprising powers that seek to revise if not overthrow the existing regional order, which is often characterised as 'rules-based'. Interested Western governments and observers often anticipate that traditionally non-aligned states in the region will inevitably prioritise what may appear to be their long-term security interests by aligning more closely with the US and the West as their confrontation with China and other revisionist powers intensifies. Although there has been some indication of movement in this direction, there is no region-wide trend towards alignment with the US.

Australia stands out in the region because of its population (still largely European in its ethnic origins), its lively liberal democracy and, crucially – notwithstanding its long-term investment in developing strong economic,

Table 0.1: **Asian countries' votes on Ukraine-related UN General Assembly resolutions, 2022–23**

Country	1	2	3	4	5	6
Australia	Yes	Yes	Yes	Yes	Yes	Yes
Bangladesh	Abstention	Yes	Abstention	Yes	Abstention	Abstention
Bhutan	Abstention	Yes	Abstention	Yes	Abstention	Yes
Brunei	Yes	Abstention	Abstention	Yes	Abstention	Yes
Cambodia	Yes	Yes	Abstention	Yes	Abstention	Yes
China	Abstention	Abstention	No	Abstention	No	Abstention
India	Abstention	Abstention	Abstention	Abstention	Abstention	Abstention
Indonesia	Yes	Yes	Abstention	Yes	Abstention	Yes
Japan	Yes	Yes	Yes	Yes	Yes	Yes
Laos	Abstention	Abstention	No	Abstention	Abstention	Abstention
Malaysia	Yes	Yes	Abstention	Yes	Yes	Yes
Maldives	Yes	Yes	Abstention	Yes	Yes	Yes
Mongolia	Abstention	Abstention	Abstention	Abstention	Abstention	Abstention
Myanmar*	Yes	Yes	Yes	Yes	Yes	Yes
Nepal	Yes	Yes	Abstention	Yes	Abstention	Yes
North Korea	No	No	No	No	No	No
Pakistan	Abstention	Abstention	Abstention	Abstention	Abstention	Abstention
Philippines	Yes	Yes	Yes	Yes	Yes	Yes
Singapore	Yes	Yes	Yes	Yes	Yes	Yes
South Korea	Yes	Yes	Yes	Yes	Yes	Yes
Sri Lanka	Abstention	Abstention	Abstention	Abstention	Abstention	Abstention
Thailand	Yes	Yes	Abstention	Yes	Abstention	Yes
Timor-Leste	Yes	Yes	Yes	Yes	Abstention	Yes
Vietnam	Abstention	Abstention	No	Abstention	Abstention	Abstention

Legend: Yes — No — Abstention

1. Resolution ES-11/1   demanding Russia withdraw forces from Ukraine and reverse recognition of Donetsk and Luhansk people's republics, 2 March 2022
2. Resolution ES-11/2   demanding again Russian forces' withdrawal, and condemning attacks on civilian populations and infrastructure, 24 March 2022
3. Resolution ES-11/3   suspending Russia's membership of the UN Human Rights Council, 7 April 2022
4. Resolution ES-11/4   declaring Russia's claimed annexations of the Donetsk, Kherson, Luhansk and Zaporizhzhia oblasts invalid under international law, 12 October 2022
5. Resolution ES-11/5   calling for Russia to pay war reparations to Ukraine, 14 November 2022
6. Resolution ES-11/6   calling for a 'comprehensive, just and lasting peace in Ukraine' and demanding again Russian forces' withdrawal, 23 February 2023

*Myanmar's votes reflect its ambassador to the UN being aligned with the ousted democratic government rather than with the military one that has de facto replaced it.

Source: UN Digital Library, digitallibrary.un.org

political and security links throughout Asia – its strategic alignment with the West and particularly the US through a bilateral alliance. This security relationship has been underscored by the trilateral AUKUS security arrangement, which also involves the UK and has as its primary initial goal the provision of a nuclear-submarine capability to Australia. This capability will constitute an essential part of Australia's effort to expand its military power – specifically its long-range capabilities – in response to what it assesses to be a deteriorating regional security environment, largely due to China's growing military power and

The three AUKUS leaders – Australian Prime Minister Anthony Albanese, US President Joe Biden and UK Prime Minister Rishi Sunak – meet at Naval Base Point Loma in California, US, 13 March 2023

(Tayfun Coskun/Anadolu Agency via Getty Images)

strategic extroversion. In mid-March 2023, the three AUKUS governments announced details of Australia's nuclear-submarine programme, clarifying that the Royal Australian Navy is expected to receive its first 'SSN–AUKUS', a trilaterally developed submarine incorporating technology from all three countries (including cutting-edge US submarine technologies), in the early 2040s. In addition, starting in the early 2030s, pending US congressional approval, the US will sell to Australia up to five *Virginia*-class submarines.[3]

No regional country has closer security ties with the US than Australia. Notably, India has participated more fully in the Quad (as the Quadrilateral Security Dialogue, the regional security dialogue also involving Australia, Japan and the US, is now usually called) since 2020 following a deterioration in India–China relations after armed clashes along their un-demarcated land border in the Galwan Valley. However, India's refusal to condemn or sanction Russia in response to its invasion of Ukraine in February 2022 (Table 0.1 highlights India's abstentions on Ukraine-related UN General Assembly resolutions) was disappointing from a Western perspective and seemed to vindicate the scepticism of some observers about the extent to which New Delhi is willing to move away from its traditionally non-aligned posture. It raised the important question of whether, if its foreign policy was at odds with the West elsewhere, India could still play a significant burden-sharing security role in the Indian Ocean region (in the face of a growing Chinese challenge there) and thereby support the Indo-Pacific strategies of the US and its allies. Over the following year, the answer to this question seems to be a cautious affirmative. Despite New Delhi maintaining a largely uncritical stance towards Russia's behaviour in relation to Ukraine (which is partly explained by India's heavy reliance on Russian arms supplies), the country has continued to play a full role in the Quad. In March 2022, Prime Minister Narendra Modi participated in a virtual summit of Quad leaders, while in May and September he joined in-person summits in Tokyo and Washington DC, respectively. In March 2023, India hosted a meeting of Quad foreign ministers. And, significantly, as Nick Childs notes in his chapter, India is coordinating its naval activities more closely with its Quad partners.

Although a formal ally of the US, South Korea under its former government led by president Moon Jae-in pursued security-related policies that diverged significantly from those of the US in at least three important areas. Under Moon, Seoul's posture towards North Korea was more accommodating than that of Washington, emphasising dialogue, peaceful coexistence and economic incentives even after the failure of talks on denuclearisation between then US president Donald Trump and North Korean leader Kim Jong-un in 2019. The Moon administration also showed itself reluctant to mend relations with the other US ally in Northeast Asia, Japan, despite their common interest with Washington in deterring North Korea. Moreover, the Moon administration followed an approach of 'choice avoidance' in its relations with the US and China, developing a 'strategic cooperative partnership' with Beijing alongside its alliance with the US.[4] It also established 'three noes' (no deployment of new Terminal High-Altitude Area Defense (THAAD) missile batteries in South Korea; no trilateral US–Japan–South Korea missile-defence system; and no trilateral US–Japan–South Korea security alliance) to appease Beijing. The Moon administration thought this was necessary partly because of a perceived need to encourage Beijing to act as a restraining influence on North Korea. However, the fact that South Korea's economy depends heavily on exports to China (see Figure 0.2) also provided an important rationale for maintaining close, cooperative ties with Beijing.

The election in May 2022 of President Yoon Suk-yeol, who had emphasised in his election campaign the need for a 'comprehensive strategic alliance' with the US and tougher policies towards North Korea and China, was widely expected to bring significant changes to Seoul's regional security policies. However, the Yoon administration has not adopted a significantly tougher line towards Pyongyang. In his inauguration speech in May, the new president signalled South Korea's willingness to present an 'audacious initiative' to boost North Korea's economy, providing the latter embarked on denuclearisation. Under Yoon, Seoul is trying to improve political and security relations with Japan. South Korea published its Strategy for a Free, Peaceful, and Prosperous Indo-Pacific Region in December 2022, which stated that with Japan, South Korea would 'seek a forward-looking

Figure 0.2: **Selected Asia-Pacific trade with China and the US, 2021**

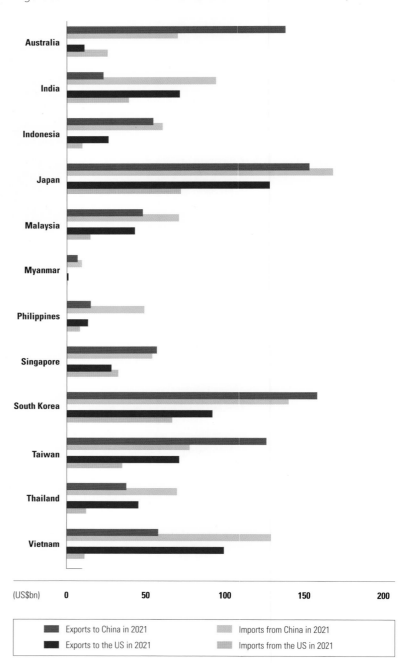

(US$bn)

Exports to China in 2021 · Imports from China in 2021
Exports to the US in 2021 · Imports from the US in 2021

Note: In the context of this figure, 'China' refers to mainland China only, excluding Hong Kong, Macao and Taiwan.

Source: Observatory of Economic Complexity, oec.world

partnership that supports our common interests and values' and that improved relations with Japan were 'essential for fostering cooperation and solidarity among like-minded Indo-Pacific nations'.[5] In the same vein, in March 2023 Yoon stated that 'Japan has transformed from a militaristic aggressor of the past' into a 'partner that shares the same universal values'.[6] South Korea's posture towards China has not changed significantly, however. Its Indo-Pacific strategy described China as a 'key partner for achieving prosperity and peace in the Indo-Pacific region' and pledged to 'nurture a sounder and more mature relationship'.[7] Yoon abandoned an

A Samsung plant that manufactures semiconductors – a key South Korean export to China – in Hwaseong, South Korea, 5 October 2022

(SeongJoon Cho/Bloomberg via Getty Images)

election promise to deploy new THAAD missile batteries and has followed his predecessor's stance of avoiding involvement in any US-led regional missile-defence system. Seoul has also continued to distance itself from US positions on Taiwan: for example, Yoon refused to meet Pelosi when she visited South Korea after her trip to Taipei.[8] Moreover, reflecting South Korea's economic interests, Seoul has continued to avoid becoming enmeshed in US efforts to 'decouple' from China.

Across Southeast Asia, strong traditions of non-alignment, flexible diplomacy and omnidirectional scepticism regarding major powers' intentions have combined with economic self-interest to produce a sub-regional strategic culture characterised by a persistent aversion to choosing between China and the US in strategic terms. Beijing's assertive behaviour in the security sphere – notably in the South China Sea, where it has physically expanded for military purposes some of the features it occupies – has impacted the attitudes of some Southeast Asian governments. Importantly, following May 2022 presidential elections that brought to power the new government led by President Ferdinand Marcos Jr, the Philippines – a US treaty ally and one of the rival territorial claimants to China in the South China Sea – has strengthened security relations with the US. The previous administration led by president Rodrigo Duterte had pursued closer relations with Beijing and sometimes adopted anti-American postures, including issuing threats to abrogate the Philippines–US Enhanced Defense Cooperation Agreement (EDCA), agreed in 2014 and intended to provide a framework for revived bilateral security cooperation. Under Marcos, Manila's relations with Washington have stabilised, and in February 2023 they announced plans to 'accelerate the full implementation' of the EDCA and expand the US military presence in the Philippines.[9]

Elsewhere in Southeast Asia, governments have largely continued to avoid significant changes in their national strategic postures. For example, Vietnam – a country with a history of conflict with China and, in effect, Beijing's most important rival in the South China Sea – has not shown great enthusiasm for developing the security dimension of its relations with the US and, meanwhile, has been looking forward to the positive economic impacts expected to follow China's return to normality after the removal of COVID-19-related restrictions. Tellingly, while China's Comprehensive Strategic Cooperative Partnership with Vietnam is at the apex of Hanoi's hierarchy of international partnerships, the US languishes in the low-level 'Comprehensive Partnership' category, placing it in the same group as Brunei, Myanmar and South Africa, among other countries.[10] Important changes in Hanoi's leadership in late 2022 and early 2023 are unlikely to affect Vietnam's international orientation significantly. Meanwhile, Singapore has remained a close military and economic partner of Washington and announced in March 2023 that it would

Philippines President Ferdinand Marcos Jr speaking at the 126th anniversary of the Philippines Army's founding, at Fort Bonifacio in Metro Manila, 22 March 2023

(Ezra Acayan/Getty Images)

purchase an additional batch of F-35B combat aircraft from the US.[11] However, the city-state has eschewed alliance relations with the US, and in February Minister for Foreign Affairs Vivian Balakrishnan stated that it would not be a 'proxy or a stalking horse for any superpower'. He went on to reiterate that, like other countries in its region, Singapore did 'not wish to be forced to choose sides'.[12] Such caution over the potential costs of closer alignment with one or another superpower continues to dominate the outlooks of many – even most – Asian governments. Largely because of their specifically vulnerable national predicaments in relation to Chinese pressure on their territorial claims, some states – notably India and the Philippines – have shown tentative signs of closer alignment with the US. However, there remain limits on alignment in every case, particularly in the economic sphere; these apply even to Washington's closest Asian ally, Japan, which, while increasingly concerned over Beijing's regional behaviour, has continued to value economic cooperation with China, shown by Tokyo's engagement in the Regional Comprehensive Economic Partnership (which came into effect at the start of 2022).

ASEAN AND THE CONFLICT IN MYANMAR

Of course, not all security concerns in the Asia-Pacific involve rivalries and tensions between states. Some – particularly those in South and Southeast Asia and in the South Pacific – are focused at the domestic level. The final chapter in this volume analyses the armed conflict in Myanmar, which has emerged since the military coup there in February 2021 as the most potentially consequential violent internal dispute in Southeast Asia. The conflict is both long-running – in that some of the country's ethnic minorities have been in rebellion against the central government since the country became independent in 1948 – and relatively new because, since the most recent coup, it has also involved large numbers of supporters of the so-called National Unity Government, which is opposed to the State Administration Council (SAC) installed by the Myanmar Armed Forces. As Aaron Connelly and Shona Loong explain in their chapter, since the coup, 310 of Myanmar's

330 townships (third-level administrative divisions) have experienced armed violence, resulting in the largest humanitarian crisis in Southeast Asia since the end of the Cold War. The authors' analysis points to seven distinct conflict theatres, which they group into three broad categories: 'borderland resistance strongholds', where ethnic armed organisations (EAOs) collaborate with newly formed anti-SAC forces; 'central contested areas', where anti-SAC forces have been fighting with relatively little support from EAOs; and 'non-aligned areas', where EAOs hold territory but stand aloof from the broader resistance to the coup.

Myanmar's coup and its violent aftermath prompted a range of responses internationally. Most Western countries imposed sanctions, though to little practical effect. Some Asia-Pacific countries were less hostile to the military regime, with Bangladesh, China and India seeking to 'build bridges to the SAC'. Australia, Japan and South Korea condemned the coup but have been 'reluctant to completely isolate the junta'. Developments in Myanmar have created a major problem for the governments of other Southeast Asian states and for ASEAN, which since 2007 has claimed 'centrality' for itself as the main force for regional cooperation in Southeast Asia and also the wider Asia-Pacific. ASEAN has faced important challenges in living up to this role, having been notably unable, for example, to foster a coherent Southeast Asian response to China's activities in the South China Sea over the last decade. Following the 2021 coup in Myanmar, the foreign ministers of ASEAN's nine other member states quickly called for a 'return to normalcy'. In April 2022, these countries' leaders met the chairman of Myanmar's SAC, Senior General Min Aung Hlaing, in Jakarta and agreed a 'Five-Point Consensus' calling, most importantly, for a ceasefire and an ASEAN-sponsored dialogue aimed at securing a 'peaceful solution'. As Connelly and Loong point out, while the Five-Point Consensus has so far failed to achieve its explicit objectives, it has successfully bridged a divide among ASEAN members between those favouring isolating the military regime and those arguing for closer engagement with it. However, national elections planned by the regime for late 2023 could reopen divisions over Myanmar within ASEAN and more widely, as some governments may view them as 'an opportunity to turn the page' while others may see them as justification for stronger sanctions.

CHANNELS OF COMMUNICATION

With the range and seriousness of pressing security challenges in the Asia-Pacific being as great as they have been since the end of the Cold War – and with the calamity of the war in Ukraine serving as an ongoing case study of what can happen in a worst-case scenario where defence and diplomacy fail – the responsibilities of those charged with maintaining peace and security in the region are huge. Keeping open channels of communication between policymakers and those who may influence policy constructively will be critical if defence and security establishments in the region are to play their parts effectively. The IISS Shangri-La Dialogue, which will convene for the 20th time in June 2023, has proven vital in facilitating such communications through both its public and private elements. It was on the sidelines of the Shangri-La Dialogue in 2022 that the US and Chinese defence chiefs met in person for the first time and agreed to more talks. As ever, the IISS intends that the analysis contained within the *Asia-Pacific Regional Security Assessment* will support a fruitful exchange of views at the Dialogue on regional challenges and how best to manage them, and thereby contribute to the making of effective policies for maintaining security in the Asia-Pacific, during the current year and beyond.

DR TIM HUXLEY

Senior Adviser, IISS–Asia
Editor, *Asia-Pacific Regional Security Assessment*

DR LYNN KUOK

Shangri-La Dialogue Senior Fellow for Asia-Pacific Security, IISS
Editor, *Asia-Pacific Regional Security Assessment*

NOTES

1   Agence France-Presse, 'China's Warplane Incursions into Taiwan Air Defence Zone Doubled in 2022', *Guardian*, 2 January 2023, https://www.theguardian.com/world/2023/jan/02/chinas-warplane-incursions-into-taiwan-air-defence-zone-doubled-in-2022.

2   Todd H. Hall and Alanna Krolikowski, 'Making Sense of China's Belt and Road Initiative: A Review Essay', *International Studies Review*, vol. 24, no. 3, September 2022, https://academic.oup.com/isr/article/24/3/viac023/6654852.

3   White House, 'Joint Leaders Statement on AUKUS', 13 March 2023, https://www.whitehouse.gov/briefing-room/statements-releases/2023/03/13/joint-leaders-statement-on-aukus-2/.

4   Scott Snyder, 'China–South Korea Relations Under South Korea's New Yoon Administration: The Challenge of Defining "Mutual Respect"', *Forbes*, 11 May 2022, https://www.forbes.com/sites/scottasnyder/2022/05/11/china-south-korea-relations-under-south-koreas-new-yoon-administration-the-challenge-of-defining-mutual-respect/?sh=e49012345cd7.

5   South Korea, Ministry of Foreign Affairs, 'Strategy for a Free, Peaceful, and Prosperous Indo-Pacific Region', 28 December 2022, p. 14, https://www.mofa.go.kr/eng/brd/m_5676/view.do?seq=322133.

6   Jesse Johnson, 'In Push to Mend Ties, South Korea's Yoon Says Japan Has Gone from "Aggressor to Partner"', *Japan Times*, 1 March 2023, https://www.japantimes.co.jp/news/2023/03/01/national/yoon-anniversary-speech-japan-partner/.

7   South Korea, Ministry of Foreign Affairs, 'Strategy for a Free, Peaceful, and Prosperous Indo-Pacific Region', p. 14.

8   James Park, 'South Korea's Enduring Restraint Toward China', *Diplomat*, 18 February 2023, https://thediplomat.com/2023/02/south-koreas-enduring-restraint-toward-china/.

9   US, Department of Defense, 'Philippines, US Announce Four New EDCA Sites', 1 February

2023, https://www.defense.gov/News/Releases/
Release/Article/3285566/philippines-us-
announce-four-new-edca-sites/.

10 See 'Arming Vietnam: Widened International-
security Relations in Support of Military-capability
Development', IISS Research Paper, 20 March
2023, p. 12, https://www.iiss.org/research-
paper//2023/03/arming-vietnam.

11 Davina Tham, 'Singapore to Acquire 8
More F-35B Fighter Jets, Growing Fleet
to 12', CNA, 24 February 2023, https://

www.channelnewsasia.com/singapore/
f35-fighter-jet-mindef-saf-rsaf-air-force-
military-defence-3302941.

12 Dewey Sim and Kimberly Lim, 'Singapore
Will Feel "Spillover" Effect of Growing US–
China Tensions but Won't Be a "Proxy":
Foreign Minister', *South China Morning
Post*, 27 February 2023, https://www.scmp.
com/week-asia/politics/article/3211688/
singapore-will-feel-spillover-effect-growing-us-
china-tensions-wont-be-proxy-foreign-minister.

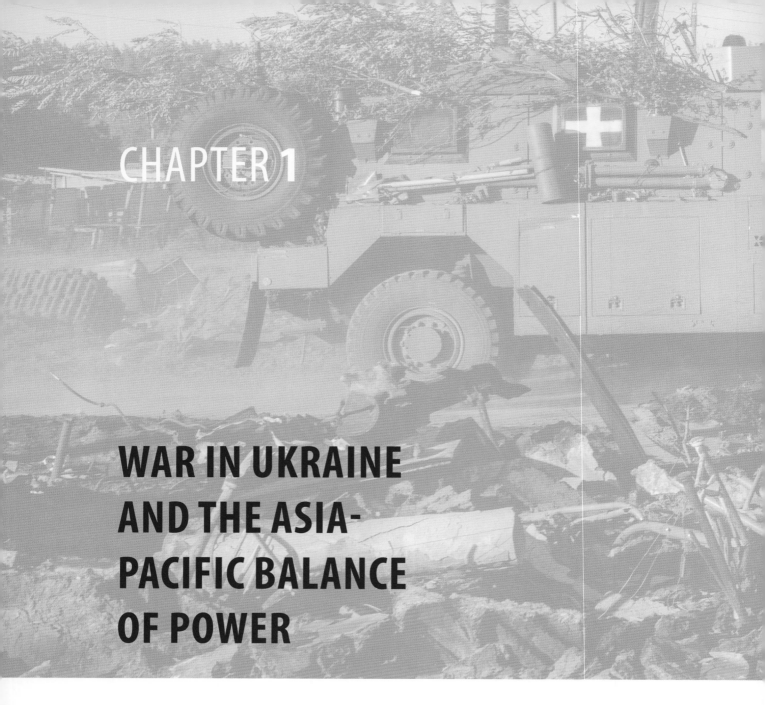

CHAPTER 1

WAR IN UKRAINE AND THE ASIA-PACIFIC BALANCE OF POWER

JAMES CRABTREE

Executive Director, IISS–Asia

DR EUAN GRAHAM

Shangri-La Dialogue Senior Fellow
for Indo-Pacific Defence and Strategy, IISS

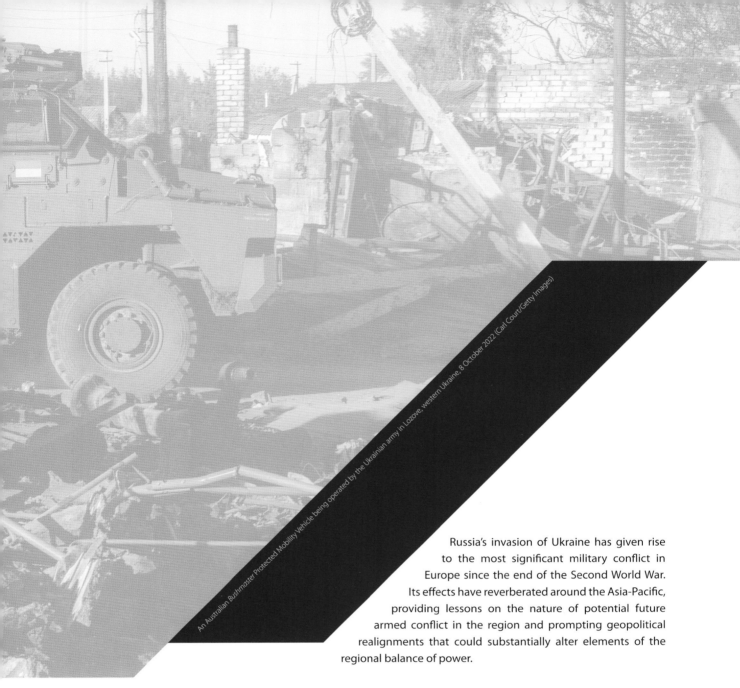

An Australian Bushmaster Protected Mobility Vehicle being operated by the Ukrainian army in Lozove, western Ukraine, 8 October 2022 (Carl Court/Getty Images)

Russia's invasion of Ukraine has given rise to the most significant military conflict in Europe since the end of the Second World War. Its effects have reverberated around the Asia-Pacific, providing lessons on the nature of potential future armed conflict in the region and prompting geopolitical realignments that could substantially alter elements of the regional balance of power.

DIPLOMATIC AND STRATEGIC LESSONS

The diplomatic response to the conflict has revealed a series of global geopolitical fault lines and raised issues from the potential use of nuclear weapons and the effectiveness of deterrence to the use of pre-emptive intelligence disclosure in the run-up to conflicts.

OPERATIONAL AND TACTICAL LESSONS

The war offers potentially important lessons for future conflicts in Asia, in areas including maritime security, information warfare, logistics and military capacity-building, among others.

GEOPOLITICAL IMPLICATIONS AND THE REGIONAL BALANCE

Russia's military fortunes in Ukraine have implications for its status as an Asia-Pacific security actor. Its rapidly deepening relationship with China and its changing military ties to countries like India and Vietnam could affect the regional balance of power.

THE US AND EUROPE IN THE ASIA-PACIFIC

The Ukraine war has sharpened concerns about the ability of the United States and its European partners to manage commitments in both the Euro-Atlantic and Asia-Pacific theatres.

Japanese Prime Minister Kishida Fumio used his keynote address at the 19th IISS Shangri-La Dialogue in June 2022 to deliver a warning about Russia's invasion of Ukraine, arguing that 'Ukraine today may be East Asia tomorrow'.[1] Since the conflict's outbreak in February 2022, defence establishments across the Asia-Pacific have watched it closely to glean operational and strategic lessons and assess consequences for the global and regional balance of power. This chapter provides a preliminary analysis of those lessons and consequences. The fact that the war is ongoing means any lessons must be

Japanese Prime Minister Kishida Fumio addressing the IISS Shangri-La Dialogue in Singapore, 10 June 2022

(Roslan Rahman/AFP via Getty Images)

drawn with caution; its implications, both in Europe and in the Asia-Pacific, will depend on whether Russia or Ukraine is ultimately seen to have prevailed. Moreover, there are obvious differences between the two theatres, not least the fact that the conflict in Ukraine is largely land-based while many Asia-Pacific flashpoints are maritime in nature. Broadly speaking, however, the lessons offered by the Ukraine war that are relevant to Asia-Pacific states may be divided into four categories. Firstly, there are diplomatic and strategic lessons – regarding the role of deterrence, nuclear signalling, capacity-building and intelligence disclosure. Secondly, there are operational and tactical lessons, including in the maritime and information domains. Thirdly, there is the geopolitical impact of the war with respect to Russia's ties to India and China. In the case of the latter, there are also possible implications with respect to Taiwan. Finally, there is the likely impact of the war on the Asia-Pacific strategies of the United States and larger European countries, including France, Germany and the United Kingdom.

DIPLOMATIC AND STRATEGIC LESSONS

Linkages between European and Asia-Pacific security were being asserted in Western policy debates long before Russia's invasion of Ukraine.[2] The war has generally strengthened such convictions, including concerns about international precedent regarding the future use of military force and territorial annexation. However, it has also sharpened pre-existing concerns about the ability of the US and its European partners to apportion finite defence resources between the Euro-Atlantic and Asia-Pacific regions. A few non-aligned countries in the region, notably Singapore, have drawn links between Russia's actions and their own defence security – and have therefore supported sanctions against Moscow.[3] Japan and South Korea – both US allies – sent logistical and humanitarian support to Ukraine (see Table 1.1).[4] Australia and New Zealand went further, providing defence equipment (in Australia's case) and training to Ukrainian forces.[5] Although Seoul has not sent arms to Ukraine, in 2022 it concluded a US$5.8 billion deal to sell 180 K2 tanks, 212 K9 self-propelled howitzers and 48 FA-50 jet aircraft to Poland.[6]

Asia-Pacific countries' varying stances on the war came to light at the United Nations via a number of Ukraine-related resolutions, including one in early March 2022 criticising Russian 'aggression' that passed with backing from 141 states.[7] Many in the region

Table 1.1: **Major pledges of assistance to Ukraine by non-NATO Asia-Pacific governments**

Country	Assistance provided
Australia	Australia has provided A$475 million (US$317m) in military assistance to Ukraine. This includes 90 *Bushmaster* IMV armoured utility vehicles, 28 M113AS4 armoured personnel carriers and demining equipment, six M777A2 155mm towed artillery and howitzer ammunition, anti-armour ammunition and weapons, tactical decoys, uninhabited aerial and uninhabited ground systems, rations and medical supplies, as well as other ammunition and missiles. Australia will also train Ukrainian troops in the United Kingdom in 2023. Australia has further provided A$65m (US$43m) in humanitarian assistance to Ukraine, as well as 70,000 tonnes of coal and 60 pallets of medical supplies and other personal protective equipment.
New Zealand	In May, August and November 2022, New Zealand announced three separate deployments of personnel to the UK to train Ukrainian military personnel. New Zealand has provided NZ$22.19m (US$13.78m) worth of military fuel, access to commercial satellite imagery, weapons, and ammunition procurement, as well as an additional NZ$12.78m (US$7.94m) in humanitarian aid for Ukraine.
Japan	As of January 2023, Japan had pledged or contributed around US$703.12m worth of humanitarian aid to Ukraine, including generators, medical supplies, food and recovery funds. It has also provided Ukraine with civilian vans and other supplies of unspecified value.
South Korea	In 2022, South Korea provided a total of US$100m worth of aid to Ukraine, including generators, vaccines and medical equipment. In 2023, another US$130m in humanitarian aid is pledged.
China	In March 2022, China announced a humanitarian aid package worth CNY5m (US$822,000) for Ukraine via the Red Cross Society of China, plus another CNY10m (US$1.64m) worth of humanitarian supplies to Ukraine.
Pakistan	Pakistan sent 7.5 tonnes of humanitarian cargo to Ukraine in June 2022. It had previously sent 15 tonnes of humanitarian aid to Ukraine in March 2022.
Mongolia	In April 2022, Mongolia announced a humanitarian aid package worth US$200,000 for Ukraine.
Vietnam	In May 2022, Vietnam announced US$500,000 in humanitarian aid for Ukraine, to be provided through the Ukrainian Red Cross and UN agencies.
Singapore	In June 2022, Singapore announced humanitarian assistance consisting of nine ambulances and two fire engines, as well as an assortment of firefighting protective gear, rescue equipment, mine detectors and medical supplies, to aid Ukraine.
India	As of September 2022, India had sent over 97.5 tonnes of humanitarian aid to Ukraine in 12 separate consignments.
Cambodia	In January 2023, Cambodia, in cooperation with the Japanese government, trained a group of Ukrainian deminers.

Source: IISS

abstained, including China, India, Laos, Mongolia, Pakistan, Sri Lanka and Vietnam. Generally, most states in South and Southeast Asia have hedged their positions and are wary of criticising Moscow. A number of countries, including Cambodia, China, India and Indonesia, have sent humanitarian aid to Ukraine. However, there is also sympathy in some regional security establishments for the Russian position that NATO's eastward expansion constituted a strategic provocation to Moscow, alongside distrust of Western motivations and actions, including military support for Ukraine.[8]

Although fought with conventional weapons, the war in Ukraine has raised significant questions relating to nuclear weapons, with implications for the Asia-Pacific. Moscow's repeated nuclear threats set an ominous prec-edent at odds with the Soviet Union's largely responsible approach to nuclear doctrine.[9] The threat of a nuclear confrontation with Russia – personally reinforced in a warning issued by Russian President Vladimir Putin on the eve of the invasion – is likely the most important consideration that has prevented NATO countries from undertaking a direct combat role in Ukraine.[10] Nuclear deter-rence has worked in Russia's favour in this regard. Notably, however, Ukraine has not

A UN General Assembly special session takes place at the UN headquarters in New York City, US to discuss two resolutions related to the conflict in Ukraine, 23 March 2022

(Michael M. Santiago/Getty Images)

been deterred from attacking military targets inside Russia, nor have NATO states and other countries been discouraged from offering increasingly potent weapons systems to Ukrainian forces, although they have supplied arms with caution.[11]

China has publicly expressed its opposition to the use of nuclear weapons and nuclear threats in Ukraine.[12] The significance of these declarations is unclear, given that Russia would determine nuclear-weapon use according to its own calculus. Viewed more broadly, Moscow's aggression can be seen as one element of a broader challenge to the existing global order posed by a 'triple entente' of geographically contiguous authoritarian states – China, North Korea and Russia. This growing alignment is particularly concerning given that all three states possess nuclear weapons. Based on the precedent established by Russia in Ukraine, in a future crisis or war both China and North Korea could be tempted to issue their own nuclear threats to ward off third-party intervention. For China, this could apply to contingencies involving Taiwan, which – like Ukraine – has no formal security guarantees from the US. In general, the war's momentum appears to be driving closer rela-tions between not only Russia and China but also Russia and North Korea.[13] In December 2022, Washington accused Pyongyang of directly supplying arms to the Wagner Group, a Russian private military company operating in Ukraine.[14]

The failure to deter Russia's invasion is likely to lead to a re-examination of the United States' (and its partners') approaches to China as they seek new methods to deter Beijing – including over the use of force against Taiwan.[15] This development could have a positive influence on regional stability providing US allies and partners are persuaded to increase investment in conventional defence capabilities.[16] Conversely, Russia's nuclear threats over Ukraine may have compounded existing doubts about the long-term viability of the United States' extended nuclear-deterrence framework in the Asia-Pacific. In January 2023, Yoon Suk-yeol became the first sitting South Korean president to warn publicly that Seoul could develop its own nuclear weapons in extremis.[17] Seoul's strategic anxiety should be read primarily as a response to North Korea's accelerating nuclear-weapons and ballistic-missile capabilities.[18] However, Russia's nuclear brinkmanship and its erosion of nuclear taboos adds further pressure to the global non-proliferation regime, including in Northeast Asia.

Ukraine's military successes suggest a further, potentially preventive lesson for the Asia-Pacific: Western military training and capacity-building efforts – as provided to

Ukraine after 2014 – can bear strategic fruit. While media attention has focused on the provision of weapons systems since the invasion,[19] Ukraine's armed forces benefitted from US- and UK-led training, equipment and skills transfer in the pre-war phase, thus forestalling a rapid Russian fait accompli in 2022. Ukraine may come to be seen as one of the most successful cases in recent history of military capacity-building prior to full-scale hostilities – with potential lessons for Taiwan.[20] In this regard, developments in Ukraine contrast starkly with those in Afghanistan, where the Western-trained and -equipped Afghan National Security and Defence Forces promptly collapsed following the departure of Western forces from the country. While some commentators have complained that Ukraine has drawn military assistance away from Taiwan and other US regional partners and therefore undermined deterrence, post-Afghanistan, military-assistance programmes in the Asia-Pacific might have been less politically supportable in the US absent the galvanising experience of Ukraine.[21]

Finally, many in the Asia-Pacific will learn from the successful pre-emptive intelligence-based assessments of the US and its security partners – and their public disclosure – which highlighted Russia's aggressive intentions and its pre-invasion military build-up.[22] This was a high-risk strategy for Western governments given the reputational consequences had Russia's build-up turned out to be a bluff, or had the disclosures themselves changed Putin's mind about mounting an invasion. The fact that these warnings were proven accurate spurred a robust diplomatic response in Europe – despite the scepticism of some European NATO member states' governments right up to the invasion.[23] Reportedly having discounted Western warnings, some Asian governments were caught off guard by the invasion and had to hurriedly evacuate diplomatic staff and nationals.[24] The Ukraine war has helped to rehabilitate the international credibility of Western intelligence organisations, which had been seriously hampered by intelligence failures in the lead-up to the invasion of Iraq in 2003. Although Western intelligence-based warnings did not prevent Russia's invasion in February 2022, a clear lesson for would-be aggressors in Asia is that large-scale military preparations are virtually impossible to disguise, with surprise very likely to be unattainable except in the case of small-scale operations. As a result of the Ukraine experience, pre-emptive intelligence disclosure is likely to be factored into the Asia-Pacific strategies of the US and its allies – for deterrence purposes but also with a view to shaping the diplomatic environment during a major regional security crisis.

OPERATIONAL AND TACTICAL LESSONS

The war in Ukraine has yielded a multitude of military lessons at the operational and tactical levels. While many are specific to the geography of Ukraine, a few are transposable to other regions. One example is Ukraine's ability to adapt its military strategy and tactics to changing battlefield circumstances while integrating a diverse plethora of donated equipment. Following announcements by the German, UK and US governments (as well as others) in January 2023, the Ukrainian army is now in line to receive three different Western-made main battle tanks (MBT) – the UK's *Challenger* II, the US-made M1A2 *Abrams* and the German-made *Leopard* 2A6 – adding to the ex-Soviet tanks it currently operates (as well as a number of new T-90 MBTs captured from Russia).[25] Some *Challenger*s and *Leopard*s have already arrived in Ukraine, with deliveries of *Abrams* to start later in 2023. Ukraine's eclectic stock of MBTs provides an extreme example of the integration and logistics challenges it faces, though the long-term trend points towards the country adopting NATO-standard equipment across its inventory. This ability to integrate mixed-origin equipment – and its experience of the process of transitioning away from Russian/Soviet designs – is likely to be of interest to India, Vietnam and some other countries in Southeast Asia.

A *Bushmaster* vehicle bound for Ukraine is loaded onto a C-17A transport aircraft at RAAF Base Amberley, Australia, 8 April 2022

(Dan Peled/Getty Images)

The war in Ukraine has been predominantly fought on land and it is in this domain that the conflict's outcome is most likely to be decided. That said, the naval war in the Black Sea, although some way off the war's centre of gravity, arguably has more relevance for many Asia-Pacific countries, not least because instances of actual naval combat on any scale have been rare in recent history. The naval war has featured a Russian blockade of Ukrainian ports and the use of sea mines by both sides. Most strikingly, in April 2022, Ukraine sank the flagship of Russia's Black Sea Fleet, the cruiser *Moskva*, with coast-based, domestically developed *Neptune* anti-ship missiles. *Moskva* is the largest warship to be sunk in combat since the Falklands War in 1982. In October 2022, Ukraine also mounted a long-range strike against Russia's fleet base at Sevastopol in Crimea using small low-observable remote surface vessels. Ukraine recaptured the strategically located Snake Island despite losing most of its small navy in the early stages of the conflict. While ships and submarines from Russia's Black Sea Fleet have continued to launch missiles into Ukraine with relative impunity, the naval war has demonstrated the viability of improvised, asymmetric 'sea-denial' capabilities and served as a reminder of the potential vulnerability of surface ships to land-based missiles. These are important considerations for force concepts and force design that will be of relevance to several armed forces in the Asia-Pacific, including those of China and the US.

Turkiye's ability to control naval movements through the Bosporus Strait during wartime, under the 1936 Montreux Convention, has become relevant in the Ukraine conflict – a reminder of the strategic importance of choke-point straits and the leverage that third-party littoral states can bring to bear through legal as well as military instruments.[26] Ukraine's partial success in countering Russia's blockade during 2022 required a subtle blend of diplomatic and military pressure, demonstrating that non-combatants – in this case including the US and its partners – can exert meaningful influence through non-military means.[27] Russia has conducted unopposed amphibious operations to support its offensive against the port of Mariupol on the Sea of Azov.[28] More significantly, however, Russia has not attempted landings anywhere along Ukraine's Black Sea coast, despite Odesa being earmarked as one of Moscow's original military objectives.[29] The various elements that have shaped the naval war in Ukraine are all potentially relevant to the Asia-Pacific, where blockade is widely assumed to be one of China's most likely actions – against Taiwan directly, or against smaller features in the South China Sea.[30]

One clear lesson from the battlefields of Ukraine that is being absorbed by Taiwan's armed forces, among others in the Asia-Pacific, is the importance of reserves for regenerating combat forces during a protracted conflict.[31] Without its effective reserve structure, Ukraine's armed forces would have struggled to adjust to the early loss of experienced personnel, which in turn would have made it much harder to launch rapid offensive operations in areas like Kharkiv and Kherson.[32] The logic here is broadly similar to the importance of maintaining a 'deep magazine' of munitions stocks – a need highlighted by the

Speaking at a press conference in Taipei, Taiwanese President Tsai Ing-wen announces the extension of military service in Taiwan, 27 December 2022

(Lam Yik Fei/Bloomberg via Getty Images)

prodigious consumption rates of both sides in Ukraine, particularly with regard to artillery. However, trained soldiers, sailors and air-force personnel are much harder to reconstitute than equipment once hostilities commence unless reserves are already in place. In late December 2022, Taiwan's President Tsai Ing-wen referenced Ukraine when she announced a force-realignment plan, extending the minimum term of conscription in Taiwan from four months to one year and creating a 'standing garrison force'.[33]

For several of Asia's smaller countries and armed forces, the difficulty of resupply is likely to be compounded by the far greater distances involved compared to those in Europe. For some, their circumstances mean exclusive reliance on seaborne and airborne supplies. The risk of regional armed forces being obliged to fight for the duration with the forces and stocks in place from a conflict's outbreak is significantly greater than in Ukraine, which has benefitted enormously from land borders with NATO countries. Before the war, this vulnerability had already been acknowledged, with Australia for example seeking to increase investment in onshore weapons storage and production.[34] The war in Ukraine has further underlined the importance of a national defence-industrial base for winning a protracted, high-intensity conflict. It has also highlighted the related risk that the United States' defence industries may not be able to meet the demands of its allies, especially if there are concurrent conflicts occurring in different regions.[35]

Finally, in addition to kinetic exchanges on the battlefield, Ukraine's information-warfare techniques are certain to be studied and perhaps widely emulated, including in Asia. This has emerged as another notable and perhaps unexpected strength of Ukraine, helping Kyiv to garner and maintain international support at the level of the general public as well as among elites. President Volodymyr Zelenskyy's personal leadership style and commitment to public communication has clearly been a singular asset in this regard, as was the pre-war existence in Ukraine of a large advertising industry, which the government has been able to mobilise in order to prosecute a sophisticated communications strategy, making highly effective use of social media. The Ukrainian government's mastery of the information domain has been augmented by a mass of online supporters and sympathisers – adding a spontaneous and self-organising dynamic to Ukraine's information operations.[36]

Russia's information-warfare efforts have appeared clumsy, antiquated and self-defeating by comparison, though Moscow continues to invest in disinformation and misinformation campaigns that find some purchase internationally, including in the Asia-Pacific.[37] Ukraine's success in the information domain suggests that this could actually be an area of comparative advantage for democratic systems (over authoritarian systems) under the unifying conditions of an unprovoked external attack, in sharp contrast to the peacetime trend of open societies more often appearing vulnerable to information warfare. If this is indeed a conclusion from Ukraine, it should be of particular interest to Taiwan and South Korea with regard to their relations with China and North Korea respectively, where in both contexts the information 'battlespace' is already well developed and where – akin to the Russia–Ukraine dynamic – relations are characterised not simply by the dichotomy between democracy and dictatorship but also by a high degree of linguistic and cultural familiarity.

Indonesian President Joko Widodo meeting his Ukrainian counterpart Volodymyr Zelenskyy in Kyiv and Russia's Vladimir Putin in Moscow, 29 and 30 July 2022

(L: Volodymyr Tarasov/ Ukrinform/Future Publishing via Getty Images. R: Contributor/Getty Images)

Russian Minister of Foreign Affairs Sergei Lavrov meets his Indian counterpart Subrahmanyam Jaishankar in New Delhi, 1 April 2022

(Indian Ministry of External Affairs/Handout/Anadolu Agency via Getty Images)

GEOPOLITICAL IMPLICATIONS AND THE REGIONAL BALANCE

Russia's military fortunes in Ukraine have implications for its status as an Asia-Pacific security actor. Its military power has been degraded due to battlefield attrition, while organisational weaknesses and incompetence have been exposed. As Russia is an Asia-Pacific power, these developments will impact the conventional military balance in the region. It remains militarily active in its Far East region, where activities in 2022 post-invasion have included conducting exercises in the southern Kuril Islands[38] and mounting long-range aviation and naval deployments in the vicinity of Japan, South Korea and, occasionally, further into the Western Pacific.[39] Some of Russia's Pacific units have already been deployed to Ukraine, raising the possibility that its regional military posture (or at least its ground-force elements) will become hollowed out as the conflict continues.[40]

Beyond its own defence requirements, Russia's regional influence has long rested on its role as an energy and weapons exporter. Moscow's strongest defence-supplier relationships in the Asia-Pacific are with India and Vietnam, alongside others including China, Indonesia, Malaysia and Myanmar.[41] While China imports weapons from Russia, the value of those imports has generally decreased in recent decades, meaning Beijing is rarely reliant on Moscow for supplies.[42] By contrast, India's and Vietnam's diplomatic caution over the Ukraine war – indicated by abstentions on Ukraine-related UN votes – is likely influenced by their ongoing dependence upon Russia for imported equipment (see Figure 1.1).[43] Moscow's position as a prime supplier was already under pressure prior to the invasion, as its partners sought more diverse sources of equipment. For instance, for many decades Hanoi bought almost all its weapons systems from Russia; in the five years to 2021, this proportion fell to two-thirds.[44] The conflict in Ukraine will likely accelerate this trend in Vietnam, India and other regional countries. Russia's weak performance in Ukraine has also undermined the reputation of its armed forces, while the difficulties it has encountered in replenishing its forces have generated supplier-reliability concerns.[45] In addition, Western sanctions have made it much harder for Russian contractors to source components – a development that will hamper future deal financing.

The aftermath of Moscow's invasion has generated difficult questions for India's strategic positioning between Russia and the West. New Delhi and Moscow have long enjoyed a 'Special and Privileged Strategic Partnership'.[46] More recently, as its concerns about China have grown, India has drawn closer to the West.[47] In the Asia-Pacific this is seen via its membership in the Quad grouping alongside Australia, Japan and the US. Many in Western capitals assumed these ties would lead New Delhi to join in the international condemnation of Moscow's actions. Instead, Prime Minister Narendra Modi stuck to a carefully calibrated strategy, avoiding criticism of Russia and abstaining in UN votes (see Figure 1.2, for example). India has also been robustly critical of assumptions regarding its stance on the conflict, especially from European capitals.[48]

Figure 1.1: **Selected equipment operated by India's and Vietnam's militaries by country of origin, 2002–22**

INDIA

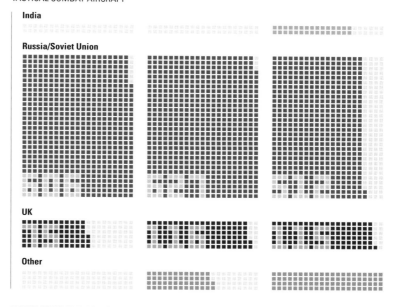

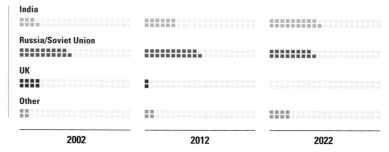

VIETNAM

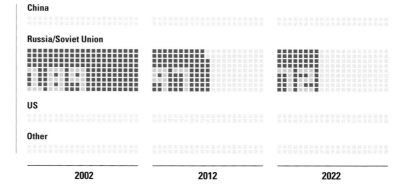

Source: IISS

India's position on the Ukraine war also reflects a calculation of strategic interests. India and Russia share some geopolitical assumptions, including support for a future multipolar global order featuring a less dominant US. Putin made a rare visit to New

On 2 March 2022, the United Nations General Assembly overwhelmingly voted in favour of a resolution demanding that Russia immediately cease its military operations in Ukraine

Total Asia-Pacific countries **37**

8
1
28

Yes   No   Abstention

©IISS

Delhi in late 2021 designed to shore up bilateral ties. India welcomed Russian Foreign Minister Sergei Lavrov for a high-profile visit in April 2022. New Delhi continues to assess China to be its primary security threat and is particularly concerned by the risk of further, more intense clashes in disputed areas along India's long Himalayan border. A future confrontation with China would be especially challenging for India without supplies of Russian arms. Viewed from New Delhi, any Russian defeat in Ukraine would be likely to push Moscow and Beijing closer together. Maintaining ties with Moscow might blunt that risk by providing Moscow with options for geopolitical partnership beyond its reliance on Beijing. India has also benefitted from purchases of discounted Russian oil since the invasion of Ukraine.[49]

New Delhi's ambivalent reaction to Russia's invasion rekindled doubts among Western strategists about both India's reliability and its willingness to be part of a balancing coalition against China.[50] These concerns should not be overplayed, however. Excessive reliance on Russian arms curtails India's strategic autonomy with respect to China, a fact many policymakers in New Delhi recognise. Russia's share of Indian arms imports had already dropped from a recent high of 77% in 2018 to around one-third in 2021.[51] India has reportedly suspended plans to purchase Russian systems, including helicopters. Delays to some existing weapons orders, including temporary hold-ups for a batch of S-400 surface-to-air missiles, have raised reliability concerns.[52] Although New Delhi currently remains reliant on Russian equipment, it is likely to try to reduce its dependence over time, both by seeking alternative suppliers and by boosting domestic defence production wherever practicable.[53] India's patience with Russia has its limits too: in December 2022, Modi cancelled a planned meeting with Putin following concerns in New Delhi over Russia's war conduct.[54]

Figure 1.2: **Asia-Pacific countries' votes on UN General Assembly Resolution ES-11/1 ('Aggression against Ukraine'), 2 March 2022**

Country	Vote	Country	Vote	Country	Vote	Country	Vote
Australia	●	Indonesia	●	Nauru	●	Solomon Islands	●
Bangladesh	●	Japan	●	Nepal	●	South Korea	●
Bhutan	●	Kiribati	●	New Zealand	●	Singapore	●
Brunei	●	Laos	●	North Korea	●	Sri Lanka	●
Cambodia	●	Malaysia	●	Pakistan	●	Thailand	●
China	●	Maldives	●	Palau	●	Timor-Leste	●
Federated States of Micronesia	●	Marshall Islands	●	Papua New Guinea	●	Tonga	●
Fiji	●	Mongolia	●	Philippines	●	Tuvalu	●
India	●	Myanmar*	●	Samoa	●	Vanuatu	●
						Vietnam	●

*Myanmar's vote reflects its ambassador to the UN being aligned with the ousted democratic government rather than with the military one which has de facto replaced it.

Source: UN Digital Library, digitallibrary.un.org

Russia's deepening relationship with China since the invasion of Ukraine also carries potentially far-reaching strategic implications. Chinese President Xi Jinping and Putin unveiled a manifesto for broader cooperation in February 2022. The document stated: 'Friendship between the two States has no limits, there are no "forbidden" areas of cooperation.'[55] In the conflict's early stages, political leaders in Europe and the US harboured hopes that China might be persuaded to distance itself from Russia. Indeed, Washington launched various diplomatic overtures, first asking China to dissuade Russia from invading and then attempting to dissuade Beijing from sending military equipment to support Russia's war aims.[56] Beijing, however, generally refused to condemn Moscow. Although China has mostly avoided providing to Russia the kind of material and military support that might trigger US-led sanctions,[57] in January 2023 the US imposed sanctions on a Chinese company for allegedly supplying satellite imagery of Ukraine for use by the Wagner Group, via a Russian third party.[58] Media reports subsequently alleged that Chinese companies were supplying defence equipment to Russia, including via trans-shipment through third countries.[59] China has called for peace talks while blaming the West and NATO expansion for starting the war.[60]

Russia's invasion has at times strained bilateral ties with China. While Beijing has provided diplomatic support at the UN, it is still not clear to what extent China's leadership supports Russia's war aims.[61] There has been debate within China's ruling elite about how much Beijing should embrace or distance itself from Moscow.[62] China's dilemma relates in part to Beijing's long-standing declaratory support for claims of national territorial integrity, while Russia's weak battlefield performance has also put Beijing in the awkward position of supporting a military operation that has failed to achieve its central objectives. China is also concerned about Putin's nuclear brinkmanship.[63] Moreover,

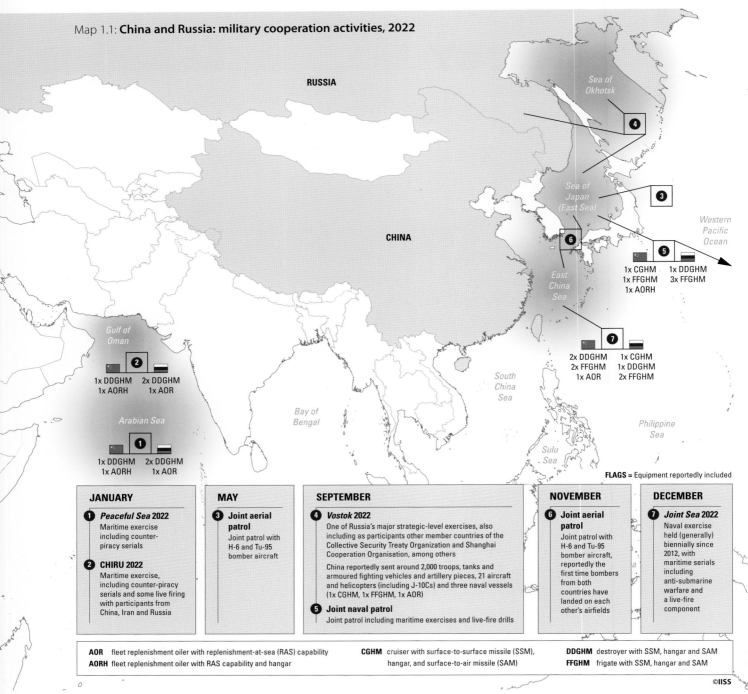

Map 1.1: **China and Russia: military cooperation activities, 2022**

FLAGS = Equipment reportedly included

JANUARY

1 *Peaceful Sea 2022*
Maritime exercise including counter-piracy serials

2 **CHIRU 2022**
Maritime exercise, including counter-piracy serials and some live firing with participants from China, Iran and Russia

MAY

3 **Joint aerial patrol**
Joint patrol with H-6 and Tu-95 bomber aircraft

SEPTEMBER

4 *Vostok 2022*
One of Russia's major strategic-level exercises, also including as participants other member countries of the Collective Security Treaty Organization and Shanghai Cooperation Organisation, among others

China reportedly sent around 2,000 troops, tanks and armoured fighting vehicles and artillery pieces, 21 aircraft and helicopters (including J-10Cs) and three naval vessels (1x CGHM, 1x FFGHM, 1x AOR)

5 **Joint naval patrol**
Joint patrol including maritime exercises and live-fire drills

NOVEMBER

6 **Joint aerial patrol**
Joint patrol with H-6 and Tu-95 bomber aircraft, reportedly the first time bombers from both countries have landed on each other's airfields

DECEMBER

7 *Joint Sea 2022*
Naval exercise held (generally) biennially since 2012, with maritime serials including anti-submarine warfare and a live-fire component

AOR fleet replenishment oiler with replenishment-at-sea (RAS) capability
AORH fleet replenishment oiler with RAS capability and hangar

CGHM cruiser with surface-to-surface missile (SSM), hangar, and surface-to-air missile (SAM)

DDGHM destroyer with SSM, hangar and SAM
FFGHM frigate with SSM, hangar and SAM

©IISS

Source: IISS

existing Sino-Russian pledges to co-develop new technological capabilities have made little progress and are now likely to be further hampered by sanctions and export controls on semiconductors and other technologies.

Whatever qualms Xi may harbour about Putin's modus operandi in Ukraine, Beijing's bottom line is that it does not want to see Russia defeated or Putin replaced by a new Russian leader less amenable to Chinese interests.[64] Despite occasional bilateral strains, China and Russia have also deepened their partnership in several ways since the start of the war. In economic terms, sanctions have forced Russia to increase its dependence on its neighbour, which now consumes a larger portion of Russian energy exports.[65] Military cooperation has also deepened (see Map 1.1). In May 2022, the two countries flew a joint bomber sortie close to Japan, signalling displeasure at a leader-level Quad summit being held in Tokyo on the same day.[66] In early November 2022, they flew bombers to each other's air bases for the first time during joint military exercises, hinting at future reciprocal access arrangements that could extend their respective operational reach in the Northwest Pacific.[67] The two countries have also conducted joint live-fire exercises in the East China Sea, while the People's Liberation Army (PLA) participated in Russia's *Vostok* 2022 military exercises.

A Chinese H-6 bomber landing at a Russian air base as part of the Russian-organised International Army Games, 2018

(Artyom Anikeev/Stocktrek Images via Getty Images)

Asia-Pacific leaders remain concerned that Russia's actions in Ukraine have lowered the threshold for armed conflict in Asia – an argument clearly embraced by Japan's Prime Minister Kishida. Such worries centre most obviously on China and the prospect that Beijing might be emboldened to use armed force against Taiwan or its other neighbours. China's willingness to pressure Taiwan militarily has grown in 2022 and early 2023, most clearly evident in its military response to then-speaker of the US House of Representatives Nancy Pelosi's visit to the island in August 2022. Assessing Beijing's strategic intentions with any precision remains difficult, however.

At one level it seems reasonable to conclude that Russia's battlefield frustrations in Ukraine would give pause to those in Beijing who might be mulling military adventures of their own. Chinese officials rarely comment on such matters in public, however, so there is little conclusive evidence as to how Russia's 'special operation' against Ukraine will affect the odds of any possible future Chinese invasion of Taiwan. Instead of focusing on the potential for China to engage in military adventurism, it may be more profitable to examine the broader developmental lessons that the PLA might take from the performance of Russia's and Ukraine's armed forces. In many cases those lessons are likely to support existing PLA priorities and modernisation plans, for instance concerning the importance of developing greater expertise in combined arms or joint operations, and how to integrate new technologies in innovative ways.[68] The onus placed on new technologies – such as drones – in Ukraine also chimes with China's existing modernisation plans.[69]

THE US AND EUROPE IN THE ASIA-PACIFIC

The administration of US President Joe Biden has long denied any tension between US activities in Europe and its aim of increasingly focusing resources on the Asia-Pacific and China. The US National Security Strategy published in October 2022 underlined China as Washington's primary focus, as did the related National Defense Strategy released in the same month.[70] Senior US officials claim that developments in Ukraine have not altered their focus.[71] In many ways, Ukraine's military success has bolstered the United States' reputation in the Asia-Pacific. Indeed, while the chaotic military drawdown from Afghanistan in 2021 dented perceptions of Washington's competence, in contrast, the Ukraine war has highlighted US strengths in alliance management, technological leadership, equipment provision and intelligence disclosure. When US Secretary of Defense Lloyd Austin noted in April 2022 that the US 'want[s] to see Russia weakened', the reasoning was presumably that Washington would then be more able to focus on China.[72] Pushing back against Russia's challenge to the international order could enhance the credibility of US security guarantees in Asia (although the opposite is likely to be the result if Ukraine loses the war despite US assistance).

US Secretary of Defense Lloyd Austin speaks at the launch of the 2022 National Defense Strategy – which focuses on China as the 'pacing challenge' for the US despite the war in Ukraine – in Virginia, US, 27 October 2022

(Kevin Dietsch/Getty Images)

Nonetheless, the war risks distracting Washington from its focus on the Asia-Pacific. Ukraine is a drain on US finances, munitions and policy bandwidth. The US has reportedly ordered some of its military equipment stockpiled in South Korea to be moved to Ukraine.[73] Washington's allies in the Asia-Pacific have long watched carefully for signals that the US may not be able or willing to deliver on its existing security guarantees. Successive US administrations have pledged greater US focus on and resources to the Asia-Pacific for more than a decade. That shift has happened slowly,[74] although one senior US defence official recently predicted that 2023 would be 'the most transformative year in US force posture in the region in a generation'.[75]

For European powers, the war raises similar questions pertaining to US focus and resources, albeit on a much smaller scale in terms of military presence and assets that can be deployed to the region. France, Germany and the UK have unveiled strategies for the region, although these arguably appear less sustainable following the invasion of Ukraine. In March 2023 the UK published a 'refresh' of its 2021 Integrated Review of Security, Defence, Development and Foreign Policy, the security strategy that announced its 'tilt' to the Asia-Pacific. Echoing earlier statements from officials, the refresh underlined that the UK's enhanced focus on the region will continue.[76] Other European NATO members, most notably Germany, have pledged to increase defence spending. These promised steps could provide additional resources for security engagement in the Asia-Pacific. However, fiscal constraints and the overwhelming need to focus on Ukraine make it unlikely that European states will be able to develop more ambitious approaches to the Asia-Pacific in the short to medium term. In the face of fiscal pressures and competition for extra resources in Europe, the likes of the UK and France are more likely to focus on maintaining existing and planned commitments in the region.

The Ukraine war also has implications for US partners in the Asia-Pacific. NATO's Madrid Summit in June 2022 was attended by the leaders of Australia, Japan, New

Zealand and South Korea.[77] Their decision to engage NATO more closely reflects mutual concerns over China but also interest in understanding NATO's response to Ukraine. NATO Secretary-General Jens Stoltenberg visited Japan and South Korea in January 2023, calling on the latter to do more to support Ukraine.[78] Heightened perceptions of global insecurity following Russia's invasion may be a contributing element behind increased defence spending among the United States' regional allies and partners. However, this factor should not be overemphasised: Australia, Japan, South Korea and Taiwan were all on a path

Leaders of NATO's four Asia-Pacific partner countries – Australian Prime Minister Anthony Albanese, Japanese PM Kishida Fumio, then New Zealand PM Jacinda Ardern and South Korean President Yoon Suk-yeol – with Secretary-General Jens Stoltenberg at a NATO summit in Madrid, Spain, 29 June 2022

(Pierre-Philippe Marcou/AFP via Getty Images)

to higher defence spending before the Ukraine conflict, largely reflecting their perceptions of rising threats within the region. That said, Kishida has cited the Ukraine war as one of the justifications for his government's commitment to doubling Japanese defence spending – to 2% of GDP – by 2027.[79]

CONCLUSION

Although geographically limited to Eastern Europe and the Black Sea, the war in Ukraine is a major inter-state conflict that is likely to have long-term global ramifications, including for the Asia-Pacific. One universal lesson is that unprovoked aggression and territorial conquest by major powers remains an active risk and a salient feature of international relations in the twenty-first century. Perceptions of military threat have thus deepened in the Asia-Pacific. While trends of higher defence expenditure in the region pre-dated Russia's invasion, deepening feelings of insecurity, driven in part by the war in Ukraine, may now accelerate these trends and lead to faster military modernisation and capability development. Russia's failure to achieve a quick victory in the face of Ukraine's determined and competent defence – aided by substantial assistance from Western countries – has also emerged as a fact of the war's first year. Russia has already paid a heavy price, on the battlefield and reputationally, while Ukraine's civilian and military leadership has consistently outperformed expectations. If Ukraine ultimately prevails, it will provide a considerable boost for the existing rules-based order in both Europe and the Asia-Pacific. By contrast, if Russia achieves some measure of victory, Moscow's gains in Ukraine will likely lead to a weakening of those same rules and norms in the Asia-Pacific, setting revisionist precedents from which China and North Korea are likely to benefit. While the war is unlikely to produce new flashpoints in Asia, it is already having direct impacts on regional strategic alignments, defence policies, doctrines and equipment-purchase decisions. Whatever else happens, the growing strategic interplay between the Asia-Pacific and the Euro-Atlantic looks likely to endure long after Russia's conflict in Ukraine has concluded.

NOTES

1   Japan, Prime Minister's Office, 'Keynote Address by Prime Minister KISHIDA Fumio at the IISS Shangri-La Dialogue', 10 June 2022, https://japan.kantei.go.jp/101_kishida/statement/202206/_00002.html.

2   Ben Barry et al., 'The UK Indo-Pacific Tilt: Defence and Military Implications', IISS Research Paper, 8 June 2022, https://www.iiss.org/blogs/research-paper/2022/06/the-uk-indo-pacific-tilt.

3   See Singapore, Ministry of Foreign Affairs, 'Statement by Ambassador Burhan Gafoor, Permanent Representative of Singapore, at the Emergency Special Session of the United Nations General Assembly on the Situation in Ukraine, 28 February 2022, New York', 28 February 2022, https://www.mfa.gov.sg/Overseas-Mission/New-York/Mission-Updates/General_assembly/2022/10/20220228; and Tommy Koh, 'Ukraine, International Law and the Security of Small States', *Straits Times*, 5 March 2022, https://www.straitstimes.com/asia/ukraine-international-law-and-the-security-of-small-states.

4   See 'Japan to Offer Protective Masks, Clothing, Drones to Ukraine', Kyodo News, 19 April 2022, https://english.kyodonews.net/news/2022/04/00e4cd64dc1c-japan-to-offer-protective-masks-clothing-drones-to-ukraine.html; and South Korea, Ministry of Foreign Affairs, 'Korea Sends Additional Medical Supplies to Ukraine', 20 April 2022, https://www.mofa.go.kr/eng/brd/m_5676/view.do?seq=322033.

5   Australian Government, Defence, 'Additional Support for Ukraine', 27 October 2022, https://www.minister.defence.gov.au/media-releases/2022-10-27/additional-support-ukraine; and New Zealand, Defence Force, 'Further Support to Ukraine Confirmed', 14 November 2022, https://www.nzdf.mil.nz/news/further-support-to-ukraine-continued/.

6   Soo-Hyang Choi, 'Poland Buy S.Korean Rocket Launchers After Tank, Howitzer Sales', Reuters, 19 October 2022, https://www.reuters.com/world/europe/poland-expected-buy-skorean-rocket-launchers-after-tank-howitzer-sales-2022-10-19/.

7   'Aggression Against Ukraine: Resolution / Adopted by the General Assembly', UN Digital Library, 2 March 2022, https://digitallibrary.un.org/record/3959039?ln=en.

8   Kishore Mahbubani, 'Ukraine War: Where Are the Peacemakers?', *Straits Times*, 19 March 2022, https://www.straitstimes.com/opinion/where-are-the-peacemakers.

9   Guy Faulconbridge and Felix Light, 'Putin Ally Warns NATO of Nuclear War if Russia Is Defeated in Ukraine', Reuters, 19 January 2023, https://www.reuters.com/world/europe/putin-ally-medvedev-warns-nuclear-war-if-russia-defeated-ukraine-2023-01-19/.

10 Pierre de Dreuzy and Andrea Gilli, 'Russia's Nuclear Coercion in Ukraine', *NATO Review*, 29 November 2022, https://www.nato.int/docu/review/articles/2022/11/29/russias-nuclear-coercion-in-ukraine/index.html.

11 *Ibid.*; and Steve Rosenberg and Jaroslav Lukiv, 'Ukraine War: Drone Attack on Russian Bomber Base Leaves Three Dead', BBC News, 26 December 2022, https://www.bbc.com/news/world-europe-64092183.

12 Jack Lau, 'No Nuclear Weapons Over Ukraine, Chinese President Xi Jinping Says, in Clear Message to Russia', *South China Morning Post*, 4 November 2022, https://www.scmp.com/news/china/diplomacy/article/3198505/no-nuclear-weapons-over-ukraine-chinese-president-xi-jinping-says-clear-message-russia.

13 Peter Beaumont, 'The Ukraine War Is Deepening Russia's Ties With North Korea as Well as Iran', *Guardian*, 7 November 2022, https://www.theguardian.com/world/2022/nov/07/russia-ukraine-war-iran-north-korea-arms-ties.

14 Steve Holland, 'Exclusive: US Says Russia's Wagner Group Bought North Korean Weapons for Ukraine War', Reuters, 22 December 2022, https://www.reuters.com/world/us-says-russias-wagner-group-bought-north-korean-weapons-ukraine-war-2022-12-22/.

15 Kathrin Hille et al., 'Ukraine War Hardens Washington's Asia Allies on China', *Financial Times*, 11 March 2022, https://www.ft.com/content/bcf45320-78f4-41d4-9ed3-668e29f5bdff.

16 Ted Gover, 'Commentary: Even as Taiwan Boosts Defence Spending, Its Security May Depend on How the Budget Is Spent', CNA, 27 August 2022, https://www.channelnewsasia.com/commentary/us-china-taiwan-defence-invasion-pelosi-visit-2899971.

17 Choe Sang-Hun, 'In a First, South Korea Declares Nuclear Weapons a Policy Option', *New York Times*, 12 January 2023, https://

www.nytimes.com/2023/01/12/world/asia/south-korea-nuclear-weapons.html.

18 IISS and Center for Energy and Security Studies, 'DPRK Strategic Capabilities and Security on the Korean Peninsula: Looking Ahead', IISS Research Paper, 14 July 2021, https://www.iiss.org/blogs/research-paper/2021/07/dprk-strategic-capabilities-security-korean-peninsula.

19 David Brown, Jake Horton and Tural Ahmedzade, 'Ukraine Weapons: What Tanks and Other Equipment Are the World Giving?', BBC News, 22 February 2023, https://www.bbc.com/news/world-europe-62002218.

20 Jerad I. Harper and Michael A. Hunzeker, 'Learning to Train: What Washington and Taipei Can Learn From Security Cooperation in Ukraine and the Baltic States', War on the Rocks, 20 January 2023, https://warontherocks.com/2023/01/learning-to-train-what-washington-and-taipei-can-learn-from-security-cooperation-in-ukraine-and-the-baltic-states/.

21 For an example of such complaints, see Gabriel Dominguez, 'Shrinking US Munition Reserves Could Impact a Taiwan Conflict', *Japan Times*, 31 January 2023, https://www.japantimes.co.jp/news/2023/01/31/asia-pacific/us-munitions-shortage-taiwan/. On the galvanising impact of the Ukraine war on military-assistance programmes in the Asia-Pacific, see, for example, Demetri Sevastopulo, 'US's Taiwan Security Bill Spurs Debate on Level of Support for Taipei', *Financial Times*, 13 September 2022, https://www.ft.com/content/a48ee082-a617-472f-bff2-83f8c6fb2dd9.

22 Jake Harrington, 'Intelligence Disclosures in the Ukraine Crisis and Beyond', War on the Rocks, 1 March 2022, https://warontherocks.com/2022/03/intelligence-disclosures-in-the-ukraine-crisis-and-beyond/.

23 Shane Harris et al., 'Road to War: US Struggled to Convince Allies, and Zelensky, of Risk of Invasion', *Washington Post*, 16 August 2022, https://www.washingtonpost.com/national-security/interactive/2022/ukraine-road-to-war/.

24 Vishnu Som, 'Embassy in Ukraine Shuts After Attempts to Evacuate Indians From Kyiv', NDTV, 1 March 2022, https://www.ndtv.com/india-news/indian-embassy-in-ukraines-capital-kyiv-shuts-down-sources-2797584; and Hadi Azmi, 'Ukraine Invasion: Malaysian Diplomats Flee Kyiv by Road as Government Draws Flak for Evacuation Bungling', *South China Morning Post*, 26 February 2022, https://www.scmp.com/week-asia/politics/article/3168507/ukraine-invasion-malaysian-diplomats-flee-kyiv-road-government.

25 On the Western-made tanks, see Ellen Francis et al., 'Who's Sending What to Ukraine: A New Wave of Western Weapons Explained', *Washington Post*, 2 February 2023, https://www.washingtonpost.com/world/2023/02/02/ukraine-weapons-tanks-leopard-abrams/. On the captured T-90s, see Jake Epstein, 'Retreating Russian Troops Are Arming Ukraine With Modern T-90 Tanks as Putin's Army Digs 60-year-old Armor Out of Storage, Ukraine's Military Says', Business Insider, 13 October 2022, https://www.businessinsider.com/ukraine-armed-with-modern-t-90-tanks-captured-from-russians-2022-10.

26 Mark Nevitt, 'The Russia–Ukraine Conflict, the Black Sea, and the Montreux Convention', Just Security, 28 February 2022, https://www.justsecurity.org/80384/the-russia-ukraine-conflict-the-black-sea-and-the-montreux-convention/.

27 Ali Kucukgocmen and Pavel Polityuk, 'Ukraine Grain Export Deal Back on Track as Russia Resumes Participation', Reuters, 1 November 2022, https://www.reuters.com/article/ukraine-crisis-idAFKBN2RR3VX.

28 Dan Sabbagh and Peter Beaumont, 'Where Has Fighting Been Focused on Day Two of Russia's Invasion of Ukraine?', *Guardian*, 25 February 2022, https://www.theguardian.com/world/2022/feb/25/fight-for-kyiv-russian-forces-ukraine-capital-war.

29 Murat Sofuoglu, 'Art of War: What Does the Russian Withdrawal From Kherson Signify?', TRT World, 11 November 2022, https://www.trtworld.com/magazine/art-of-war-what-does-the-russian-withdrawal-from-kherson-signify-62472.

30 Chris Buckley et al., 'How China Could Choke Taiwan', *New York Times*, 25 August 2022, https://www.nytimes.com/interactive/2022/08/25/world/asia/china-taiwan-conflict-blockade.html.

31 Ben Blanchard, 'Ukraine War Gives Taiwan's Military Reservist Reform New Impetus', Reuters, 12 March 2022, https://www.reuters.com/world/asia-pacific/ukraine-war-gives-taiwans-military-reservist-reform-new-impetus-2022-03-12/.

32 Henry Foy et al., 'The 90km Journey That Changed the Course of the War in Ukraine',

Financial Times, 28 September 2022, https://ig.ft. com/ukraine-counteroffensive/.

33   Taiwan, Office of the President, 'President Tsai Announces Military Force Realignment Plan', 27 December 2022, https://english.president.gov. tw/NEWS/6417.

34   Australian Government, Defence, 'Morrison Government Accelerates Sovereign Guided Weapons Manufacturing', 31 March 2021, https://www.minister. defence.gov.au/media-releases/2021-03-31/ morrison-government-accelerates-sovereign- guided-weapons-manufacturing-0.

35   Joe Gould, 'US Defense Industry Unprepared for a China Fight, Says Report', Defense News, 23 January 2023, https://www.defensenews.com/ industry/2023/01/23/us-defense-industry- unprepared-for-a-china-fight-says-report/.

36   Peter Suciu, 'Ukraine Is Winning on the Battlefield and on Social Media', *Forbes*, 13 October 2022, https://www. forbes.com/sites/petersuciu/2022/10/13/ ukraine-is-winning-on-the-battlefield-and-on- social-media/?sh=e0707ab40082.

37   Hadi Azmi, 'Ukraine War: How the Battle on Malaysia's Social Media Has Become a Propaganda Tool for Russia and Ukraine', *South China Morning Post*, 19 March 2022, https:// www.scmp.com/week-asia/article/3171049/ ukraine-war-battle-malaysias-social-media- propaganda-tool-russia-and.

38   Lidia Kelly, 'Russia Conducts Military Drills on Isles Disputed With Japan', Reuters, 26 March 2022, https://www.reuters.com/world/europe/ russia-conducts-military-drills-isles-disputed- with-japan-media-2022-03-26/.

39   Julian Ryall, 'Russia Ramps Up Military Activities Around Japan in "Sabre-rattling" Move as Tokyo Faces Energy Security Dilemma', *South China Morning Post*, 14 March 2022, https://www.scmp.com/week-asia/ politics/article/3170413/russia-ramps-mili- tary-activities-around-japan-sabre-rattling; Hyonhee Shin, 'South Korea Scrambles Jets as China, Russia Warplanes Enter Air Defence Zone', Reuters, 30 November 2022, https:// www.reuters.com/world/asia-pacific/china- russia-warplanes-temporarily-entered-south- korea-air-defence-zone-yonhap-2022-11-30; and 'Russia Says Its Navy in Joint Patrols With China in Pacific', Reuters, 15 September 2022, https://www.reuters.com/world/

russian-chinese-navies-conduct-joint-patrols- pacific-russian-defence-ministry-2022-09-15.

40   John Paul Rathbone, Sam Jones and Daniel Dombey, 'Military Briefing: Why Russia Is Deploying More Troops to Ukraine', *Financial Times*, 17 March 2022, https://www.ft.com/ content/d721718e-37cd-4113-8c2f-489f930991fb.

41   Ian Storey, 'The Russia–Ukraine War and Its Potential Impact on Russia's Arms Sales to Southeast Asia', *ISEAS Perspective*, no. 47, 5 May 2022, https:// www.iseas.edu.sg/articles-commentaries/ iseas-perspective/2022-47-the-russia-ukraine- war-and-its-potential-impact-on-russias-arms- sales-to-southeast-asia-by-ian-storey/.

42   See Stockholm International Peace Research Institute (SIPRI), 'SIPRI Arms Transfers Database', https://www.sipri.org/databases/armstransfers.

43   Christophe Jaffrelot and Aadil Sud, 'Indian Military Dependence on Russia', Institut Montaigne, 5 July 2022, https://www. institutmontaigne.org/en/analysis/indian- military-dependence-russia; and Mike Yeo, 'Vietnam Expo Displays Declining but Ongoing Dependence on Russian Arms', Defense News, 12 December 2022, https:// www.defensenews.com/industry/2022/12/12/ vietnam-expo-displays-declining-but-ongo- ing-dependence-on-russian-arms/.

44   Le Hong Hiep, 'Will Vietnam Be Able to Wean Itself Off Russian Arms?', *Fulcrum*, 4 April 2022, https://fulcrum.sg/will-vietnam-be-able-to- wean-itself-off-russian-arms/.

45   Sarosh Bana, 'India's Russian Arms Imbroglio', *Strategist*, Australian Strategic Policy Institute, 1 November 2022, https://www.aspistrategist.org. au/indias-russian-arms-imbroglio/.

46   Embassy of India in Moscow, Russia, 'Bilateral Relations: India–Russia Relations', https:// indianembassy-moscow.gov.in/bilateral- relations-india-russia.php.

47   Jim Garamone, 'US, India Ties Continue to Strengthen, Austin Says', US Department of Defense, 26 September 2022, https://www. defense.gov/News/News-Stories/Article/ Article/3170929/us-india-ties-continue-to- strengthen-austin-says/.

48   Sourav Roy Barman, 'Europe Has to Grow Out of Mindset That Its Problems Are World's Problems: Jaishankar', *Indian Express*, 4 June 2022, https://indianexpress.com/article/ india/europe-has-to-grow-out-of-mindset-

that-its-problems-are-worlds-problems-jaishankar-7951895/.

49 Shivam Patel and Krishna N. Das, 'India Says Russia Oil Deals Advantageous as Yellen Visits Delhi', Reuters, 8 November 2022, https://www.reuters.com/business/energy/buying-russian-oil-is-indias-advantage-foreign-minister-2022-11-08/.

50 Mihir Sharma, 'India Should Stand With the West Against Russia', Bloomberg, 22 February 2022, https://www.bloomberg.com/opinion/articles/2022-02-22/india-should-stand-with-the-west-against-russia-in-ukraine-crisis.

51 SIPRI, 'SIPRI Arms Transfers Database'. See 'Importer/exporter TIV tables'.

52 Bana, 'India's Russian Arms Imbroglio'.

53 Devjyot Ghoshal and Aftab Ahmed, 'India, World's Biggest Buyer of Russian Arms, Looks to Diversify Suppliers', Reuters, 18 May 2022, https://www.reuters.com/world/india/india-worlds-biggest-buyer-russian-arms-looks-diversify-suppliers-2022-05-18/.

54 Sudhi Ranjan Sen, 'Modi to Skip Annual Putin Summit Over Ukraine Nuke Threats', Bloomberg, 9 December 2022, https://www.bloomberg.com/news/articles/2022-12-09/modi-to-skip-annual-summit-with-putin-over-ukraine-nuke-threats.

55 Tony Munroe, Andrew Osborn and Humeyra Pamuk, 'China, Russia Partner Up Against West at Olympics Summit', Reuters, 4 February 2022, https://www.reuters.com/world/europe/russia-china-tell-nato-stop-expansion-moscow-backs-beijing-taiwan-2022-02-04/.

56 Edward Wong, 'US Officials Repeatedly Urged China to Help Avert War in Ukraine', New York Times, 25 February 2022, https://www.nytimes.com/2022/02/25/us/politics/us-china-russia-ukraine.html.

57 Amanda Lee and Wendy Wu, 'US Sanctions Threat if China Aids Russia Stirs Fear in Beijing About Forex Assets', South China Morning Post, 7 April 2022, https://www.scmp.com/economy/china-economy/article/3173273/us-sanctions-threat-if-china-aids-russia-stirs-fear-beijing.

58 Kelly Ng, 'Ukraine: US Sanctions Chinese Firm Helping Russia's Wagner Group', BBC News, 27 January 2023, https://www.bbc.com/news/world-asia-china-64421915.

59 Ian Talley and Anthony DeBarros, 'China Aids Russia's War in Ukraine, Trade Data Shows', Wall Street Journal, 4 February 2023, https://www.wsj.com/articles/china-aids-russias-war-in-ukraine-trade-data-shows-11675466360.

60 For example, China's Foreign Ministry Spokesperson Zhao Lijian said that 'NATO's continuous expansion in Europe has led to the Ukraine crisis. Now it is seeking to reach beyond its geographical confines and mission scope by stoking bloc confrontation in the Asia-Pacific.' China, Ministry of Foreign Affairs, 'Foreign Ministry Spokesperson Zhao Lijian's Regular Press Conference on July 8, 2022', 8 July 2022, https://www.fmprc.gov.cn/mfa_eng/xwfw_665399/s2510_665401/202207/t20220708_10717764.html.

61 Kathrin Hille, 'Xi Pursues Policy of "Pro-Russia Neutrality" Despite Ukraine War', Financial Times, 27 February 2022, https://www.ft.com/content/bf930a62-6952-426b-b249-41097094318a.

62 Yan Xuetong, 'China's Ukraine Conundrum: Why the War Necessitates a Balancing Act', Foreign Affairs, 2 May 2022, https://www.foreignaffairs.com/articles/china/2022-05-02/chinas-ukraine-conundrum.

63 Geoffrey Smith, 'China's Xi Warns Putin Not to Use Nuclear Weapons in Ukraine', Yahoo! News, 4 November 2022, https://sg.news.yahoo.com/chinas-xi-warns-putin-not-073636312.html.

64 Iliya Kusa, 'China's Strategic Calculations in the Russia–Ukraine War', Wilson Center, 21 June 2022, https://www.wilsoncenter.org/blog-post/chinas-strategic-calculations-russia-ukraine-war.

65 Chen Aizhu, 'Russian Oil Supplies to China Up 22% on Year, Close Second to Saudi – Data', Reuters, 24 October 2022, https://www.reuters.com/business/energy/russian-oil-supplies-china-up-22-year-close-second-saudi-data-2022-10-24/.

66 Takahashi Kosuke, 'China, Russia Fly 6 Bombers Near Japan Amid Quad Summit', Diplomat, 25 May 2022, https://thediplomat.com/2022/05/china-russia-fly-6-bombers-near-japan-amid-quad-summit/.

67 Mike Yeo, 'Chinese, Russian Long-range Bombers Make Reciprocal Base Visits', Defense News, 1 December 2022, https://www.defensenews.com/air/2022/12/01/chinese-russian-long-range-bombers-make-reciprocal-base-visits/.

68 Michael Raska, 'The Russia–Ukraine War: Lessons for Northeast Asia', S. Rajaratnam School of International Studies, IDSS paper, 12 January 2023, https://www.rsis.edu.sg/

rsi-publication/idss/ip23007-the-russia-ukraine-war-lessons-for-northeast-asia/#.Y9tWMexBzdo.

69 Meia Nouwens, 'China's Military Modernisation: Will the People's Liberation Army Complete Its Reforms?', IISS Analysis, 7 December 2022, https://www.iiss.org/blogs/analysis/2022/12/strategic-survey-2022-chinas-military-modernisation.

70 Antony J. Blinken, 'Release of the President's National Security Strategy', US Department of State, 12 October 2022, https://www.state.gov/release-of-the-presidents-national-security-strategy/; and C. Todd Lopez, 'DOD Releases National Defense Strategy, Missile Defense, Nuclear Posture Reviews', United States Department of Defense, 27 October 2022, https://www.defense.gov/News/News-Stories/Article/Article/3202438/dod-releases-national-defense-strategy-missile-defense-nuclear-posture-reviews/.

71 Mara Karlin and Ryan Evans, 'Talking Strategy With Assistant Secretary of Defense Mara Karlin', War on the Rocks, 31 January 2023, https://warontherocks.com/2023/01/talking-strategy-with-assistant-secretary-of-defense-mara-karlin/.

72 Missy Ryan and Annabelle Timsit, 'US Wants Russian Military "Weakened" From Ukraine Invasion, Austin Says', *Washington* Post, 25 April 2022, https://www.washingtonpost.com/world/2022/04/25/russia-weakened-lloyd-austin-ukraine-visit/.

73 Christy Lee, 'Experts: Arming Ukraine via US Could Worsen South Korea's Ties With Russia', VOA News, 26 January 2023, https://www.voanews.com/a/experts-arming-ukraine-via-us-could-worsen-south-korea-s-ties-with-russia-/6934625.html.

74 Ashley Townshend and James Crabtree, 'US Indo-Pacific Strategy, Alliances and Security Partnerships', in IISS, *Asia-Pacific Regional Security Assessment 2022: Key Developments and Trends* (Singapore: KHL Printing for the IISS, 2022), pp. 12–37, https://www.iiss.org/publications/strategic-dossiers/asia-pacific-regional-security-assessment-2022/aprsa-chapter-1.

75 Christopher Woody, 'The US Military Is Planning for a "Transformative" Year in Asia as Tensions With China Continue to Rise', Business Insider, 27 December 2022, https://www.businessinsider.com/us-military-transform-indo-pacific-force-posture-in-2023-2022-12?op=1.

76 UK, Prime Minister's Office, 'Prime Minister: The UK Will Be a Firm Friend to the Indo-Pacific', 15 November 2022, https://www.gov.uk/government/news/prime-minister-the-uk-will-be-a-firm-friend-to-the-indo-pacific; UK, Foreign, Commonwealth and Development Office, 'UK Minister Travels to Australia for Talks on the Indo-Pacific', 26 November 2022, https://www.gov.uk/government/news/uk-minister-travels-to-australia-for-talks-on-the-indo-pacific ; and UK, Cabinet Office, 'Integrated Review Refresh 2023: Responding to a more contested and volatile world', 13 March 2023, https://www.gov.uk/government/publications/integrated-review-refresh-2023-responding-to-a-more-contested-and-volatile-world/integrated-review-refresh-2023-responding-to-a-more-contested-and-volatile-world.

77 NATO, 'NATO Leaders Meet With Key Partners to Address Global Challenges, Indo-Pacific Partners Participate in a NATO Summit for the First Time', 29 June 2022, https://www.nato.int/cps/en/natohq/news_197287.htm.

78 Matthew Mpoke Bigg, 'NATO's Chief Hints That South Korea Should Consider Military Aid for Ukraine, a Move Seoul Has Resisted', *New York Times*, 30 January 2023, https://www.nytimes.com/2023/01/30/world/europe/south-korea-ukraine-nato.html.

79 'Japan Boost Defence Spending, More Acquisition Plans in the Works', *Asian Defence Journal*, 26 December 2022, https://adj.com.my/2022/12/26/japan-boost-defence-spending-more-acquisition-plans-in-the-works/.

CHAPTER **2**

STRAINED US–CHINA RELATIONS AND THE GROWING THREAT TO TAIWAN

NIGEL INKSTER

Senior Adviser for Cyber Security and China, IISS

Military helicopters carrying Taiwanese flags conduct a flypast rehearsal ahead of Taiwan's Double Ten Day celebrations in Taipei, 7 October 2021 (Watcharit Praihirun/Getty Images)

US–China relations have become progressively more strained in the past decade, with each state increasingly convinced that the other is seeking to undermine it. This situation was thrown into stark relief during the Trump administration, which initiated the United States' trade and technology wars with China and enhanced relations with Taiwan. While both countries are seeking to put a floor under their deteriorating relationship, the prospects for sustained improvement are remote given their differences in ideology, values and geopolitical ambitions.

NO CHANGE UNDER BIDEN

The Biden administration has not merely maintained the policies of the previous US administration: it has systematically sought to build alliance relations in the Indo-Pacific to constrain China's room for manoeuvre.

TECHNOLOGY WARS

The US president has also imposed major restrictions on the sale to China of advanced semiconductors – and the equipment required to manufacture them – in order to maintain US dominance in technologies deemed critical for national security. Decoupling is a reality, although its pace and impact remain unclear.

TAIWAN: THE PLACE WHERE IT ALL COMES TOGETHER

Sino-American tensions have become focused on Taiwan, a critical source of advanced semiconductors, with Beijing perceiving Washington's increased engagement with the island as hollowing out the United States' long-standing 'One China' policy and reducing the prospects for peaceful reunification.

The US–China relationship has been characterised by cultural and political misperceptions and mismatches of expectations ever since the two countries first came into contact in the mid-nineteenth century. The result has been a dynamic that has seesawed between periods of close approximation and intense antagonism. Even during the best of times, relations were never straightforward; as China has grown in wealth and power it has become increasingly competitive and confrontational, while the US perceives China's rise as a threat to its global standing. The 2008 global financial crisis proved to be a major tipping point in the relationship

Chinese President Xi Jinping and US President Joe Biden meet at the G20 summit in Bali, Indonesia, 14 November 2022

(Saul Loeb/AFP via Getty Images)

as Beijing sought, not without justification, to blame Washington for failing to prevent it while overlooking its own role in precipitating the crisis through mercantilist behaviours that led to an unmanageable global savings glut.

The second major tipping point was the 2012 appointment of Xi Jinping as secretary-general of the Chinese Communist Party (CCP). Shortly after assuming office, Xi made it clear that China had effectively abandoned Deng Xiaoping's policy of keeping a low profile ('hide and bide') in favour of a more assertive posture commensurate with the country's growing wealth and power.[1] Xi began promoting internationally the concept of a 'Community of Common Destiny for Mankind', a deliberately vague formulation first used in 2012 by then Chinese president and CCP secretary-general Hu Jintao that amounts to a significant revision of the post-Second World War US-led global order in ways favourable to China's interests. Such a revision would include recognition of the validity of different political and values systems and would preclude the establishment of alliances and blocs based on shared political and values systems – a feature of the US-led global order.[2] The trope that 'the East is rising, the West is in decline' began to feature in leadership speeches, reflecting the belief in historical determinism and Chinese exceptionalism that form the basis of 'Xi Jinping Thought on Socialism with Chinese Characteristics for a New Era', an amalgamation of Marxism–Leninism with aspects of traditional Chinese concepts of statecraft.

While believing that the West (and particularly the US) is in terminal decline, Chinese leaders are also seized of the conviction that this decline may translate into ever more desperate actions by the US to maintain its hegemonic status. A particular concern is the threat of subversion through US attempts to encourage 'peaceful evolution' and to promote colour revolutions in authoritarian states. This concern was articulated by Hu in a 2011 speech in which he stated that 'hostile foreign powers are intensifying strategies and plots to Westernize and divide our country, the ideological and cultural sphere is the focus sphere in which they conduct long-term infiltration'.[3] This message was reiterated in a video produced by China's National Defence University in 2013 with the title 'Jiaoliang Wusheng – Silent Contest', which focuses on the West's supposed unremitting hostility to China and its determination to subvert it through the introduction of Western values.[4] Moreover, the CCP's Central Party Document Number Nine, formally entitled 'Briefing on the Current Situation in the Ideological Realm', amounted to a comprehensive rejection of universal values.[5]

MATTERS COME TO A HEAD

After a long period during which both Washington and Beijing played down their differences, matters came to a head midway through the tenure of US president Donald Trump. Though Trump's initial attitude to China was ambivalent, by the end of 2017 his administration had published a National Security Strategy that described a new era of great-power competition and characterised

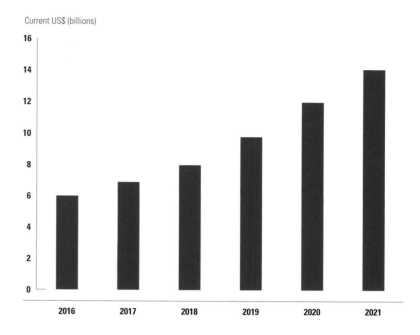

Figure 2.1: **US semiconductor sales to China, 2016–21**

Current US$ (billions)

Note: In the context of this figure, 'China' refers to mainland China only, excluding Hong Kong, Macao and Taiwan.

Source: Enodo Economics, www.enodoeconomics.com

China as the United States' primary strategic threat. It was followed in 2018 by the imposition of 25% tariffs on some Chinese imports, with the threat of more tariffs to come. Washington's behaviour was driven by frustration with Beijing's perceived gaming of the international trading system to the detriment of the US economy, as well as China's pervasive acquisition of US intellectual property (IP) both through industrial-scale cyber espionage and by compelling US and other Western companies to hand over proprietary technology as a condition of access to Chinese markets. Trump sought to address both the chronic US trade deficit in goods with China (see Figure 2.2) and the decline in US domestic manufacturing. According to a report by the Economic Policy Institute, the growing trade deficit with China resulted in the loss of 3.7 million US jobs between 2001 and 2018.[6]

Though arguably incoherent in both conception and execution, the Trump approach to China reflected a growing perception within the US policy community that engagement with Beijing had been a failure. Far from bringing China more in line with Western norms of behaviour and values, engagement was perceived as having empowered an authoritarian regime that was irremediably hostile to such norms and values in ways detrimental to US interests.[7] China seems either to have been unaware of such sentiments or to have discounted them in the conviction that the gravitational pull of Chinese markets would prove irresistible to Western entrepreneurs and investors. And it was and remains the case that Silicon Valley and Wall Street are heavily invested in maintaining the best possible relations with China, for understandable reasons. In the case of the former, in 2020, 15 publicly traded US chip manufacturers derived, on average, 31% of their revenues from sales to China; in the following year, the US sold US$14 billion worth of semiconductors to China (see Figure 2.1).[8] Also in 2021, major US financial institutions, including Goldman Sachs, Blackstone and JP Morgan, made substantial investments in China's financial sector.[9]

(Frederic J. Brown/Pool/AFP via Getty Images)

Senior Chinese and US officials meet
in Alaska, US, 18 March 2021

A Phase One trade agreement signed between the two countries at the beginning of
2020 did little to address the underlying causes of tension, which were themselves a function of profound differences of ideology and values – differences that had always been
present but which had been brought into sharp relief by China's growing geostrategic
ambitions. Nor would it prove to make a significant difference to the US trade deficit
with China. Relations were further exacerbated by the coronavirus pandemic, the effect
of which on a hitherto buoyant US economy cast doubt on Trump's re-election prospects.
Thereafter relations entered what appeared to be an uncontrollable downward spiral:
the US sanctioned China's actions in Xinjiang and Hong Kong; imposed restrictions on
Chinese technology companies, notably Huawei; promoted the concept of 'clean' networks
(networks free from Chinese technology); restricted visas for Chinese students, journalists
and CCP members; and closed China's Houston consulate, which stood accused of acting
as a collection hub within the US for stolen US technology.

By the end of the Trump administration, senior US officials, including then-secretary of
state Mike Pompeo and then-deputy national security adviser Matt Pottinger, were making
speeches that sought to distinguish between the CCP and the Chinese people in ways that
Beijing interpreted as a policy of regime change.[10] The hawks in the Trump administration
appeared determined to put US–China relations beyond any possibility of recovery. Meanwhile,
Congress achieved a rare consensus on the need to get tough on Beijing, initiating a range of
anti-China and pro-Taiwan legislation, an approach that was to continue under President Joe
Biden. By late 2020, China's leaders were convinced that the Trump administration – in a 'final
stage of madness', to quote the state-backed *Global Times*[11] – was using its last days in office to
provoke Beijing, and it subsequently transpired that China feared the US military would seek
to provoke the People's Liberation Army (PLA) into launching an armed attack on US forces.[12]

Figure 2.2: **US trade balance with and goods imports from China, 1994–2021**

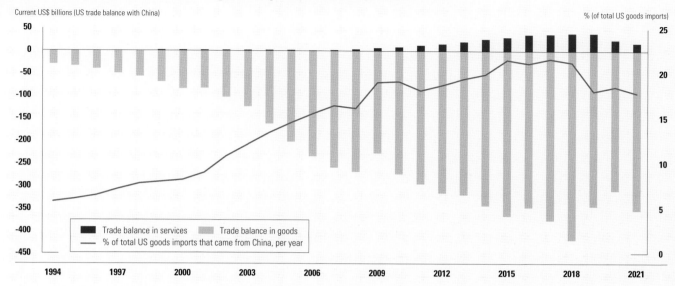

Note: In the context of this figure, 'China' refers to mainland China only, excluding Hong Kong, Macao and Taiwan.

Source: Enodo Economics, www.enodoeconomics.com

NO CHANGE UNDER BIDEN

Chinese leaders did not expect the relationship to improve following Biden's arrival in office. Veteran US watcher Yuan Peng, the president of the China Institutes of Contemporary International Relations – a respected think tank that is also the open-source research institute of China's Ministry of State Security – had provided the Chinese leadership with a series of analytical pieces on US–China relations in which he compared the US to the United Kingdom after the First World War: diminished and unable to exercise effective hegemony but still powerful enough to prevent any would-be competitor from displacing it.[13] In the US–China context this analysis high-lighted the risk that relations could tip over into confrontation. In an initially unreported exchange with a provincial cadre in early 2021, Xi referred to the US as the biggest threat to China's security.[14]

Early interactions between Biden's top national-security and foreign-policy staff and their Chinese counterparts amounted to little more than a recital of each country's griev-ances with the other. At a March 2021 meeting in Alaska between senior US and Chinese officials, in a departure from standard protocols, Secretary of State Antony Blinken upbraided China in front of the assembled press corps. State Counsellor Yang Jiechi responded by publicly accusing the US of abusing 'so-called notions of national security to obstruct normal trade exchanges, and incite some countries to attack China'.[15] The Chinese position was that the US should revert to 'correct' behaviour, with Beijing offering no concessions. Biden indicated that he was in no hurry to lift the Trump-era tariffs and tech-nology restrictions. He stated in his first press conference as president that he would not allow China to become the world's leading and wealthiest country.[16] It became apparent that Biden, whose room for manoeuvre was limited by the hawkish stance of Congress and

the Republican Party, would essentially continue Trump's policies but in a more struc-
tured and focused way (Figure 2.3 highlights the continuity in US legislation on China
across the administrations).

Over the course of 2021 China became progressively more vocal and specific in setting
out its grievances with the US and demanding action to address them. In July 2021, then
minister of foreign affairs Wang Yi told US Deputy Secretary of State Wendy Sherman
that 'the US must not challenge, slander or even attempt to subvert the path and system
of socialism with Chinese characteristics'.[17] That same month, Vice-Foreign Minister Xie
Feng presented Sherman with two sets of demands: a 'List of US Wrongdoings that Must
Stop', and a 'List of Key Individual Cases that China Has Concerns With'. These included
demands that the US revoke visa restrictions on CCP members and their families; revoke
sanctions imposed on Chinese leaders over Xinjiang and Hong Kong; cease suppressing
Confucius Institutes; revoke the requirement for Chinese media organisations to register
as foreign agents; and revoke the extradition request for Huawei's chief financial officer,
Meng Wanzhou (who is also the daughter of Huawei's founder), whose detention on
alleged breaches of US sanctions on Iran had become a cause célèbre.[18]

In March 2021 the Biden administration published its Interim National Security
Strategy. In his introductory message, the president spoke of a world at an inflection
point involving a contest between democracy and authoritarianism. He continued that for
democracy to prevail at a global level the US would need to

build back better our economic foundations; reclaim our place in international institutions; lift up our values at home and speak out to defend them around the world;

Figure 2.3: **US legislation on China and Taiwan, 2018–22**

01 2018: the Taiwan Travel Act
This act encourages and permits US officials
at all levels to travel to Taiwan to meet their
Taiwanese counterparts and permits high-
level Taiwanese officials to travel to the US
and conduct meetings with US counterparts.

02 2018: the Asia Reassurance Initiative Act
This is a broad-ranging act dealing with
US policy in the Indo-Pacific region, with
a particular focus on the promotion of
democracy, civil society, human rights, the
rule of law and transparency. Though not
expressly directed at it, China has seen this
act as a provocation.

**03 2019: the Taiwan Allies International Protection
and Enhancement Initiative (TAIPEI) Act**
Signed into law in 2020, this act aims to
increase the scope of US relations with
Taiwan and incentivise other states and
international organisations to strengthen
their official and unofficial ties with Taiwan.

**04 2019: the Hong Kong Human Rights and
Democracy Act**
Signed into law following protests in
Hong Kong against the introduction of an
extradition law, this act requires the US
State Department to determine annually
whether Hong Kong retains enough
autonomy from China to justify the
favourable trading terms with the US it
has enjoyed since 1997.

05 2021: the US Innovation and Competition Act
This act makes broad-ranging provisions
to enhance US competitiveness in areas of
technology where China poses a challenge
to US dominance. The Chinese government
has characterised it as a direct challenge
and has threatened unspecified retaliation.

06 2021: the Uyghur Forced Labor Prevention Act
Signed into law in 2021, this act
stipulates that all goods manufactured
in China's Xinjiang region are to be

considered the product of forced labour
unless the Commissioner for US Customs
and Border Protection determines
otherwise. It also provides for sanctions
on individuals who knowingly benefit
from forced labour in Xinjiang.

07 2021: the Taiwan Fellowship Act*
Also incorporated into the 2023
National Defense Authorization Act,
this act provides support for ten US
federal-government employees per year
to undertake two-year language and
regional-issues studies in Taiwan.

**08 2022: the Taiwan Enhanced Resilience Act
(formerly entitled the Taiwan Policy Act)**
A version of this act, introduced to the
Senate in 2022 by senators Marco Rubio
and Chris Smith, was incorporated into
the United States' National Defense
Authorization Act for Fiscal Year 2023. It
authorises US$10 billion in military aid

modernize our military capabilities, while leading first with diplomacy; and revitalize America's unmatched network of alliances and partnerships.[19]

These points were broadly repeated in the 2022 National Security Strategy released in November that year, which stated: 'The People's Republic of China harbors the intention and, increasingly, the capacity to reshape the international order in favor of one that tilts the global playing field to its benefit, even as the United States remains committed to managing the competition between our countries responsibly.' The strategy also repeated the juxtaposition between democracy and authoritarianism.[20]

ALLIANCE RELATIONS

Though the Biden administration placed the reinvigoration of US alliances at the heart of its security policy, it was Trump who initiated this policy – despite his professed disdain for alliances. His administration's Indo-Pacific Strategy, declassified in 2020 years ahead of normal schedules, advocated the creation of a latticework of alliance and partnership relations as a means to contain China. The strategy involved a reactivation of the Quadrilateral Security Dialogue (the Quad), bringing together Australia, Japan, India and the US in a loose partnership. This grouping has subsequently held two summits, one virtual and another face to face. The Quad was first launched in 2007 and followed the four countries' cooperative response to the 2004 Indian Ocean tsunami. However, the format did not progress in subsequent years due to Australian fears that China would see its existence as provocative. While its revival was made possible in large measure by India's desire to develop closer links with the US to hedge against China's more assertive posture – particularly in the wake of the 2020 Sino-Indian border clashes – New Delhi has been at pains to ensure that the Quad presents itself not as a military alliance but as a means of ensuring security and stability in the Indo-Pacific region.[21]

Another major alliance initiative by the Biden administration was the AUKUS pact, which aims (among other objectives) to provide Australia with

for Taiwan (including US$2bn in annual grants for 2023–27), US$2bn in loans for arms, and a regional contingency stockpile for Taiwan of up to US$100 million a year in munitions for use in the event of a conflict.

09   **2022: the CHIPS (Creating Helpful Incentives to Produce Semiconductors) and Science Act***
Signed into law in August 2022, this act provides for US$280bn to promote domestic research and manufacturing of semiconductors and related technologies. The act addresses the challenge posed by China to US technology dominance and is designed to enable decoupling in key areas of technology and to reduce dependence on Chinese manufacturing.

*Held in abeyance until incorporated into the 2023 National Defense Authorization Act
Note: Years appearing before the title of a piece of legislation indicate when it was first introduced as a bill to Congress.

Source: IISS

(Kiboecontor via Pixabay)

nuclear-powered submarines. Washington's maladroit handling of the initiative, which saw Canberra terminate a 2016 deal – worth US$60bn – with Paris to supply it with 12 conventionally powered submarines, had the unintended effect of alienating France, a consequential Indo-Pacific power in its own right.[22] The AUKUS project goes far beyond just the provision of nuclear submarines, which are unlikely to be operational until well into the 2030s; it extends to uninhabited underwater vehicles, quantum sensing, artificial intelli-

Quad leaders – Australian Prime Minister Anthony Albanese, US President Joe Biden, Japanese Prime Minister Kishida Fumio and Indian Prime Minister Narendra Modi – meet in Tokyo, 24 May 2022

(Zhang Xiaoyu/Xinhua/Bloomberg via Getty Images)

gence (AI), cyber capabilities, hypersonic weapons and electronic warfare. The ultimate goal is to provide Australia with a comprehensive advanced defence-industrial capability such that it can meet its own defence requirements and contribute to wider regional security.[23]

The Biden administration's engagement with allies has contributed to public shifts in position by Japan and Australia, with leaders in both countries expressing concern regarding China's more confrontational posture and identifying Taiwan as key to their national security.[24] The government of Japanese Prime Minister Kishida Fumio aspires to double Tokyo's defence budget – from 1% to 2% of GDP – by 2027 and, in a significant departure from decades of pacifism, to develop counterstrike capabilities.[25] European states have also been encouraged by the US to undertake assertions of maritime rights and freedoms in waters claimed by China, namely the South China Sea and the Taiwan Strait. Meanwhile, China has become a more pressing issue on the agendas of both the European Union and NATO.

China's relationship with the EU has undergone a significant deterioration since 2019, driven by Europe's frustration over its restricted access to Chinese markets and China's predatory efforts to acquire European technology. Values have also come to the fore, driven by China's repressive policies in Xinjiang and Hong Kong, resulting inter alia in the European Parliament's refusal to ratify a Comprehensive Agreement on Investment with China that had taken years to negotiate. Such collective decisions, however, mask significant disparities between individual EU member states over China policy, a situation Beijing has sought to exploit by urging Europe to exercise 'strategic autonomy' – code for divergence from US positions.[26]

More consequential than the EU's changing policy has been NATO's new focus on China. At a June 2021 summit, for the first time the Alliance acknowledged that 'China's stated ambitions and assertive behaviour present systemic challenges to the rules-based international order'.[27] A year later, NATO's 2022 Strategic Concept identified China, together with Russia, as a major strategic challenge. The Strategic Concept stated that NATO would

work together responsibly, as Allies, to address the systemic challenges posed by the PRC [People's Republic of China] to Euro-Atlantic security and ensure NATO's enduring ability to guarantee the defence and security of Allies. We will boost our shared awareness, enhance our resilience and preparedness, and protect against the

PRC's coercive tactics and efforts to divide the Alliance. We will stand up for our shared values and the rules-based international order, including freedom of navigation.[28]

This shift in focus can be seen as a product of US efforts to indicate that continued American commitment to European security – NATO's fundamental *raison d'être* – will henceforth be a function of the organisation's willingness to provide concrete support for US objectives in the Indo-Pacific.

TECHNOLOGY WARS

Technology has become a critical issue area in US–China relations and one that is inextricably linked with the other primary source of contention: Taiwan. Prior to the Trump administration, the US had adopted a broadly collaborative approach with regard to providing technology to China. This policy was to some degree based on a complacent and – as it proved – mistaken conviction that China could copy US technology but not innovate.[29] The Trump administration's efforts to constrain China's technical development appeared to be somewhat haphazard and lacking in coherence but did serve to recognise and begin to address the challenges China presented.

The United States' initial focus was China's efforts to become the dominant global force in fifth-generation (5G) mobile technology. This reflected the fact that China's national telecommunications champions Huawei and ZTE had assumed a globally leading position in 5G manufacture and systems integration while the US, though responsible for much of the technology that enabled 5G, had nothing comparable to offer. Through a combination of applying pressure on US allies to exclude China from their 5G networks and denying the likes of Huawei and ZTE access to US technologies by placing them on the US Department of Commerce Entities List, the business models of these companies were substantially eroded, buying time for the US to concentrate on the development of alternative 5G solutions, such as Open-RAN.[30]

The Trump administration applied a variety of instruments to constrain China's technology development. Chinese technology companies were added to the Entities List on the basis that their technologies might have military applications. The result was that US companies wishing to export to these companies had to apply for an export licence – with a presumption of denial. Other measures adopted by the Trump administration included application of the Foreign Direct Product Rule, first introduced in 1959 to control trading of US technologies, to limit the amount of US technology in any given system that Chinese firms could acquire; a more rigorous application of Committee on Foreign Investment in the US (CFIUS) rules, to limit Chinese acquisitions of US technology companies; visa restrictions imposing limits on the number of Chinese graduate and research students and denying access to those with links to China's civil–military fusion programmes; and law enforcement, in the form of an ill-conceived and since abandoned effort to identify and prosecute US-based academics involved in unauthorised research collaborations with Chinese institutions.[31]

The Biden administration's early focus was addressing the United States' own shortcomings through investment in human capital and the creation of incentives for US companies to 're-shore' or 'friend-shore' manufacturing capabilities to reduce exposure to China. The most egregious example of the latter policy was the CHIPS and Science Act of 2022, which made provision for US$280bn in spending between 2023 and 2027. Of this, US$200bn is slated for scientific research and development (R&D) and commercialisation, while US$52.7bn is allocated for semiconductor manufacturing, R&D and workforce development. US$24bn is earmarked for chip production – in the form of tax credits. Moreover, US$3bn has been allotted for programmes focused on leading-edge tech-

A TSMC facility under construction in Arizona, US, 6 December 2022

(Caitlin O'Hara/Bloomberg via Getty Images)

nology and wireless supply chains.[32] Other initiatives included persuading the Taiwan Semiconductor Manufacturing Company (TSMC) to invest approximately US$40bn to build two advanced microprocessor foundries in Arizona.[33]

Initially, Biden did little to impact the situation he had inherited from his predecessor, beyond adding some Chinese technology companies to the Entities List. However, a debate between his administration's security and economic constituencies was, over the course of 2022, resolved in favour of the former. A series of statements by senior US officials followed. In May 2022, Blinken gave a speech at George Washington University entitled 'The Administration's Approach to the People's Republic of China', stating that because the US could not change China, 'so we will shape the strategic environment around Beijing'.[34] In September 2022, in a speech to the Special Competitive Studies Project established by former Google chairperson Eric Schmidt, National Security Advisor Jake Sullivan identified export controls as a strategic tool of national security:

> On export controls, we have to revisit the longstanding premise of maintaining 'relative' advantages over competitors in certain key technologies. We previously maintained a 'sliding-scale' approach that said we need to stay only a couple of generations ahead. That is not the strategic environment we are in today. Given the foundational nature of certain technologies, such as advanced logic and memory chips, we must maintain as large of a lead as possible.[35]

The practical application of the approach outlined by Sullivan became clear the following month when the US Department of Commerce's Bureau of Industry and Security issued new rules restricting the sale of advanced semiconductors – and the equipment needed to make them – to Chinese entities. The rules restricted specifically the sale of logic chips with non-planar transistor architectures (i.e., FinFET or GAAFET) of 16 nanometres or 14 nm, or below; dynamic random-access memory (DRAM) chips of 18 nm half-pitch or less; and NAND flash memory chips with 128 layers or more.[36] In effect, the US government was not only making it impossible for China to acquire or produce semiconductors at the most advanced production nodes but also making it impossible for the country to maintain existing production at less advanced nodes.

The new regulations targeted in particular the sale of advanced graphics processing units used to train and run AI algorithms and enable small-scale high-performance computing applications. As a result, they will significantly restrict China's ability to become a major AI power. The new regulations also prohibited 'US persons' – not merely citizens or green-card holders but anyone resident in the US – from assisting China in the development of advanced semiconductors, a move that resulted in the immediate repatriation of hundreds of US engineers working on projects in China.

The new regulations, accompanied by a decision to place a further 31 Chinese companies on the Entities List, targeted a key Chinese vulnerability. For all the talk within China's leadership of the need for technological self-sufficiency – a focus reiterated in Xi's work report to the CCP's 20th Party Congress – China has consistently lagged behind the most technically advanced economies in the production of advanced semiconductors, most of which are designed in the US and manufactured in Taiwan and South Korea. In early 2022, a report produced by Peking University's Institute of International and Strategic Studies, which was removed from the internet after just a few days, assessed China's competitiveness and weakness – relative to the US – in information technology, AI and aerospace. The report concluded that in the event of a technology decoupling between the US and China, both sides would lose but China would suffer more: 'In the future, China may narrow the technological gap with the U.S. and achieve "autonomous control" in some key sectors. But China faces a long uphill battle surpassing the US in technology.'[37]

In recent years, China has spent in excess of US$100bn trying to stimulate its indigenous semiconductor industry, with at best mixed results.[38] China's flagship initiative for promoting indigenous semiconductor manufacture – the China Integrated Circuit Industry Investment Fund (CICF, also known as the 'Big Fund') – is a case in point. Set up in 2014 and backed by the Ministry of Finance, the Big Fund has received over US$40bn of capitalisation. A 2022 review conducted by Vice Premier Liu He confirmed that there was little to show for this investment. Those heading the fund are now under investigation for corruption. Notwithstanding this failure, it has been reported that the Chinese government is preparing an investment of US$143bn to develop China's indigenous semiconductor industry, though this has not yet been officially confirmed.[39]

China's efforts have not been totally without success. It has achieved significant progress in areas such as memory-chip design, produces substantial quantities of less sophisticated semiconductors (24 nm upwards) and has effectively cornered the global market in semiconductor assembly, testing and packaging. One of the country's national champions, the Semiconductor Manufacturing International Corporation, has managed to produce semiconductors at the 7 nm node, although it has done so only in small quantities using a highly laborious process that is unlikely to prove commercially viable.[40] These achievements being acknowledged, the US retains a stranglehold on the production of electronic design automation tools (EDAs), while the amount of US IP that informs the most advanced etching tools – extreme ultraviolet lithography (EUV) machines, for which the Dutch company ASML has a global monopoly – means that Washington is able to veto their export to China.

Even if China were able to circumvent the US embargo and acquire EUV machines, it would still need to address a shortage of skilled workers. It would also lack access to a complex supply chain of chemicals that have to be refined to the highest levels of purity, as well as valves, pipes, lenses and mirrors machined to the highest levels of precision (99.9999% is the industry standard). These considerations would apply in the event that China was, by invading Taiwan, able to secure control of TSMC, whose 'pure-play' foundries (foundries that only manufacture to clients' designs) account for roughly

TSMC headquarters in Hsinchu, Taiwan, 12 October 2022

(Bloomberg via Getty Images)

50% of global semiconductor production.[41] This share rises to 92% in the case of the most advanced production nodes.[42] In 2020, the US and China accounted for 60% and 20% of all TSMC sales, respectively.[43] The fact that the TSMC foundries are situated just 150 kilometres off China's coastline has led to speculation that the opportunity to acquire them might constitute an incentive for Beijing to invade sooner rather than later. However, for the reasons outlined above, that is an unlikely prospect and fails to consider what are likely to be the real drivers for Beijing to take such action – China's perception that the recovery of Taiwan is necessary to restore a sense of national honour impugned by the 'century of humiliation' and, more pragmatically, the CCP's need to be seen by the Chinese people to deliver on its commitment to realise the 'great rejuvenation of the Chinese nation'. Conversely, Taiwan's globally dominant role in semiconductor production has been cited by Taiwanese leaders as a reason why the US and its allies would have to intervene to prevent China's occupation of the island – the so-called 'silicon shield' – a perception that is likely to prove equally misplaced.[44] Beijing may well conclude that if it cannot benefit from the TSMC foundries then no one can, and that without them China would still be in a relatively strong global position by virtue of its ability to manufacture lower-end semiconductors at a scale others cannot match.

The effectiveness of the United States' new technology-containment measures will depend on Washington's ability to persuade other major Western technology powers to apply similar sales embargoes. For example, though the precise details have yet to be announced, both the Netherlands and Japan have agreed to match US restrictions and it has become clear that this outcome was never in serious doubt. However, it remains to be seen whether other states, notably South Korea, will follow suit. US technology companies are manifestly unhappy with the new measures, which will deprive them of significant revenues and have implications for their ability to invest in innovation. While the US has seen the beginnings of a move away from 'fabless' semiconductor production – which has seen design taking place in the US and manufacture outsourced overseas – towards indigenous manufacture, the limited scale of these efforts means they are unlikely to prove an effective substitute for current arrangements. Nor will it be straightforward to decouple from the

US–China technology relationship, which has developed over the course of several decades and is characterised by deep entanglement.

To date, China's reaction to the US restrictions has been relatively restrained. A case has been brought before the World Trade Organization alleging that the US is guilty of protectionism.[45] However, Beijing has not brought to bear a range of Chinese legislation developed in recent years to counter the effect of sanctions and embargoes, including the Anti-Foreign Sanctions Law, which empowers the Chinese state to seize the assets of entities implementing sanctions against China and imposes liabilities on

Employees work on the production line of solar panels for export at a factory in Hefei, Anhui province, China, 24 December 2021

(Visual China Group via Getty Images)

firms that refuse to help the country counter sanctions; an Unreliable Entity List, similar to that of the US; and the Rules on Counteracting Unjustified Extra-territorial Application of Foreign Legislation and Other Measures, which bar Chinese persons and companies from complying with extraterritorial applications of foreign laws. Nor has China yet sought to embargo the sale of rare earths to the US and its allies, possibly mindful of its earlier efforts to apply such an embargo against Japan, which proved counterproductive and simply reduced China's market share as Japan found alternative sources of supply. China has however declared a ban on the export of solar-energy technology (a field in which China already occupies a dominant position) – an action which may have been intended as a retaliatory measure, although it was not announced as such.

The US has made it clear that in addition to advanced computing-related technologies, biotechnology and clean technology are also viewed as '"force-multipliers" throughout the technology eco-system', such that 'leadership in each of these is a national security imperative'.[46] It therefore seems likely that – notwithstanding China's efforts to pose as an advocate of globalisation and open trade – a degree of US–China technology decoupling has become both a reality and an inevitability. The US approach to decoupling has been described as 'small yard, high fence', meaning that small amounts of key technologies should be heavily protected while trade in less sensitive technologies continues as normal.[47] It is unclear how effective this approach will prove, especially given that in biotechnology and clean technology there is no obvious single point-of-failure technology that equates to advanced semiconductors. Nor is it clear how far the process of decoupling will go or what its practical effects will prove to be.

TAIWAN: THE PLACE WHERE IT ALL COMES TOGETHER

Geopolitical rivalry and technology competition between the US and China have become focused on Taiwan, which since 1949 has been a de facto independent entity but which has always been claimed by the PRC. Since the US and China established diplomatic relations in 1979 the status of Taiwan has been the subject of a diplomatic fudge whereby the United

States' 'One China' policy acknowledges – but does not recognise – China's claim to the island. Per the 1979 Taiwan Relations Act, Washington has maintained a commitment to supply Taiwan with arms for its own defence while maintaining a policy of strategic ambiguity regarding its readiness to come to the island's assistance in the event of a conflict with China.

Then-speaker of the US House of Representatives Nancy Pelosi and Taiwanese President Tsai Ing-wen meet in Taipei, 3 August 2022

(Chien Chih-Hung/Office of The President via Getty Images)

Until relatively recently the prospects of such a conflict were not high. Though tensions had arisen following Taiwan's transition to democracy and the emergence of the pro-independence Democratic Progressive Party during the 1990s, China has remained committed to peaceful reunification on the basis of Deng Xiaoping's 'one country, two systems' model, a commitment most recently repeated by Xi in his 2022 work report to the 20th Party Congress. However, there are indications that Xi may have concluded that this model is no longer viable and has charged CCP Politburo Standing Committee member and chief ideologue Wang Huning with devising a new theoretical framework for reunification.

Concurrently, China has refused to renounce the use of force to achieve reunification and has implemented a major military-modernisation strategy that has, at its heart, the development of the capabilities needed to keep US forces out of theatre long enough for China to accomplish a military takeover of Taiwan.[48] As a result, the PLA has developed a broad suite of military capabilities that comprehensively overmatch those of Taiwan. Moreover, in some areas, such as numbers of naval and paramilitary vessels and ballistic and cruise missiles, these capabilities exceed those of the US. The PLA has also focused relentlessly on practising the kind of joint operations it would need to conduct to invade Taiwan, while also building up amphibious-assault capabilities that involve the use of civilian roll-on roll-off ferries.

What has arguably been more consequential in altering the long-standing status quo over Taiwan has been the shift in Washington's level of engagement with the island. Since establishing relations with the PRC in 1979, the US has effectively served as a guarantor of peace in the Taiwan Strait, reining in Taiwanese ambitions to declare independence while providing reassurances to successive Taiwanese administrations in relation to the island's defence needs. This pattern ended in 2018 when the Trump administration began using Taiwan as a means to antagonise and undermine China, introducing a succession of measures that have been continued under Biden. These measures have included enhanced political relations through high-level visits to Taiwan by both congressional delegations and senior US officials, most notably then-speaker of the House of Representatives Nancy Pelosi in August 2022, and an invitation to Taiwanese President Tsai Ing-wen to speak at the December 2021 Summit for Democracy; legislation designed to enhance Taiwan's international space; a major increase in levels of military assistance (the Trump administration provided US$18bn in arms over four years, while Biden has made provision in the 2023 National Defense Authorization Act for US$10bn in arms sales over five years[49]); and regular freedom-of-navigation transits by US and allied warships through the Taiwan Strait.

For China, the cumulative effect of such actions is seen as a 'hollowing out' of the US 'One China' policy calculated to encourage Taiwan in the direction of independence.[50] In interactions with US counterparts, Chinese leaders – most recently Xi during his meeting with Biden on the margins of the Bali G20 summit – have emphasised that Taiwan is 'at the very core of China's core interests … and the first red line that must not be crossed in China–US relations'.[51] More consequentially, China has responded to US actions by progressively ratcheting up its 'grey-zone'

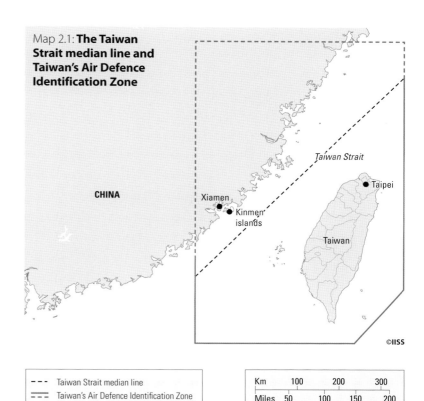

Map 2.1: **The Taiwan Strait median line and Taiwan's Air Defence Identification Zone**

- - - Taiwan Strait median line
= = = Taiwan's Air Defence Identification Zone

Km	100	200	300
Miles	50	100	150	200

Sources: IISS

pressure on Taiwan via cyber attacks, selective trade embargoes, military incursions into Taiwanese airspace and naval exercises in the waters around the island that have included simulations of a naval blockade. These developments have resulted in a 'new normal' whereby the PLA Air Force now regularly dispatches large contingents of fighters, strategic bombers and aerial-reconnaissance aircraft across the median line into Taiwan's Air Defence Identification Zone (see Map 2.1) with the aim of both intimidating Taiwan and imposing attrition on Taiwan's air force and air-defence systems.

The increased military activity around Taiwan carries obvious risks of accidents leading to escalation, although it is worth noting that, to date, China has never allowed itself to be drawn into a conflict unless it was ready for one. Whether it is ready now remains a moot point. It has long been an article of faith that the attainment of China's second centennial goal of 'becoming a strong, democratic, civilised, harmonious and modern socialist country by 2049' is dependent on achieving national reunification.[52] However, realistically, achieving this by 2049 can only be an aspiration; there is no evidence that China has a fixed timetable for invading Taiwan. US military leaders have claimed that China may move as early as 2027 or even 2023 – though such statements appear to have been based not on firm intelligence but rather on an assessment of the date by which China will have in place all the military capabilities it will need.[53] In fact, a decision on whether to achieve reunification by force is likely to be a function not just of military capability but also of a calculation of likely US and allied sanctions and non-military responses, in particular with regard to the potential impact of economic and financial sanctions on China's economy. Chinese leaders will be aware that military defeat or a pyrrhic victory could prove terminal for their hold on power.

US civilian leaders, most recently Biden following his November 2022 meeting with Xi, have played down the risk of military action.[54] Nor is there any evidence to indicate that Russia's invasion of Ukraine in February 2022 has altered Chinese thinking on the timescale or methodology for attacking Taiwan. It is clear that Chinese military thinkers have analysed both the implications of Western support for Ukraine – in the form of weaponry, enhanced cyber defences, intelligence sharing, information operations and the imposition of economic and financial sanctions – and the factors that have contributed to Russia's poor military performance.[55] However, Taiwan is seen as a separate case on the basis that the Chinese leadership has always considered it to be part of China's national territory. Therefore, Chinese officials bridle at the suggestion that there may be any similarity between the Ukraine war and a potential invasion of Taiwan.

It is impossible to determine whether China will use force to take Taiwan at some point in the future. Such force might take a variety of forms, ranging from a contested amphibious assault to concerted missile attacks and bombardments or a naval blockade. China has prepared for all these options, including via 'lawfare' by claiming that the Taiwan Strait is not an international waterway.[56] In any case, the decision on whether to resort to armed force is arguably no longer just in China's hands; rather, it has become a function of the dynamic that has evolved between Beijing and Washington. As such, the US must walk a fine line, taking measures to reduce the risk of a Taiwan conflict while avoiding actions that either encourage Beijing to conclude that peaceful reunification is no longer an option or back China into a corner such that it feels obliged to strike out. This context may well account for Washington's reluctance to abandon its long-standing policy of strategic ambiguity in relation to an intervention in Taiwan despite the fact that a US military intervention is considered a given in PLA planning. The formal abandonment of US strategic ambiguity may well be the action that tips China over the edge. The stakes are high, not just for the region but for the world as a whole: Rhodium Group has estimated that a war in the Taiwan Strait would result in an immediate US$2 trillion hit to the global economy as a result of massive disruption of global supply chains, with the most serious disruptions being to supplies of semiconductors from Taiwan.[57]

CONCLUSION

Towards the end of 2022, the US and China took steps to renew top-level communications with the explicit aim of putting a floor beneath the rapid deterioration in their relations. However, it is difficult to envisage how such a tactical pause can address the intractable issues that divide these two major powers. When presidents Biden and Xi met in November 2022, each sought to reassure the other: Biden that the US did not seek to constrain China, and Xi that China did not seek to displace the US. Both statements were at odds with objective reality, begging the question of whether the two countries can find a modus vivendi without tipping into conflict.

NOTES

1　China, Ministry of Foreign Affairs, 'The Central Conference on Work Relating to Foreign Affairs Was Held in Beijing', 29 November 2014, https://www.fmprc.gov.cn/eng/wjb_663304/ zzjg_663340/xws_665282/xgxw_665284/201412/ t20141201_600270.html.

2　Jacob Mardell, 'The "Community of Common Destiny" in Xi Jinping's New Era', *Diplomat*, 25

October 2017, https://thediplomat.com/2017/10/the-community-of-common-destiny-in-xi-jinpings-new-era/.

3 'China Targets Entertainment TV in Cultural Purge', NPR, 11 January 2012, https://www.npr.org/2012/01/11/144994861/china-targets-entertainment-tv-in-cultural-purge.

4 The video was removed from the internet and is no longer available. However, Chinascope has produced a translation of the narrative. See 'Silent Contest II', Chinascope, 21 April 2014, http://chinascope.org/archives/6449.

5 'Document 9: A ChinaFile Translation', ChinaFile, 8 November 2013, https://www.chinafile.com/document-9-chinafile-translation.

6 Economic Policy Institute, 'The Growing Trade Deficit with China Eliminated 3.7 Million US Jobs Between 2001 and 2018', 30 January 2020, https://www.epi.org/press/growing-china-trade-deficits-eliminates-us-jobs/.

7 James Curran, 'How America's Foreign Policy Establishment Got China Wrong', *National Interest*, 17 December 2018, https://nationalinterest.org/feature/how-america%E2%80%99s-foreign-policy-establishment-got-china-wrong-39012.

8 'Mapping US Chip Company Exposure to China', Semi-Literate, 19 September 2021, https://semiliterate.substack.com/p/mapping-us-chip-company-exposure.

9 Thomas Hale et al., 'Wall Street's New Love Affair with China', *Financial Times*, 28 May 2021, https://www.ft.com/content/d5e09db3-549e-4a0b-8dbf-e499d0606df4.

10 Speech by then US secretary of state Michael R. Pompeo, 'Communist China and the Free World's Future', US Department of State, 23 July 2020, https://2017-2021.state.gov/communist-china-and-the-free-worlds-future/index.html.

11 Hu Xijin, 'China Fully Prepared, Including Militarily, for Any Final Trump Madness', *Global Times*, 6 December 2020, https://www.global-times.cn/page/202012/1209086.shtml.

12 Kyle Morris, 'Milley Secretly Called Chinese Officials Out of Fear Trump Would "Attack" in Final Days, Book Claims', Fox News, 14 September 2021, https://www.foxnews.com/politics/milley-secretly-called-chinese-officials-out-of-fear-trump-would-attack-in-final-days-book-claims.

13 Yuan Peng, 'Yuan Peng: xinguan yiqing yu bainian bianju' 袁鹏：新冠疫情与百年变局 [Yuan Peng: The new coronavirus epidemic and changes (not

seen) in the past hundred years], Aisixiang, 17 June 2020, http://www.aisixiang.com/data/121742.html.

14 Mark Moore, 'Xi Jinping Calls US "Biggest Threat" to China's Security', *New York Post*, 3 March 2021, https://nypost.com/2021/03/03/xi-jinping-calls-us-biggest-threat-to-chinas-security/.

15 'US and China Trade Angry Words at High-level Alaska Talks', BBC News, 19 March 2021, https://www.bbc.co.uk/news/world-us-canada-56452471.

16 Robert Delaney, 'Biden Pledges to Prevent China from Becoming the World's "Leading" Country', *South China Morning Post*, 26 March 2021, https://www.scmp.com/news/china/diplomacy/article/3127051/biden-pledges-prevent-china-becoming-worlds-leading-country.

17 Xinhua, 'Chinese FM Meets US Deputy Secretary of State, Urging Rational China Policy', China.org.cn, 27 July 2021, http://www.china.org.cn/world/2021-07/27/content_77653268.htm.

18 'China Puts Forward Two Lists During Talks with Visiting US Deputy Secretary of State', China.org.cn, 26 July 2021, http://www.china.org.cn/world/2021-07/26/content_77652538.htm.

19 White House, 'Interim National Security Strategic Guidance', March 2021, p. 3, https://www.whitehouse.gov/wp-content/uploads/2021/03/NSC-1v2.pdf.

20 White House, 'National Security Strategy', October 2022, p. 3, https://www.whitehouse.gov/wp-content/uploads/2022/11/8-November-Combined-PDF-for-Upload.pdf.

21 Akshay Ranade, 'How India Influences the Quad', *Diplomat*, 30 May 2022, https://thediplomat.com/2022/05/how-india-influences-the-quad. See also Tanvi Madan, 'India and the Quad', in International Institute for Strategic Studies, *Asia-Pacific Regional Security Assessment 2022: Key Developments and Trends* (Hampshire: Hobbs The Printers for the IISS, 2022), pp. 198–221.

22 Zoya Sheftalovich, 'Why Australia Wanted Out of Its French Submarine Deal', *Politico*, 16 September 2021, https://www.politico.eu/article/why-australia-wanted-out-of-its-french-sub-deal/.

23 Andrew I. Park and Steven Wills, 'The Land Down Under the Sea: AUKUS Is About Submarines, not Bombers', *Hill*, 27 November 2022, https://thehill.com/opinion/national-security/3747130-the-land-down-under-the-sea-aukus-is-about-submarines-not-bombers/.

24 See Japan, Ministry of Defense, 'Defense of Japan 2021', July 2021; and Demetri Sevastopulo, 'Australia Vows to Help US Defend Taiwan from

Chinese Attacks', *Financial Times*, 13 November 2021, https://www.ft.com/content/231df882-6667-4145-bc92-d1a54bccf333.

25 Japan, Ministry of Defense, 'National Defense Strategy', 16 December 2022, https://japan.kantei.go.jp/content/000120034.pdf.

26 'China Urges Europe to Uphold Strategic Autonomy, Practice True Multilateralism', Xinhua, 6 December 2021, https://english.news.cn/europe/20211015/C9A06E8593D000018138F31D1F3A17B3/c.html.

27 NATO, 'Brussels Summit Communiqué', 14 June 2021, https://www.nato.int/cps/en/natohq/news_185000.htm.

28 NATO, 'NATO 2022 Strategic Concept', p. 5, https://www.nato.int/strategic-concept/index.html.

29 Regina M. Abrami, William C. Kirby and F. Warren McFarlan, 'Why China Can't Innovate', *Harvard Business Review*, March 2014, https://hbr.org/2014/03/why-china-cant-innovate.

30 Brandon Vigliarolo, 'US Defense Department Wants to Fund Open, Interoperable 5G', *Register*, 10 April 2022, https://www.theregister.com/2022/04/10/us_govt_has_3m_to/.

31 Jon Bateman, 'Opinion: The Fevered Anti-China Attitude in Washington Is Going to Backfire', *Politico*, 15 December 2022, https://www.politico.com/news/magazine/2022/12/15/china-tech-decoupling-sanctions-00071723.

32 'The CHIPS and Science Act: Here's What's In It', McKinsey, 4 October 2022, https://www.mckinsey.com/industries/public-and-social-sector/our-insights/the-chips-and-science-act-heres-whats-in-it.

33 TSMC, 'TSMC Announces Updates for TSMC Arizona', 6 December 2022, https://pr.tsmc.com/english/news/2977.

34 US, Department of State, 'The Administration's Approach to the People's Republic of China', 26 May 2022, https://www.state.gov/the-administrations-approach-to-the-peoples-republic-of-china/.

35 White House, 'Remarks by National Security Advisor Jake Sullivan at the Special Competitive Studies Project Global Emerging Technologies Summit', 16 September 2022, https://www.whitehouse.gov/briefing-room/speeches-remarks/2022/09/16/remarks-by-national-security-advisor-jake-sullivan-at-the-special-competitive-studies-project-global-emerging-technologies-summit/.

36 US, Department of Commerce, Bureau of Industry and Security, 'Commerce Implements New Export Controls on Advanced Computing and Semiconductor Manufacturing Items to the People's Republic of China (PRC)', 7 October 2022, p. 3, https://www.bis.doc.gov/index.php/documents/about-bis/newsroom/press-releases/3158-2022-10-07-bis-press-release-advanced-computing-and-semiconductor-manufacturing-controls-final/file.

37 'Jishu lingyu de zhongmei zhanlue jingzheng: fenxi yu zhanwang' 技术领域的中美战略竞争与展望 [US–China strategic competition in the field of technology: analysis and perspectives], Peking University International and Strategic Studies Institute report no. 123, 30 January 2022.

38 Figure is author's rough approximation of the combined spending by central government, provincial and municipal administrations.

39 Julie Zhu, 'Exclusive: China Readying $143 Billion Package for Its Chip Firms in Face of US Curbs', Reuters, 14 December 2022, https://www.reuters.com/technology/china-plans-over-143-bln-push-boost-domestic-chips-compete-with-us-sources-2022-12-13/.

40 Nigel Inkster, Emily S. Weinstein and John Lee, 'Ask the Experts: Is China's Semiconductor Strategy Working?', LSE Blogs, 1 September 2022, https://blogs.lse.ac.uk/cff/2022/09/01/is-chinas-semiconductor-strategy-working/.

41 Yen Nee Lee, '2 Charts Show How Much the World Depends on Taiwan for Semiconductors', CNBC, 15 March 2021, https://www.cnbc.com/2021/03/16/2-charts-show-how-much-the-world-depends-on-taiwan-for-semiconductors.html.

42 Antonio Varas et al., 'Strengthening the Global Semiconductor Supply Chain in an Uncertain Era', Boston Consulting Group and Semiconductor Industry Association, April 2021, https://bcgxsia-strengthening-the-global-semiconductor-value-chain-april-2021.pdf.

43 Eleanor Olcott, 'TSMC Faces Pressure to Choose a Side in US–China Tech War', *Financial Times*, 16 April 2021, https://www.ft.com/content/b452221a-5a82-4f5d-9687-093b9707e261.

44 Christopher Vassallo, 'The Silicon Shield Is a

Danger to Taiwan and America', *National Interest*, 15 May 2022, https://nationalinterest.org/feature/%E2%80%98silicon-shield%E2%80%99-danger-taiwan-and-america-202363.

45 Arjun Kharpal, 'China Brings WTO Case Against US and Its Sweeping Chip Export Curbs as Tech Tensions Escalate', CNBC, 14 December 2022, https://www.cnbc.com/2022/12/13/china-brings-wto-case-against-us-chip-export-restrictions.html.

46 White House, 'Remarks by National Security Advisor Jake Sullivan at the Special Competitive Studies Project Global Emerging Technologies Summit'.

47 Du Zhihang and Matthew Walsh, 'US Shifts from "Decoupling" to "Small Yard, High Fence" on China', Nikkei Asia, 16 February 2021, https://asia.nikkei.com/Spotlight/Caixin/US-shifts-from-decoupling-to-small-yard-high-fence-on-China.

48 Aaron L. Friedberg, *Beyond Air–Sea Battle: The Debate over US Military Strategy in Asia*, IISS *Adelphi*, no. 444 (Abingdon: Routledge for the IISS, 2014), pp. 20–38.

49 'Trump's Ten Arms Sales to Taiwan, Military Rebalance in the Taiwan Strait', Institute for National Policy Research, http://inpr.org.tw/m/412-1728-93.php?Lang=en; and 'Taiwan in the National Defense Authorization Act (NDAA), 2023', Taiwan Defense & National Security, 23 December 2022, https://www.ustaiwandefense.com/taiwan-in-the-national-defense-authorization-act-ndaa-2023/.

50 'US on Collision Course if It Keeps Hollowing Out One-China Principle: China Daily Editorial', *China Daily*, 26 December 2022, https://www.chinadaily.com.cn/a/202212/26/WS63a980a7a31057c47eba63a4.html.

51 'China's Xi Tells Biden: Taiwan Issue Is "First Red Line" That Must Not Be Crossed', Reuters, 14 November 2022, https://www.reuters.com/world/asia-pacific/chinas-xi-tells-biden-taiwan-issue-is-first-red-line-that-must-not-be-crossed-2022-11-14/.

52 'CPC Q&A: What Are China's Two Centennial Goals and Why Do They Matter?', Xinhua, 17 October 2017, http://www.xinhuanet.com/english/2017-10/17/c_136686770.htm.

53 Mallory Shelbourne, 'China's Accelerated Timeline to Take Taiwan Pushing Navy in the Pacific, Says CNO Gilday', USNI News, 19 October 2022, https://news.usni.org/2022/10/19/chinas-accelerated-timeline-to-take-taiwan-pushing-navy-in-the-pacific-says-cno-gilday; and Mallory Shelbourne, 'Davidson: China Could Try to Take Control of Taiwan In "Next Six Years"', USNI News, 9 March 2021, https://news.usni.org/2021/03/09/davidson-china-could-try-to-take-control-of-taiwan-in-next-six-years.

54 See Mark Moore and Steven Nelson, 'Biden Says Taiwan Invasion by China Not "Imminent" After Xi Meeting', *New York Post*, 14 November 2022, https://nypost.com/2022/11/14/biden-says-taiwan-invasion-by-china-not-imminent-after-xi-meeting/.

55 Exchanges between author and Chinese scholars, September 2022; and Thomas Corbett, Ma Xiu and Peter W. Singer, 'What Is China Learning from the Ukraine War?', Defense One, 3 April 2022, https://www.defenseone.com/ideas/2022/04/what-lessons-china-taking-ukraine-war/363915/.

56 Peter Martin, 'China Alarms US with Private Warnings to Avoid Taiwan Strait', Bloomberg, 12 June 2022, https://www.bloomberg.com/news/articles/2022-06-12/china-alarms-us-with-new-private-warnings-to-avoid-taiwan-strait?sref=EgYNCHYw&leadSource=uverify%20wall.

57 Charlie Vest, Agatha Kratz and Reva Goujon, 'The Global Economic Disruptions from a Taiwan Conflict', Rhodium Group, 14 December 2022, https://rhg.com/research/taiwan-economic-disruptions/.

CHAPTER **3**

ASIA-PACIFIC NAVAL AND MARITIME CAPABILITIES: THE NEW OPERATIONAL DYNAMICS

NICK CHILDS

Senior Fellow for Naval Forces and Maritime Security, IISS

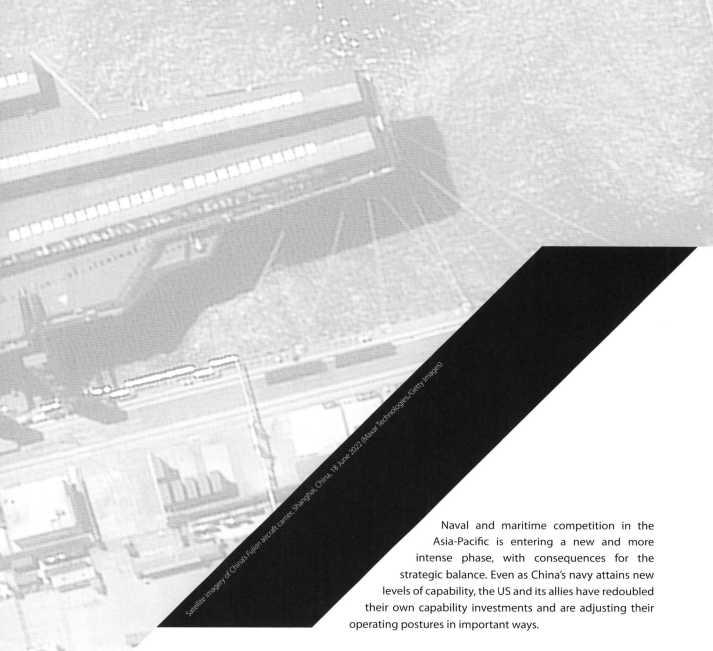

Satellite imagery of China's Fujian aircraft carrier, Shanghai, China, 18 June 2022 (Maxar Technologies/Getty Images)

Naval and maritime competition in the Asia-Pacific is entering a new and more intense phase, with consequences for the strategic balance. Even as China's navy attains new levels of capability, the US and its allies have redoubled their own capability investments and are adjusting their operating postures in important ways.

THE PACING MARITIME ARENA

Notwithstanding the war in Ukraine, which, though broadly perceived as a land war, has significant maritime aspects, the Asia-Pacific remains the 'pacing' maritime arena in terms of technological change, as well as the scale and scope of capability and operational development across the spectrum of activities at sea by navies and other maritime forces.

MANOEUVRING FOR ADVANTAGE

Capability developments in the Asia-Pacific are imposing new operational requirements and patterns of activity on naval forces. These new requirements and patterns are themselves having a strategic effect, adding to the complexity of managing naval competition in the coming years.

AN ASIA-PACIFIC MARITIME PARADOX?

The growth of China's maritime power has been remarkable and continues apace. However, the US and its allies and partners may be clawing back some significant advantages – with the result being that the Chinese navy may find it needs to adjust its ambitions and programmes.

A new phase of naval and maritime competition is under way in the Asia-Pacific. Among the most attention-grabbing regional naval developments of 2022 was the 17 June launch of China's third aircraft carrier, *Fujian*. The event was notable because the vessel is Beijing's first fully indigenous carrier design. It will also be considerably more capable than its two predecessors in service with the People's Liberation Army Navy (PLAN). As a result, it represents a major step in the transformation of the PLAN's overall capabilities and aspirations.

When *Fujian* enters operational service – probably in 2024 or 2025 – it will likely find itself in a regional maritime environment that is in the midst of a significant transformation. As well as the continuing dramatic develop-

The launch ceremony for China's third aircraft carrier, *Fujian*, in Shanghai, 17 June 2022

(Li Tang/VCG via Getty Images)

ment of the PLAN and Beijing's other maritime forces, perhaps equally important are step changes in the naval and maritime capabilities and postures of other regional countries. Greater interactions, interoperability and even integration have all been notable, especially since 2021 and into 2023. As a result, a naval balance that may have appeared to some to be shifting inexorably in China's favour may be starting to swing back towards the United States and its allies and partners. However, assessing how these dynamics are developing – and how to judge their impact on regional stability and the broader Asia-Pacific strategic balance – is a significant analytical challenge.

Notwithstanding the geopolitical storm raging in the Euro-Atlantic area as a result of Russia's full-scale invasion of Ukraine in February 2022 – and the lessons being learned, including in the naval sphere, from the grim conflict that has ensued – in the long term it is China's rise that will continue to make the strategic weather. The latest version of the United States' National Defense Strategy, the public version of which appeared in October 2022, continues to focus on China as the 'pacing challenge' for the US Department of Defense.[1] Likewise, the Asia-Pacific remains the 'pacing maritime arena'. That is true not only in terms of potential high-intensity confrontation but also in the 'grey zone' of competition short of armed conflict. Meanwhile, rapid technological change and shifting strategic dynamics are adding to the potential unpredictability of an increasingly complex regional maritime domain. These dynamics are generating new and challenging capability requirements as well as novel operational patterns.

China's rise as a competitor and potential adversary presents structural challenges for the US that it has not experienced since the Second World War, particularly because in important areas – such as shipbuilding infrastructure – China can outmatch the US (see Figure 3.1). Consequently, the path ahead for the US Navy remains the subject of heated debate in Washington. The role of the United States' allies and partners may well change the game in the maritime arena, as these actors readjust their policies and plans and seek to integrate these more closely with the US and each other.

In the past, Washington has occasionally paid little more than lip service to the notion of cooperation with allies and partners; the inverse has also sometimes been true. However, there is a new understanding in the US that these partnerships are now critical, especially those with Australia, Japan and South Korea. Further, these three states share this understanding and are themselves growing closer together.[2] US officials have asserted that such cooperation can provide an asymmetric advantage (although at present, efforts to assert this advantage remain a work in progress).

Perhaps the most striking new instrument in service of the United States' reinvigorated approach to regional cooperation is the strategic capability agreement between Australia, the United Kingdom and the US known as AUKUS. Announced in September 2021, the agreement's centrepiece is an ambition to jointly deliver a nuclear-powered submarine capability to the Royal Australian Navy. AUKUS also involves a second pillar of collaboration – on key emerging defence tech-

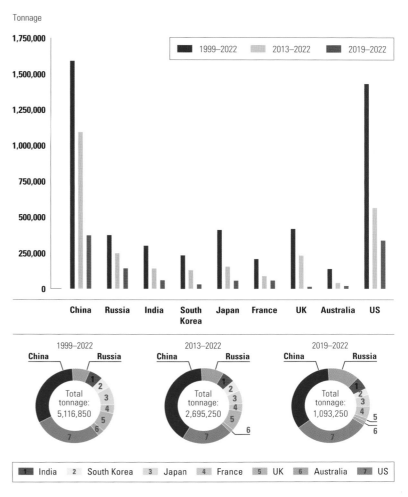

Figure 3.1: **Major new naval tonnage launched for selected navies active in the Asia-Pacific, 1999–2022**

Notes: Tonnage figures are based on approximate full-load displacements. Vessel categories included are submarines, principal surface combatants, corvettes, principal amphibious ships, mine-countermeasures vessels and minelayers, and fleet-replenishment auxiliaries. The UK's figures include *Tide*-class replenishment tankers built in South Korea. Australia's figures include *Canberra*-class LHDs and *Supply*-class replenishment ships built in Spain.

Source: IISS

nologies, many of them central to maritime-domain operations – which could ultimately prove at least as important as the submarine pillar.

The extent to which this potential tapestry of increasingly interoperable and even interchangeable allies and partners comes together in the face of significant challenges and potential frictions will be critical for the regional naval and maritime balance over the next several decades. In this context, extra-regional players, especially European powers, may also prove to have crucial roles – in a way that might not have been envisaged even a few years ago.

The expectation across the region, as well as in Washington and Beijing, is that competition between China and the US will intensify.[3] Meanwhile, the Biden administration's new National Security Strategy, announced in October 2022, describes the world as being in the early years of a 'decisive decade'.[4] All this suggests an added urgency in terms of naval and maritime capability developments, which is a factor that represents a major challenge, including for regional states, given the traditionally long-term character and slow progress of naval procurement. In what will almost inevitably become a more complex and highly charged maritime environment, managing the evolving naval balance is also likely to become even more challenging.

THE PACING MARITIME ARENA

The war in Ukraine has caused a profound security shock in the Euro-Atlantic area and beyond. Perhaps most notably, it has prompted a paradigm shift in perceptions of the likelihood of the return of major war. It is also delivering important operational lessons that are being analysed globally, including in the naval and maritime sphere. And while the conflict is most broadly perceived as predominantly a land war on Europe's doorstep, its maritime aspects are significant.

The naval and maritime lessons include the underscoring of the interconnectedness of the global trading system and its reliance on maritime arteries or sea lines of communication, and therefore the continuing relevance and effectiveness of naval blockade, as witnessed by the swirl of international concern around the blocking of Ukrainian grain exports. The dramatic loss in April 2022 of the Russian Black Sea Fleet flagship *Moskva* – although possibly in part the result of some very particular operating circumstances – was a reminder for maritime forces (including major navies) of the risks of operating in littoral areas in the presence of even relatively modest but accurate anti-ship systems and the means to target such forces. This set of capabilities continues to proliferate among both state and non-state actors, including some in the Asia-Pacific.[5]

Equally, Ukraine's combined use of uninhabited aerial vehicles (UAVs) and uninhabited surface vessels (USVs) to strike at the Black Sea Fleet in its Sevastopol base on 29 October 2022 set alarm bells ringing in naval circles worldwide, even if it may have simply involved the leveraging of emerging technology in pursuit of age-old asymmetric tactics.[6] More broadly, its human tragedy apart, the war in Ukraine has provided a reminder of the cost of high-intensity conflict in material terms – in the inevitable loss of and damage to key platforms and equipment, the very high expenditure of weaponry, and the huge requirements for sustainment and supply. All this clearly has applicability in the Asia-Pacific context, not least in the maritime domain.[7]

Notwithstanding all the lessons that have emerged from Ukraine, it is still the Asia-Pacific that is setting the pace of development of maritime competition. Whether it is in the scale and comprehensive nature of capability development, the reach of precision systems that can hold naval formations at risk or the speed of technical change, it is in this region that benchmarks are being set. Perhaps most notably, China has been developing anti-ship ballistic missile (ASBM) capabilities in the shape of the DF-21D and the DF-26B systems, which have estimated maximum ranges of 1,500 kilometres and 3,000 km, respectively.[8] Beijing is also fielding an array of other long-range anti-ship capabilities, such as the YJ-18 cruise missile, which arms surface ships,

An Australian *Collins*-class submarine and, behind it, the visiting UK nuclear-powered attack submarine HMS *Astute*, at the Royal Australian Navy Base HMAS Stirling in Perth, 29 October 2021

(Richard Wainwright/AAP/PA Images)

submarines and aircraft. Meanwhile, because for many years much of the attention of the US and its allies and partners was diverted to fighting wars in Afghanistan and Iraq, they have to some extent been playing catch-up in this area of military technology.[9]

The introduction of increasingly comprehensive intelligence, surveillance and reconnaissance (ISR) networks – including space-based systems – and thus more formidable and far-reaching targeting capabilities, combined with the prospect of applying artificial intelligence (AI) to systems and data analytics, implies that more capable anti-ship missiles will pose increasing challenges to naval formations, especially those that are forward deployed. For maritime forces, determining the most effective balance between delivering operational effect and the risks involved is becoming ever more difficult.

These developments could change the character of at least the opening exchanges of a future naval confrontation. Indeed, they have been prompting debate on whether the lethality and reach of the threats facing forward-deployed naval forces in particular are so changed that countries now require a different set of capabilities to deliver effect on and from the sea. This debate extends even to the question of whether naval forces themselves are the most effective instruments, at least in the initial stages of any confrontation, or whether alternatives – such as long-range, land-based airpower – could be a major part of the solution.[10]

Compounding these challenges is the advent of new types of hypersonic-weapons capabilities and the threats they pose in a naval context. This new operating environment may have been heralded with the reported first test of a hypersonic weapon from one of the PLAN's new Type-055 *Renhai*-class cruisers in April 2022.[11] The US Navy, for its part, has confirmed that it is pressing ahead with plans to modify its *Zumwalt*-class cruisers to accommodate hypersonic weapons from 2025 and to deploy them aboard its *Virginia*-class nuclear-powered guided-missile submarines from 2029.[12]

Adding to the proliferation of faster, more precise, more manoeuvrable and longer-range anti-ship weapons is the trend towards increased use of uninhabited or autonomous systems, including their employment in swarming tactics. They may be used especially in the increasingly contested and significant underwater and seabed spaces. China is building a range of uninhabited and autonomous systems, including 'glider' submersibles, to gather general information on the maritime environment but also increasingly for more active surveillance as part of a network of deployable and fixed sensor systems.[13] Here, China is to some extent following in the footsteps of the US, which has also been developing its uninhabited underwater vehicle (UUV)-based capabilities. In addition to China and the US, other countries, such as Australia, India, Japan and South Korea, are developing or considering increasingly sophisticated UUVs in response to elevated threat perceptions and the prospects offered by new technology, including AI.[14] This trend goes hand in hand with the continuing development of submarine capabilities. These developments highlight the sub-surface domain's increased strategic significance in regional naval and maritime calculations.

The Asia-Pacific has been setting the pace of challenge not only in terms of high-end naval capability development efforts and confrontation but also in the context of grey-zone operations just below the threshold of armed confrontation. Such operations are being undertaken to apply incremental coercive influence intended to change the maritime status quo, most notably and relentlessly in the South China Sea. This activity has been testing the doctrinal, operational and tactical approaches of maritime security forces as they seek to respond effectively. It is also driving changes in capability requirements, while technological change is also playing its part in this area of competition.

Of course, the Asia-Pacific is not a monolithic region, something which is as true in the maritime domain as it is in any other. Not all regional states see their neighbourhood through the lens of growing

The Royal Australian Navy's HMAS *Adelaide* docked at Vuna Wharf to deliver post-tsunami aid in Nuku'alofa, Tonga, 26 January 2022

(Mary Lyn Fonua/Matangi Tonga/AFP via Getty Images)

major-power competition, or at least they still seek to avoid choosing sides and prefer to pursue regionally orientated solutions. Many have a very different perspective on what are the critical security priorities.

For some regional states, the overarching security concerns relate to the environment and the impact of climate change. The Asia-Pacific is among the regions most affected by this challenge. The US intelligence community and many analysts and commentators identify the small island states of the Pacific as highly vulnerable,[15] and the Asia-Pacific will be in the vanguard of naval adaptation to climate change in terms of the development of capabilities and operational tasking. These capabilities will include platforms to support disaster relief that are able to operate in more extreme conditions, comply with environmental and emissions targets and be crewed and tasked with an increasing focus on environmental response. Tackling climate and environmental challenges and their impacts will also provide opportunities for greater international collaboration. However, it could also be an area where competitive impulses play out: international responses to the January 2022 tsunami in Tonga provided a case study of the challenges, shortfalls, cooperative opportunities and risks of competition.[16]

THE SHIFTING NAVAL BALANCE

The Asia-Pacific is predominantly a maritime theatre. This may not be how it appears in the threat perceptions of all regional states, nor is it always reflected in the position of naval forces in the hierarchy of national military establishments. However, it is in the Asia-Pacific that inter-state frictions seem more likely than ever since 1945 to flare up in the naval and maritime domain. Therefore, the regional naval balance and how it unfolds are of growing importance.

Since the turn of the century, the Asia-Pacific has been through two distinct phases of naval development. It has now entered a third. The first phase saw a striking rise in naval investment and capability development, particularly by China, and a decided shift in the global centre of gravity of naval power towards Asia, fuelled in no small part by the pendulum swing of economic power in the same direction. A second, more hard-edged phase of state-based competition became apparent in the region around 2014–15, as the PLAN's dramatic capability developments began to mature and Beijing's growing assertiveness was becoming increasingly manifest (not least in its spurt of island development and fortification in the South China Sea). Ambitious plans by Australia, India, Japan, South

Korea and the US to bolster their naval capacity were also beginning to deliver results, leaving the regional naval balance in flux.[17]

The third and latest phase of naval development dates from approximately the start of the present decade, signalled by the change of tone in a number of defence-strategy documents produced by the US and other countries, including Australia and Japan, as well as some shifts in plans and postures in the region. The PLAN has continued to make major strides in expanding its fleet, with new, high-capability surface units and other important platforms entering service. China's navy also seems set to move to a new level of potential capability, including the capacity to deploy as a fully fledged blue-water force beyond the island chains, perhaps with an initial focus on the Indian Ocean. Meanwhile, facing a significantly more combative political and diplomatic environment, the US and some of its key allies and partners have also increased their naval investment and operational readiness. Moreover, their efforts are coalescing in ways that could facilitate a shift in the naval balance in their favour. At the same time, all the major players' deployments and operations have become more assertive, making it harder to predict how events at sea in the region might evolve – with particular regard to deployments, the likelihood of a growing incidence of close naval encounters and prospects for elevated levels of a modern incarnation of 'gunboat diplomacy'.

Perhaps at least in part for budget-related reasons, the US Department of Defense now routinely refers to the PLAN as the largest navy in the world, at least in terms of ship numbers. The department's November 2022 report to Congress on China's military power spoke of a Chinese fleet with a 'battle force' (aircraft carriers, destroyers and other major surface combatants, submarines, amphibious ships, mine-warfare vessels and fleet auxiliaries) of some 340 vessels. By a similar measure, the US Navy currently has some 294 vessels,[18] though these tend to be larger and more capable – if older – than their Chinese counterparts. The report added that it expects the PLAN's battle force to grow to 400 ships by 2025 and 440 by 2030.[19] However, at least as significant as the number of ships is the considerable improvement in the quality and capability of PLAN units in service. It is also widely acknowledged that any assessment of Beijing's burgeoning maritime power must also factor in the China Coast Guard – numerically the largest force of its kind in the world – and the People's Armed Forces Maritime Militia (PAFMM).

China's development of ASBMs and its array of other anti-ship missiles and anti-access/area denial (A2/AD) capabilities have provided significant ammunition in the debate over the future utility of aircraft carriers in a high-intensity confrontation and, therefore, the role of the US Navy's carriers (or, indeed, other countries' carriers) in any major scenario involving China. As such, it is perhaps ironic that a major talisman of Beijing's naval ambitions has been its investment in carrier airpower.

It is just over a decade since the PLAN's first carrier, *Liaoning*, was declared operational. (It was originally built by the Soviet Union and sold by Ukraine in unfinished form to China in 2002.) Along with a slightly improved and domestically built sister ship, *Shandong*, the PLAN has been amassing carrier operating experience, including via the deployment of increasingly capable groups of accompanying warships. It has also been extending the ranges at which its carriers have been operating out into the Philippine Sea and to the edge of the Western Pacific, though still cautiously only around 1,000 km from the Chinese mainland.[20]

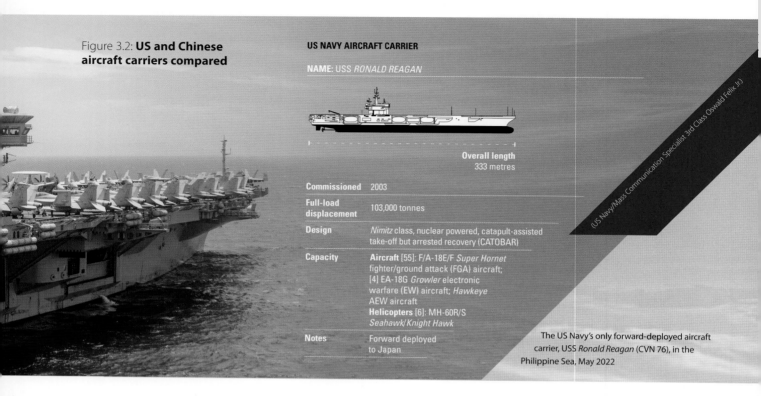

Figure 3.2: **US and Chinese aircraft carriers compared**

US NAVY AIRCRAFT CARRIER

NAME: USS *RONALD REAGAN*

Overall length
333 metres

Commissioned	2003
Full-load displacement	103,000 tonnes
Design	*Nimitz* class, nuclear powered, catapult-assisted take-off but arrested recovery (CATOBAR)
Capacity	**Aircraft** [55]: F/A-18E/F *Super Hornet* fighter/ground attack (FGA) aircraft; [4] EA-18G *Growler* electronic warfare (EW) aircraft; *Hawkeye* AEW aircraft **Helicopters** [6]: MH-60R/S *Seahawk/Knight Hawk*
Notes	Forward deployed to Japan

(US Navy/Mass Communication Specialist 3rd Class Oswald Felix Jr.)

The US Navy's only forward-deployed aircraft carrier, USS *Ronald Reagan* (CVN 76), in the Philippine Sea, May 2022

These carriers offer the prospect of the PLAN conducting enhanced independent task-group missions further afield. However, their relatively modest size of some 65,000–70,000 tonnes full-load displacement and their configuration for short take-off but arrested recovery (STOBAR) air operations limit their strike and power-projection potential. For offensive power, they would probably rely more on the missile armaments of their accompanying escort ships than on their own aircraft. The third Chinese carrier, *Fujian*, is a different proposition. It is larger than its predecessors – at an estimated 80,000 tn or more – and equipped for catapult-assisted take-off but arrested recovery (CATOBAR) operations (using electromagnetic rather than old-style steam catapults) (see Figure 3.2). The vessel will be able to accommodate a more powerful air group. It more closely resembles, albeit still at a somewhat lower level of capability, the US Navy's current force of carriers (though these are nuclear-powered).

Importantly, an even larger Chinese aircraft carrier, most likely with nuclear propulsion, is expected to follow and potentially be operational by the end of the decade, with still more possibly following. As well as significantly bolstering China's ability to present a '360-degree' challenge to Taiwan's air defences, one or more additional carriers would add considerably to the PLAN's blue-water power-projection capacity.[21] In any event, a 'break-out' of a Chinese carrier group on a significantly more far-reaching deployment – perhaps into the Indian Ocean, as a signal of intent to project greater global influence – probably cannot be delayed much longer.

In addition to the continued commissioning of highly capable principal surface combatants, such as Type-055 cruisers and Type-052D (*Luyang* III-class) destroyers, the rapid construction and induction into service of the Type-075 *Yushen*-class large-deck amphibious ships (LHDs) also suggests that China's efforts are focused on rectifying shortfalls in

CHINESE AIRCRAFT CARRIER DEVELOPMENT

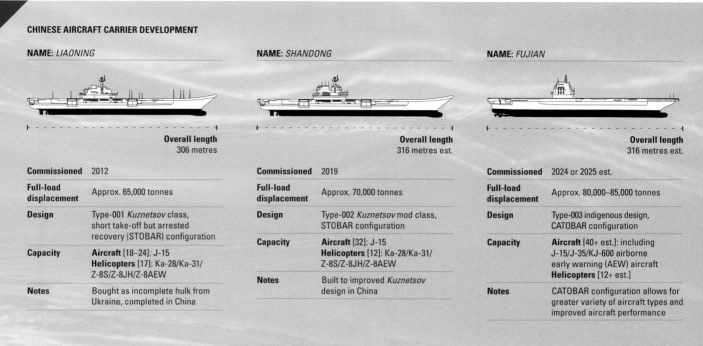

NAME: *LIAONING*

Overall length
306 metres

Commissioned	2012
Full-load displacement	Approx. 65,000 tonnes
Design	Type-001 *Kuznetsov* class, short take-off but arrested recovery (STOBAR) configuration
Capacity	**Aircraft** [18–24]: J-15 **Helicopters** [17]: Ka-28/Ka-31/ Z-8S/Z-8JH/Z-8AEW
Notes	Bought as incomplete hulk from Ukraine, completed in China

NAME: *SHANDONG*

Overall length
316 metres est.

Commissioned	2019
Full-load displacement	Approx. 70,000 tonnes
Design	Type-002 *Kuznetsov* mod class, STOBAR configuration
Capacity	**Aircraft** [32]: J-15 **Helicopters** [12]: Ka-28/Ka-31/ Z-8S/Z-8JH/Z-8AEW
Notes	Built to improved *Kuznetsov* design in China

NAME: *FUJIAN*

Overall length
316 metres est.

Commissioned	2024 or 2025 est.
Full-load displacement	Approx. 80,000–85,000 tonnes
Design	Type-003 indigenous design, CATOBAR configuration
Capacity	**Aircraft** [40+ est.]: including J-15/J-35/KJ-600 airborne early warning (AEW) aircraft **Helicopters** [12+ est.]
Notes	CATOBAR configuration allows for greater variety of aircraft types and improved aircraft performance

Sources: IISS, Military Balance+, milbalplus.iiss.org; Janes Fighting Ships; US Office of Naval Intelligence, www.oni.navy.mil

areas of relative weakness. In addition to amphibious capabilities, these shortfalls include anti-submarine warfare (ASW). Moreover, significantly, the reported US assessment that the PLAN has now equipped its Type-094 *Jin*-class nuclear-powered ballistic-missile submarines with a longer-range submarine-launched ballistic missile (SLBM) – the JL-3 – suggests that these vessels can now potentially threaten the continental US from the relative safety of a protected bastion in the South China Sea, thus altering the strategic dynamics of the underwater battlespace.[22]

While the US Navy remains overall the most capable globally by a significant margin, the gap with the PLAN has clearly narrowed, and it continues to struggle with the question of how to meet the challenge posed by China. Since around 2019, there has been an increasingly tortuous debate in the US over the desirable and achievable size and shape of the navy's future fleet given domestic shipbuilding constraints as well as priorities for capability development. The Department of Defense and the navy have often been at odds with Congress, with the navy looking to pension off older units to free up resources for new vessels and systems, while Congress has been more anxious to expand the fleet by retaining older ships as well as by seeking to add new requests for additional construction. US Chief of Naval Operations (CNO) Admiral Michael Gilday has emphasised the need to improve current readiness, including with parts and weapons stocks, and by servicing and updating the most useful current platforms.[23] Even so, the fleet still faces significant readiness and maintenance challenges.

In his updated Navigation Plan 2022, the CNO set out an ambition for a hybrid US fleet by the 2040s comprising more than 350 crewed vessels and 150 uninhabited surface and sub-surface platforms.[24] The path for achieving that target, however, remains unclear. Indeed, projections suggest that the number of ships and – most notably – submarines will continue to decline gradually until at least the early 2030s.[25] The retirement of platforms like the *Ticonderoga*-class cruisers and *Ohio*-class guided-missile-armed submarines (SSGNs) will result in a significant fall in numbers of operationally valuable vertical launch system (VLS) missile cells, which new ship construction may fail to mitigate.[26]

The US large-deck amphibious assault ship USS *Tripoli* trialling the '*Lightning* carrier' concept with 20 F-35B *Lightning* II fighters aboard, 7 April 2022

(U.S. Department of Defense Archive/Alamy Stock Photo)

However, the arming of the *Zumwalt*-class destroyers and *Virginia*-class SSGNs with hypersonic weapons is not the only offensive missile enhancement that the US Navy is urgently introducing to increase range and lethality, chiefly in response to the Chinese threat. Other enhancements include the stealthy LRASM (long-range anti-ship missile, initially an air-launched weapon) and various LRASM developments and upgrades, as well as a follow-on hypersonic air-launched offensive anti-surface warfare weapon, dubbed HALO.[27] There is also a maritime strike variant of the *Tomahawk* land-attack cruise missile.

The requirements of the Asia-Pacific theatre are also the primary motivation for another US Navy priority: extending the reach of its carrier air wings. Key to achieving this aspiration is the rapid introduction of the MQ-25 *Stingray* UAV, initially as an air-to-air refueller but potentially also for ISR missions[28] and eventually even as a weapons carrier. In another potentially significant move, the US is also exploring a more 'distributed' approach to deploying sea-based airpower with the 'Lightning Carrier' concept of operating the short take-off and vertical landing (STOVL) F-35B variant of the *Lightning* II combat aircraft from the navy's large-deck amphibious ships. To that end, during 2022 the aviation-capable amphibious assault ship USS *Tripoli* undertook a trial deployment with some 20 F-35Bs aboard.[29] This distributed approach could potentially be extended even to forward deployment of US F-35Bs aboard large-deck platforms, including those operated by US allies Australia, Japan and South Korea. Such a deployment has already been tested operationally aboard the British carrier HMS *Queen Elizabeth*.

Similarly, the requirements of the Asia-Pacific theatre are an important influence on the US Navy's effort to develop a family of directed energy weapons, such as high-energy lasers, to counter UAV and USV swarm attacks and high-speed missiles.[30] A San Diego-based destroyer has become the first operational US Navy combatant to be fitted with such a new system to counter UAVs and fast-attack craft: the high-energy laser and optical dazzler and surveillance system known as HELIOS.[31] Furthermore, it is clearly in the Asia-Pacific that the US Navy most wants to press ahead with plans to integrate USVs and UUVs into its fleet, with the aid of an experimental task force based in the Middle East to help gain support for and experience of some of these capabilities.[32]

Perhaps more profoundly, and in some ways more controversially, the US Marine Corps (USMC) is undergoing a dramatic transformation intended to create lighter, more agile and more dispersed units to provide 'stand-in' forces able to operate within China's missile engagement zones.[33] Pursuing the Expeditionary Advanced Base Operations (EABO) concept of rapidly switching between temporary footholds on islands and shorelines would refocus the USMC (absorbed for many years in counter-insurgency operations in Afghanistan and Iraq) on naval and maritime operations, enabling it to conduct anti-ship and even ASW missions.[34] As a result, the USMC is divesting itself of significant elements, such as its main battle tank units, and reorganising into lighter, more versatile formations designated as Marine Littoral Regiments, the first of which was formed in March 2022.[35] The transformation has given birth to the idea for a new light amphibious warship, a development that has led to frictions with the US Navy over shipbuilding priorities.[36] Amid doubts about whether the transformation plan can deliver the effects promised, the reforms have also prompted significant concern and criticism from some of the USMC's most senior retired officers.[37]

For the US Navy, the concept underlying its posture for countering high-intensity threats is 'distributed maritime operations', under which widely dispersed units and offensive capabilities pose challenges to an adversary.[38] At the same time, it seeks to concentrate firepower, including by undertaking more frequent multi-carrier operations involving two or three carrier strike groups (although these groups are to be sufficiently dispersed to aid survivability).[39] However, this approach poses considerable demands in terms of command and control and the need for robust networking capacity.[40]

It remains a subject of intense debate whether these measures, taken together, form a credible US response to the challenge from China. For all China's apparent capability advances, questions remain as to whether Beijing can translate these achievements fully into combat effectiveness, particularly in light of the PLA's relative lack of recent operational experience.[41] Equally, it is argued that many assessments underestimate unique US strengths, including its undersea capabilities, high-quality training and the value of its alliances.[42] Indeed, this last factor is becoming increasingly important as other major naval players in the region adjust their plans to meet a transforming strategic environment.

In 2020, Australia indicated its sense of urgency regarding developing strategic threats in the region via the publication of its Defence Strategic Update. It was released under a conservative coalition government, which was replaced by a Labor administration following the May 2022 federal elections.[43] Among the priorities identified was a need to enhance long-range-strike capabilities, a goal reinforced by the new government in pursuit of 'impactful projection'.[44] The Royal Australian Navy was already well on the way to significantly upgrading its capabilities, particularly following the commissioning of two *Canberra*-class LHDs and three *Hobart*-class *Aegis*-equipped guided-missile destroyers, thus reviving its ability to conduct power-projection missions based on task groups. In addition, highly capable *Hunter*-class frigates (built to a significantly enhanced British Type-26 design) will start entering service in the 2030s. However, the most striking signal that Canberra anticipated an increasingly challenging security environment was the September 2021 AUKUS announcement, with its central pillar of building at least eight nuclear-powered attack submarines (SSNs). The submarine delivery plan revealed on 13 March 2023 will see a phased build-up of capability leading ultimately to Australian indigenous SSN-AUKUS vessels based on a new UK SSN design. It will be hugely challenging for all the partners but should enhance submarine capability for all three, with significant potential impact for the Asia-Pacific.

Perhaps just as important as the subma-rine pillar is the agreement's focus on collaboration on other advanced defence technologies, many with a clear maritime application, including undersea capabilities, hypersonic and counter-hypersonic capa-bilities, AI and autonomy.[45] Australia has confirmed that it will buy *Tomahawk* cruise missiles for its *Hobart*-class destroyers.[46] These missiles are also likely to be fitted to the current *Collins*-class submarines pending the arrival of the new nuclear-powered boats at the end of the 2030s.

Japan's naval power on display as ships of the Maritime Self-Defense Force form the bulk of the Japanese international fleet review held in waters off Japan, 6 November 2022

(STR/JIJI Press/AFP via Getty Images)

Something of a similar step change has been under way – and gaining momentum – in the Japan Maritime Self-Defense Force (JMSDF). Tokyo set out its new defence approach in important defence and security docu-ments released in December 2022. It includes the planned introduction of enhanced stand-off counterstrike capabilities based on the purchase of *Tomahawk* cruise missiles and deployment of an extended-range version of the locally developed Type-12 surface-to-surface missile.[47]

These plans seem set to bolster further the JMSDF's transition to a force with improved defence-in-depth capabilities, greater ability to carry out independent power-projection missions at range, and greater potential to support US-led integrated operations. The JMSDF is, overall, becoming a significantly more robust and capable force in equipment terms and is pressing ahead with modification of its two largest large-deck aviation-capable platforms, the *Izumo*-class ships, to accommodate the F-35B. As a result, they will be able to operate in effect as STOVL light aircraft carriers.[48] *Izumo* itself has already carried out trials with USMC F-35Bs aboard.[49]

The JMSDF also has a formidable flotilla of eight *Aegis*-equipped cruisers and destroyers capable of undertaking ballistic missile defence (BMD).[50] The number of these ships is planned to increase to at least ten with the commissioning of two vessels being procured to replace the abandoned *Aegis* Ashore programme – though these may focus on fixed territorial-defence missions. Some of the new ships are also to be equipped with the *Standard* SM-6 missile, providing enhanced BMD capability but also a surface strike role.[51] The rapid series production of the *Mogami*-class multi-mission frigates – currently under way – will further strengthen the surface fleet.[52] It is expected that this class will ultimately number some 22 vessels. The JMSDF submarine force has also been expanding and has reached its target of 22 operational boats. The latest vessels – including the new *Taigei* class – are fitted with lithium-ion batteries for extended underwater endurance.[53]

The Republic of Korea Navy has also been significantly expanding its blue-water capa-bilities. In particular, it has been building up an impressive surface fleet, currently centred on *Sejong*-class (KDD-III) *Aegis*-equipped cruisers. A second batch of *Sejong*-class ships – able to undertake BMD – is under construction; six of these vessels are likely to be in service by the end of the decade.[54] The new *Daegu* class of frigates has also been entering service, with plans for improved ships of this class. Together, these developments represent a considerable increase in not just the tonnage but also the capability of South Korea's surface fleet.

North Korea's fleet of midget and patrol submarines poses particular challenges for South Korea and is forcing the country to improve its ASW capabilities,[55] while Pyongyang's apparent pursuit of a nuclear-armed SLBM capability is raising wider alarms in the region and beyond.[56] Seoul has made strenuous efforts to transform its submarine flotilla, including by introducing the *Chang Bogo* III (KSS-III) class outfitted with conventionally armed SLBMs. Larger and more capable variants of these submarines are under construction and planned, promising to provide Seoul with significant additional naval capability.[57]

Singapore's Prime Minister Lee Hsien Loong and German Chancellor Olaf Scholz at the naming ceremony for two new Republic of Singapore Navy Type 218SG submarines in Kiel, Germany, 13 December 2022

(Marcus Brandt/picture-alliance/dpa/AP Images)

For the time being, South Korea's ambition to procure a STOVL-equipped light aircraft carrier of around 30,000 tn under the CVX programme appears in abeyance. There are suggestions, however, that some form of carrier programme may eventually proceed, possibly involving a larger design and with a domestically developed carrier-borne combat aircraft.[58] The focus on carriers may be connected to the continued and growing interest in and commitment to carrier capabilities across the region. Moreover, further modification of the navy's plans – with renewed focus on blue-water, task-group-orientated operations – is possible given the constantly evolving regional strategic dynamics, not least in relation to China and mounting concerns about a Taiwan contingency, growing unease regarding the security of sea lines of communication, and Seoul's desire to reinforce security and defence relations with the US and even Japan.[59]

Other regional navies have also been making significant strides in modernising and enhancing their capabilities. While some belong to states anxious to avoid becoming embroiled in the increasing frictions of great-power competition, the reality of an increasingly tense regional environment is adding extra impetus to many naval procurement plans.

The potential advent during the current decade of Taiwan's first indigenous submarines,[60] combined with its growing inventory of missile-armed corvettes, will increase Taipei's sea-denial capabilities (although there are still doubts about the submarine project's viability and cost-effectiveness).[61] As well as seeking to build up its asymmetric forces, including the corvettes, Taiwan has begun to modernise its larger surface forces, with the arrival of a new and heavily armed amphibious assault ship (with others to follow) and plans for a new frigate class.[62] However, delivering on these ambitions will be challenging; again, questions abound regarding the cost-effectiveness of some of these investments in light of the challenges Taiwan faces.

Amid much fanfare, in December 2022 Germany's ThyssenKrupp Marine Systems launched the second and third of four new-generation Type 218SG submarines for

Singapore's navy.[63] Singapore is also planning to modernise its naval patrol forces with a new design of multi-role combat vessels intended to serve as motherships for various uncrewed platforms, while there is a long-standing ambition for a new Joint Multi-Mission Ship that would bolster Singapore's amphibious and power-projection capacity.[64] Indonesia, meanwhile, is planning major enhancements of its warship inventory, with orders for six Italian FREMM frigates and two UK-design *Arrowhead* 140 vessels, the latter to be built locally. Reports also indicate the possibility of ordering frigates from Japan as well as ongoing ambitions to purchase *Scorpene* submarines from France. Further enhancements in the navy's smaller patrol forces are perhaps no less significant, with continuing construction of patrol craft in considerable numbers.[65]

The Philippine Navy is also attempting to bolster its maritime-patrol and -surveillance capabilities, notably with South Korean-built vessels, including two new corvettes and six new offshore patrol ships.[66] Meanwhile, the Vietnamese Navy remains a force to be reckoned with, boasting as its main equipment six Russian-built *Improved Kilo* submarines armed with *Klub*-S anti-ship and land-attack cruise missiles, and four *Gepard* 3.9 (Project 11661E) corvettes – also supplied by Russia – with 3M24E *Uran*-E (RS-SS-N-25 *Switchblade*) anti-ship missiles.

On 2 September 2022, India commissioned its first domestically produced aircraft carrier, INS *Vikrant*, meaning it now possesses two operational carriers, although they are configured for STOBAR operations and therefore have some limits on their capacity. There are also ambitions for a third carrier to enter service within the next decade.[67] While India's naval expansion has been slow to materialise, the commissioning of the second Project 15B *Visakhapatnam*-class guided-missile destroyer in December 2022,[68] followed by its fifth *Scorpene*-type submarine in January 2023, shows that its capabilities are developing steadily, with significant implications for the naval balance in the Indian Ocean and India's potential capacity to project power further afield. Concurrently, Pakistan is undertaking a naval-modernisation programme that is raising the stakes. It includes plans to acquire a class of four Chinese-built Type-054AP frigates, four Turkish-designed *Babur*-class light frigates, and eight planned *Hangor*-class submarines (export versions of China's Type-039B *Yuan* class).[69]

MANOEUVRING FOR ADVANTAGE

When it comes to addressing and assessing changing strategic dynamics and frictions, capabilities developments are important. However, also critical (and closely connected to capability) are shifting patterns and postures of operational deployment. These have also evolved significantly in the Asia-Pacific.

Notwithstanding the relatively cautious development of the PLAN's carrier operations and the fact that the preponderance of China's naval power remains concentrated close to its coasts and within the first island chain, Beijing's naval and maritime activities – involving all China's military maritime agencies – have grown increasingly ambitious. The PLAN's continuous deployments since 2008 into the Indian Ocean, though primarily in a counter-piracy role, have long been seen as a signal of intent to extend its reach while also serving the strategic purpose of boosting its experience of long-range deployments.

Other notable indicators of Beijing's intent and the PLAN's expanding horizons include naval forays north of Alaska (on at least one occasion in company with Russian warships[70]) and increasingly in waters close to Australia – in the latter case raising particular frictions when Canberra claimed that a Chinese warship had used a laser device to dazzle the crew of a Royal Australian Air Force surveillance aircraft.[71] The security agreement forged between China and Solomon Islands in 2022 fuelled debate over potential Chinese naval-basing ambitions in the Southwest Pacific (and the attendant strategic implications).[72] The prospect of Chinese access to an enhanced base facility in Cambodia will also provide the

Chinese navy ships prepare to depart for the Gulf of Aden and the waters off Somalia to maintain Beijing's long-standing presence and escort mission in the area, 18 May 2022

(VCG/VCG via Getty Images)

PLAN's deployment capacity with additional options, including particularly into the Indian Ocean, supplementing its first foreign support facility in Djibouti.[73] Meanwhile, the increasing assertiveness and coercive tactics of the China Coast Guard and the PAFMM have also raised concern, while apprehensions remain over the China Coast Guard Law of 2021 and how Beijing might apply it to support more forceful action in waters that China disputes with others.[74]

The PLAN's patterns of activities serve an operational purpose in addition to geopolitical aims, while the increasingly complex character of its exercises is apparently intended to improve skills applicable to more complex operations.[75] The challenge for all interested parties (including Beijing's leadership) – particularly in light of what has been revealed about the performance of Russian forces in Ukraine – is assessing just how much progress is being made and how that might translate into operational performance against a peer adversary.

China has not been the only actor elevating its naval activity in the Asia-Pacific. Indeed, the transformation in the maritime posture and practice of the US and its allies and partners may prove to be equally telling in terms of how the regional naval balance will play out. The drumbeat of US Navy freedom-of-navigation operations (FONOPs) and transits of key waterways like the Taiwan Strait has been one element of this evolving posture.[76] The latest US maritime strategy, released in late 2020, notably referred to a 'continuum' of competition and highlighted the incremental, sub-threshold character of the challenges to the rules-based international order being faced at sea, calling for US naval power to adopt 'a more assertive posture' in day-to-day operations and accept calculated risk to confront 'malign behavior'.[77] This was reinforced by the published version of the 2022 US National Defense Strategy, which placed new emphasis – for all the US armed services – on a 'campaigning' approach of persistent activities to address grey-zone challenges in particular.[78] The US Third Fleet, based on the west coast of the US, is also now taking on a more operational role in support of the Seventh Fleet in the Western Pacific.[79] US Navy carrier-strike-group deployments have been enhanced to include multi-carrier exercises. The US Navy has also boosted the number of SSNs it forward deploys to Guam – to five, from two just a few years ago – and is planning to expand its facilities to support such deployments there.[80]

Nevertheless, it is a huge challenge for the US Navy to deliver an enhanced forward presence while also sustaining the fleet and seeking to transition from legacy to emerging capabilities and technologies. In this context, the third element of the regional naval-balance equation – the increasing integration of the other major regional naval players with each other and with the US – assumes greater significance.

The US uncrewed trials vessel *Sea Hunter* arrives at Pearl Harbor to take part in the *Rim of the Pacific* exercises, 29 June 2022

(U.S. Navy photo by Mass Communication Specialist 2nd Class Aiko Bongolan via AP)

While multilateral naval exercises have taken place in the region for decades, in the early 2020s they are evolving in new ways, with participants according such exercises greater significance. For example, in 2022, the US-led *Rim of the Pacific* (RIMPAC) exercise involved five large-deck aviation-capable platforms from four states – Australia, Japan, South Korea and the US. It also featured a greater number of more realistic, 'free-play' activities than previous RIMPACs. There was also a significant contribution from uncrewed vessels and other uninhabited platforms.[81] Meanwhile, the *Malabar* series of exercises has developed from a bilateral US–India arrangement into a four-state framework involving Australia and Japan, while its activities have increasingly included more complex tasks. The November 2022 *Malabar* exercise, hosted by the JMSDF and conducted off Japan in the Philippine Sea, included the USS *Ronald Reagan* carrier strike group. The exercise under-scored the increased emphasis being placed on the integration of operations between US carriers and allies and partners, including in key operating areas like the Philippine Sea.[82]

Both Australia (since 2017) and Japan (since 2019) have instigated regional task-group deployments, usually led by one of their large-deck aviation-capable warships.[83] As well as projecting influence, such deployments have enhanced participants' ability to engage in multilateral manoeuvres aimed at both training and strategic signalling. October 2022 saw a notable first, with a four-state exercise involving Australia, Canada, Japan and the US in the South China Sea.[84] In terms of dispositions, the Royal Australian Navy has drawn back from its long-standing engagement in the Middle East to concentrate on the Asia-Pacific.[85] The Royal Canadian Navy, in light of a new national Asia-Pacific strategy, aims to increase its deployment pattern in the region to three frigates during each year, ideally with a support ship also in the region.[86] Canadian vessels transited the Taiwan Strait in company with US Navy ships in October 2021 and September 2022 and there are plans for further such missions.[87] Meanwhile, growing concern about North Korea's nuclear and missile activities has seen a renewed emphasis on combined naval BMD exercises involving Japan, South Korea and the US.[88]

Another significant aspect of this trend towards greater interconnectedness and cooperation has been the growing number of support agreements between key players. Among these have been a reciprocal access agreement between Japan and Australia and a similar one between Japan and the UK, while Manila and Washington have agreed to boost base support in the Philippines for US forces under their Enhanced Defense Cooperation Agreement.[89]

The Royal Canadian Navy *Halifax*-class frigate HMCS *Vancouver* transits the Taiwan Strait in company with the US Navy guided-missile destroyer USS *Higgins*, 20 September 2022

(Mass Communication Specialist 1st Class Donavan K. Patubo/U.S.Navy via AP)

Reflecting a US campaigning approach that increasingly acknowledges that grey-zone challenges across the spectrum of competition require a response, the latest US maritime strategy emphasises the importance of integration between the US sea services, including the US Coast Guard. The profile and presence of the US Coast Guard in the Western Pacific has been increased, notably through some important demonstrative missions, again including transits of the Taiwan Strait since 2019.[90]

Nevertheless, it remains the case that the US Navy's focus (and that of some other major Western navies) on high-end war-fighting capabilities has resulted in a deficit in lower-end maritime-security capacity. While some of these deficiencies are being addressed, a number of commentators argue that the US Navy should adopt an even more disaggregated force structure and even more ubiquitous deployments, with larger numbers of smaller crewed and uncrewed platforms that can also respond more comprehensively to different levels of challenge. Another criticism is that the US strategy of periodic, high-level demonstration missions, such as FONOPs, has not produced the desired deterrent effect and that even more persistence is needed, with a range of other regional actors playing more prominent roles with the US Navy in support.[91]

Indeed, some other allies and partners may be better placed to take a leading role in areas where the great-power dynamic is second to other security concerns and where capacity-building for maritime constabulary work or disaster relief will produce more influence. Of note in this regard is Australia's Pacific Maritime Security Program, intended to generate improved maritime-security capacity, notably through the supply of new patrol craft to Pacific Islands states.[92]

HOW GREAT A GAME AT SEA?

For some observers, these evolving dynamics of naval and maritime manoeuvre and investment are starting to resemble something of a 'great game' at sea that is – while global in nature – focused particularly on the Asia-Pacific.[93] Indeed, the increasing naval engagement (or, in some cases, re-engagement) of important external players is one aspect of the broader recognition of the region's growing significance as a centre of gravity of global economic development and strategic challenge.

In this context, the return of a British naval presence to the region has perhaps attracted most attention and debate. A re-engagement was already under way before the 2021 roll-out of the UK's 'Indo-Pacific tilt', the Integrated Review of Security, Defence, Development and Foreign Policy and the accompanying Defence Command Paper: these steps reinforced an impulse that already existed.[94] Added to this was the operational debut of the UK's regenerated carrier-strike capability via the Carrier Strike Group 2021 (CSG21) deployment to the region led by the carrier HMS *Queen Elizabeth*.

In defence and particularly naval terms, the message has been that this renewed British engagement will include a mix of forces. To provide a persistent lower-level capability in the maritime arena, two *River*-class Batch 2 offshore patrol vessels have already been forward deployed – essentially for defence diplomacy. These vessels are to be supplemented by new Type-31 frigates. The UK also foresees the more periodic deployment of slightly more capable forces, such as a small amphibious formation dubbed a Littoral Response Group, and the episodic deployment of high-level capability, such as a carrier strike group. A striking feature of the CSG21 deployment was an exercise bringing together HMS *Queen Elizabeth*, two US carriers and the Japanese *Hyuga*-class ship *Ise* – a formation of four 'flat-tops' from three states.[95]

An important question is whether this revived British interest will be credible and sustainable, not least in light of the UK's other defence commitments. The ambition appears to be there, with talk even of the extended forward deployment of one of the UK's carriers, although this would probably only be possible in an even wider multinational format than the CSG21.[96] Depending on what is decided regarding Australia's new nuclear-powered submarine capability, another possibility could be the periodic forward deployment into the region of a Royal Navy *Astute*-class SSN.

A major challenge for the UK will be how to sustain the operational effectiveness of its lower-level forces as regional developments raise the bar on what constitutes minimum credible capability. This will also be an important question for France, which regards itself as a regional power in the Asia-Pacific by virtue of its territories there and maintains a significant permanent presence. The French Navy is grappling with this challenge as it seeks to renew its naval patrol and surveillance assets, not least its long-serving *Floreal*-class light frigates.[97] Following an Asia-Pacific deployment by the carrier *Charles de Gaulle* in 2019, France is aiming for a further such mission in 2025.[98] In early 2023 the carrier undertook its longest power-projection display yet, launching aircraft from the Indian Ocean to forward deploy to Singapore, a distance of 4,000 km.[99] This followed the navy's 2021 forward deployment to the region of the SSN *Emeraude* with a support ship.[100] These developments are indicators of France's ambition to expand its naval operations and presence in the Asia-Pacific.

The German Navy's dispatch of the frigate *Bayern* to the region on a seven-month deployment during 2021 and 2022 was further evidence of increased European interest and naval ambition in the Asia-Pacific. It was the first such mission for nearly two decades, with a further plan to deploy two more ships in 2024. Likewise, the Netherlands, having attached its frigate *Evertsen* to the UK's CSG21 deployment, has set out plans to deploy a warship to the Asia-Pacific every two years – a significant commitment given the Dutch navy's limited resources.[101]

In its Strategy for Cooperation in the Indo-Pacific published in September 2021, the European Union stated that it 'will explore ways to ensure enhanced naval deployments by its Member States in the region'.[102] Just what that will mean and how it might deliver it are open questions, given the limited success of the EU in the defence and security field so far and in light of the renewed focus on Euro-Atlantic security following the outbreak of the war in Ukraine. Given resource constraints and a probable lack of political consensus among EU member states regarding long-range deployments, the northwestern Indian Ocean may be the most likely area to see an enhanced European maritime security role. Furthermore, the UK has maintained a long-standing naval presence in and around the Gulf, and there is a limited European maritime monitoring operation there (European Maritime Awareness in the Strait of Hormuz – EMASOH) and an EU Naval Force mission off the Horn of Africa – EUNAVFOR *Operation Atalanta* – although the long-term sustainment of the latter may be in question.

An enhanced European maritime-security role in the northwestern Indian Ocean may not be insignificant if it relieves allies and partners of a burden, thereby allowing them to concentrate their efforts elsewhere in the region. However, for some European capitals, notably London and Paris, there is at least an implicit commitment to go further if a crisis were to erupt in the Western Pacific, although possibly by responding on a limited scale with niche capabilities. Nevertheless, their efforts could make a significant contribution in concert with the greater commitment of other regional players. For all European powers, a clue to the fact that they would need to adjust their threat perceptions – currently focused on the Euro-Atlantic area – when operating in the Asia-Pacific can be gleaned from the relative lack of magazine depth (in terms of VLS cells) of major European-design naval platforms, compared to those of the more regular Asia-Pacific naval operators (see Figure 3.3).

Figure 3.3: **Magazine depths of selected principal surface combatants**

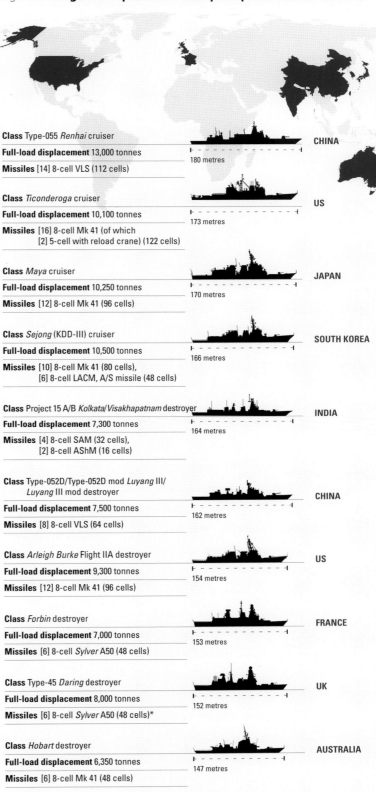

Class Type-055 *Renhai* cruiser
Full-load displacement 13,000 tonnes
Missiles [14] 8-cell VLS (112 cells)
CHINA — 180 metres

Class *Ticonderoga* cruiser
Full-load displacement 10,100 tonnes
Missiles [16] 8-cell Mk 41 (of which [2] 5-cell with reload crane) (122 cells)
US — 173 metres

Class *Maya* cruiser
Full-load displacement 10,250 tonnes
Missiles [12] 8-cell Mk 41 (96 cells)
JAPAN — 170 metres

Class *Sejong* (KDD-III) cruiser
Full-load displacement 10,500 tonnes
Missiles [10] 8-cell Mk 41 (80 cells), [6] 8-cell LACM, A/S missile (48 cells)
SOUTH KOREA — 166 metres

Class Project 15 A/B *Kolkata/Visakhapatnam* destroyer
Full-load displacement 7,300 tonnes
Missiles [4] 8-cell SAM (32 cells), [2] 8-cell AShM (16 cells)
INDIA — 164 metres

Class Type-052D/Type-052D mod *Luyang* III/ *Luyang* III mod destroyer
Full-load displacement 7,500 tonnes
Missiles [8] 8-cell VLS (64 cells)
CHINA — 162 metres

Class *Arleigh Burke* Flight IIA destroyer
Full-load displacement 9,300 tonnes
Missiles [12] 8-cell Mk 41 (96 cells)
US — 154 metres

Class *Forbin* destroyer
Full-load displacement 7,000 tonnes
Missiles [6] 8-cell *Sylver* A50 (48 cells)
FRANCE — 153 metres

Class Type-45 *Daring* destroyer
Full-load displacement 8,000 tonnes
Missiles [6] 8-cell *Sylver* A50 (48 cells)*
UK — 152 metres

Class *Hobart* destroyer
Full-load displacement 6,350 tonnes
Missiles [6] 8-cell Mk 41 (48 cells)
AUSTRALIA — 147 metres

SAM: surface-to-air missile, LACM: land-attack cruise missile, A/S: anti-submarine, AShM: anti-ship missile, VLS: vertical launch system
Note: Missile figures for each vessel are based on the number of VLS cells.
*To be fitted with additional 24 cells for *Sea Ceptor* SAM
Sources: IISS, Military Balance+, milbalplus.iiss.org; Janes Fighting Ships

Balancing these developments is the fact that Russia cannot be counted out as a Pacific naval power. Its 2022 Maritime Doctrine appears to place the Pacific second only to the Arctic in terms of priority, while Moscow has referred previously to the enormous significance of the Pacific Ocean for Russia. The new doctrine spelled out ambitions for developing Russia's naval presence and maritime industrial capacity (including, perhaps unrealistically, aspirations to construct aircraft carriers).[103] The Russian Pacific Fleet has received some significant enhancements in recent years, including submarines and modern surface vessels, although its main oceangoing surface combatants remain legacies of the Soviet era. There have been notable recent joint exercises with China, including some in waters near Japan. While these exercises may have been limited in scope and perhaps demonstrated more show than substance, signalling is important in the context of how Sino-Russian relations might develop.

In addition, the recent signs of naval cooperation between China, Iran and Russia in the northwestern Indian Ocean could prove a complicating factor in the region in the context of a crisis elsewhere in the Asia-Pacific.[104] The Iranian navy appears to be extending its own reach – with a transit by two vessels through the South Pacific as part of a long-range deployment – in another sign of the continuing changes in regional naval dynamics.[105]

AN ASIA-PACIFIC MARITIME PARADOX?

Amid the swirl of cross-currents that characterise the new phase of Asia-Pacific maritime competition, it is difficult to determine precisely where the naval balance now stands and the trajectory of its evolution. This challenge is compounded by the shadow of the Ukraine war and the need to digest the implications and lessons of that conflict, many of which have created new uncertainties. Nevertheless, it is possible to contend that although the PLAN's transformation has produced a critical mass of naval power both for operations close to home and incipiently for blue-water operations, the coming together of the plans and new postures of the US Navy and its allies and partners – combined with the increased urgency and ambition of many of their procurement programmes – may be swinging the strategic pendulum back in the latter's favour. The result is something of an Asia-Pacific maritime paradox: while China's maritime power has never been greater and the PLAN continues to grow at a remarkable rate, the US and its allies and partners may be clawing back some significant advantages such that the PLAN itself may find that it needs to adjust its own ambitions and programmes.

In the absence of recent high-intensity naval warfare, attempts to assess regional naval developments are bound to be somewhat theoretical. The fact of rapid technological change is adding another layer of complexity. Questions also remain about whether the US and its allies and partners can devise and enact the kind of comprehensive campaigning strategies that they seem to acknowledge are necessary to counter the persistent challenges to the status quo. The upshot of all these developments is a general increase of assertiveness at sea – not just by China but also by the US and others in the region – that may yet deliver strengthened deterrence but also carries increased risk and a greater danger of miscalculation.

NOTES

1 US, Department of Defense, '2022 National Defense Strategy', 27 October 2022, p. 4, https://media.defense.gov/2022/Oct/27/2003103845/-1/-1/1/2022-NATIONAL-DEFENSE-STRATEGY-NPR-MDR.PDF.

2 John Grady, 'CNO Gilday: Expanding Military Cooperation between South Korea, Japan "a Necessity"', USNI News, 13 January 2023, https://news.usni.org/2023/01/13/cno-gilday-expanding-military-cooperation-between-south-korea-japan-a-necessity.

3 See, for example, James Crabtree, 'US–China Rivalry Set to Intensify in 2023', *Straits Times*, 12 December 2022, https://www.straitstimes.com/opinion/us-china-rivalry-set-to-intensify-in-2023.

4 White House, 'National Security Strategy', October 2022, p. 6, https://www.whitehouse.gov/wp-content/uploads/2022/10/Biden-Harris-Administrations-National-Security-Strategy-10.2022.pdf.

5 Douglas Barrie and Nick Childs, 'The Moskva Incident and Its Wider Implications', IISS Military Balance Blog, 29 April 2022, https://www.iiss.org/blogs/military-balance/2022/04/the-moskva-incident-and-its-wider-implications.

6 Nick Childs, 'Ukraine: Unconventional Impact at Sea?', IISS Military Balance Blog, 11 November 2022, https://www.iiss.org/blogs/military-balance/2022/11/ukraine-unconventional-impact-at-sea.

7 See, for example, Brent D. Sadler, 'Applying Lessons of the Naval War in Ukraine for a Potential War with China', The Heritage Foundation, Backgrounder no. 3743, 5 January 2023, https://www.heritage.org/sites/default/files/2023-01/BG3743_0.pdf.

8 Office of the Secretary of Defense, US Department of Defense, 'Military and Security Developments Involving the People's Republic of China 2022', 29 November 2022, pp. 64–5, https://media.defense.gov/2022/Nov/29/2003122279/-1/-1/1/2022-MILITARY-AND-SECURITY-DEVELOPMENTS-INVOLVING-THE-PEOPLES-REPUBLIC-OF-CHINA.PDF.

9 Tim Fish, 'Decisive Development: The Build-up of Long-range Naval Missile Capabilities in the Indo-Pacific', *Jane's Defence Weekly*, 10 January 2022.

10 See, for example, Robert Haddick, 'Defeat China's Navy, Defeat China's War Plan', War on the Rocks, 21 September 2022, https://warontherocks.com/2022/09/defeat-chinas-navy-defeat-chinas-war-plan/.

11 Minnie Chan, 'Chinese Navy Shows Off Hypersonic Anti-ship Missiles in Public', *South China Morning Post*, 20 April 2022, https://www.scmp.com/news/china/military/article/3174946/chinese-navy-shows-hypersonic-anti-ship-missiles-public.

12 Sam LaGrone, 'Navy Details Hypersonic Missile Plan for Zumwalt Destroyers, Virginia Submarines', USNI News, 3 November 2022, https://news.usni.org/2022/11/03/navy-details-hypersonic-missiles-on-zumwalt-destroyers-virginia-submarines.

13 Ryan Martinson, 'Gliders with Ears: A New Tool in China's Quest for Undersea Security', Center for International Maritime Security, 21 March 2022, https://cimsec.org/gliders-with-ears-a-new-tool-in-chinas-quest-for-undersea-security/.

14 Oishee Majumdar and Nishant Kumar, 'Making It Big: Asia-Pacific's Increasing Focus on Large and Extra-large UUVs', *Jane's Defence Weekly*, 22 November 2022.

15 US, Office of the Director of National Intelligence, 'Climate Change and International Responses Increasing Challenges to US National Security Through 2040', 21 October 2021, https://www.dni.gov/files/ODNI/documents/assessments/NIE_Climate_Change_and_National_Security.pdf.

16 Joanne Wallis, Henrietta McNeil and Anna Powles, 'Tongan Disaster Highlights Lack of Co-ordination in Regional Response', *Strategist*, Australian Strategic Policy Institute, 28 January 2022, https://www.aspistrategist.org.au/tongan-disaster-highlights-lack-of-coordination-in-regional-response/.

17 See IISS, *Asia-Pacific Regional Security Assessment 2016: Key Developments and Trends* (East Sussex: Hastings Print, 2016), pp. 145–61.

18 'USNI News Fleet and Marine Tracker', USNI News, 13 February 2023, https://news.usni.org/2023/02/13/usni-news-fleet-and-marine-tracker-feb-13-2023.

19 Office of the Secretary of Defense, US Department of Defense, 'Military and Security Developments Involving the People's Republic of China 2022', p. 52.

20 Commander Michael Dahm USN (Ret.), 'Lessons from the Changing Geometry of PLA Navy Carrier Ops', US Naval Institute,

Proceedings, vol. 149/1/1,439, January 2023, https://www.usni.org/magazines/proceedings/2023/january/lessons-changing-geometry-pla-navy-carrier-ops.

21 Patrick M. Cronin, 'The Significance of China's Fujian Aircraft Carrier', *Straits Times*, 5 July 2022, https://www.straitstimes.com/opinion/the-significance-of-chinas-fujian-aircraft-carrier.

22 Anthony Capaccio, 'China Has Put Longer-range ICBMs on Its Nuclear Subs, US Says', Bloomberg, 18 November 2022, https://www.bloomberg.com/news/articles/2022-11-18/us-says-china-s-subs-armed-with-longer-range-ballistic-missiles.

23 Richard R. Burgess, 'CNO Holds Fast on Ship Decommissionings, Fleet Readiness', *Seapower Magazine*, 19 October 2022, https://seapowermagazine.org/cno-holds-fast-on-ship-decommissionings-fleet-readiness/.

24 US, Chief of Naval Operations, 'Navigation Plan 2022', 26 July 2022, p. 10, https://media.defense.gov/2022/Jul/26/2003042389/-1/-1/1/NAVIGATION%20PLAN%202022_SIGNED.PDF.

25 US, Congressional Research Service, 'Navy Force Structure and Shipbuilding Plans: Background and Issues for Congress', 21 December 2022, p. 13, https://sgp.fas.org/crs/weapons/RL32665.pdf.

26 Michael Fabey, 'USN Shipbuilding Plan Could Cut Total Number of Missile VLS Cells, CBO Says', *Jane's Navy International*, 17 September 2021.

27 Lee Willett, 'HALO Programme Accelerates US Navy Hypersonic Capability Drive', Naval News, 5 September 2022, https://www.navalnews.com/naval-news/2022/09/halo-us-navy-hypersonic-capability/.

28 Megan Eckstein, 'Boeing Demonstrates MQ-25's Utility as Surveillance Drone', *Defense News*, 16 September 2022, https://www.defensenews.com/naval/2022/09/16/boeing-demonstrates-mq-25s-utility-as-surveillance-drone/.

29 Maj. Mason Englehart, '3rd Marine Aircraft Wing, Expeditionary Strike Group 3 Demonstrate Lightning Carrier Concept', US Marine Corps, 11 April 2022, https://www.marines.mil/News/News-Display/Article/2995310/3rd-marine-aircraft-wing-expeditionary-strike-group-3-demonstrate-lightning-car/.

30 US, Congressional Research Service, 'Navy Shipboard Lasers: Background and Issues for Congress', 21 December 2022, https://sgp.fas.org/crs/weapons/R44175.pdf.

31 Joseph Trevithick, 'Here's Our First Look at a HELIOS Laser-armed Navy Destroyer', War Zone, 23 August 2022, https://www.thedrive.com/the-war-zone/heres-our-first-look-at-a-helios-laser-armed-navy-destroyer.

32 Jon Gambrell, 'US Navy Launches Mideast Drone Task Force amid Iran Tensions', AP News, 8 September 2021, https://apnews.com/article/middle-east-iran-dubai-united-arab-emirates-bahrain-fe5517a7979e037ae6e266b885cc7719.

33 US Marine Corps, 'Force Design 2030: Annual Update', May 2022, https://www.marines.mil/Portals/1/Docs/Force_Design_2030_Annual_Update_May_2022.pdf?ver=7ul-eyF6RcSq_gHU2aKYNQ%3d%3d.

34 Gen. David Berger, 'Marines Will Help Fight Submarines', US Naval Institute, *Proceedings*, vol. 146/11/1,413, November 2020, https://www.usni.org/magazines/proceedings/2020/november/marines-will-help-fight-submarines.

35 US Indo-Pacific Command, 'Redesignated: 3rd Marine Regiment Becomes 3rd Marine Littoral Regiment', 4 March 2022, https://www.pacom.mil/Media/News/News-Article-View/Article/2955826/redesignated-3rd-marine-regiment-becomes-3rd-marine-littoral-regiment/.

36 Caleb Larson, 'Kill It or Build It? Navy and Marines Don't Agree on the Light Amphibious Warship', *National Interest*, 6 October 2022, https://nationalinterest.org/blog/buzz/kill-it-or-build-it-navy-and-marines-don%E2%80%99t-agree-light-amphibious-warship-205207.

37 Jim Webb, 'Momentous Changes in the US Marine Corps' Force Organisation Deserve Debate', *Wall Street Journal*, 25 March 2022, https://www.wsj.com/articles/momentous-changes-in-the-marine-corps-deserve-debate-reduction-david-berger-general-11648217667?mod=opinion_lead_pos10.

38 See references in US, Chief of Naval Operations, 'Navigation Plan 2022'.

39 See, for example, US Navy, 'US Indo-Pacific Command Joint Force Conducts Dual Carrier Operations in South China Sea', 24 January 2022, https://www.navy.mil/Press-Office/News-Stories/Article/2910170/us-indo-pacific-command-joint-force-conducts-dual-carrier-operations-in-south-c/.

40 Bryan McGrath, 'Carrier Air Power Is Essential to Distributed Maritime Operations', 1945, 25

July 2022, https://www.19fortyfive.com/2022/07/carrier-air-power-is-essential-to-distributed-maritime-operations/.

41 See, for example, Oriana Skylar Mastro, 'China's Huge Exercises around Taiwan Were a Rehearsal, Not a Signal, Says Oriana Skylar Mastro', *The Economist*, 10 August 2022, https://www.economist.com/by-invitation/2022/08/10/chinas-huge-exercises-around-taiwan-were-a-rehearsal-not-a-signal-says-oriana-skylar-mastro.

42 US, Congressional Research Service, 'China Naval Modernization: Implications for US Navy Capabilities – Background and Issues for Congress', 1 December 2022, pp. 44–5, https://sgp.fas.org/crs/row/RL33153.pdf.

43 Australia, Department of Defence, '2020 Defence Strategic Update', 1 July 2020, https://www.defence.gov.au/about/strategic-planning/2020-defence-strategic-update.

44 Ben Packham, 'Richard Marles Has Vowed the ADF Will Get Long-range Weapons to Hold Enemies at Bay', *Australian*, 8 November 2022, https://www.theaustralian.com.au/nation/defence/richard-marles-has-vowed-the-adf-will-get-longrange-weapons-to-hold-enemies-at-bay/news-story/e154115e67fcca2135ee8c6659ee8b40.

45 White House, 'FACT SHEET: Implementation of the Australia – United Kingdom – United States Partnership (AUKUS)', 5 April 2022, https://www.whitehouse.gov/briefing-room/statements-releases/2022/04/05/fact-sheet-implementation-of-the-australia-united-kingdom-united-states-partnership-aukus/.

46 Australia, Department of Defence, 'Joint Media Statement: Australia to Pursue Nuclear-powered Submarines through New Trilateral Enhanced Security Partnership', 16 September 2021, https://www.minister.defence.gov.au/statements/2021-09-16/joint-media-statement-australia-pursue-nuclear-powered-submarines-through-new-trilateral-enhanced-security-partnership.

47 See Japan, Ministry of Defense, 'National Security Strategy of Japan', December 2022, https://www.mod.go.jp/j/approach/agenda/guideline/pdf/security_strategy_en.pdf; and Japan, Ministry of Defense, 'National Defense Strategy', 16 December 2022, https://www.mod.go.jp/j/approach/agenda/guideline/strategy/pdf/strategy_en.pdf.

48 Yoshihiro Inaba, 'F-35B Upgrades Near Completion Aboard Japanese Warship Kaga', USNI News, 29 December 2022, https://news.usni.org/2022/12/29/f-35b-upgrades-near-completion-aboard-japanese-warship-kaga.

49 Capt. Marco Valenzuela, 'Marine Corps F-35B Conducts First Landing Aboard JS Izumo', US Marine Corps, 14 October 2021, https://www.marines.mil/News/News-Display/Article/2810746/marine-corps-f-35b-conduct-first-landing-aboard-js-izumo/.

50 Kosuke Takahashi, 'JMSDF Commissions Second Maya-class Guided-missile Destroyer', *Jane's Defence Weekly*, 19 March 2021.

51 Jon Grevatt, 'Japan Plans SM-6 Deployment from 2026', *Jane's Defence Weekly*, 2 November 2022.

52 Xavier Vavasseur, 'Japan's MHI Launches "Agano" Sixth FFM Mogami-class Frigate for JMSDF', Naval News, 21 December 2022, https://www.navalnews.com/naval-news/2022/12/japans-mhi-launches-agano-%E3%80%8C%E3%81%82%E3%81%8C%E3%81%AE%E3%80%8Dsixth-ffm-mogami-class-frigate-for-jmsdf/.

53 Takahashi Kosuke, 'Japan Launches Third Taigei-class Submarine for JMSDF', *Diplomat*, 12 October 2022, https://thediplomat.com/2022/10/japan-launches-third-taigei-class-submarine-for-jmsdf/.

54 Song Sang-ho, 'S. Korea Launches New 8,200-ton Aegis Destroyer, Jeongjo the Great', Yonhap News Agency, 28 July 2022, https://en.yna.co.kr/view/AEN20220728003000325.

55 Dr Lee Willett, 'Doubling Down: North and South Korea Pursue Improved Underwater Capabilities', *Jane's Defence Weekly*, 2 November 2021.

56 Choe Sang-Hun, 'North Korea Tests a Submarine-launched Missile', *New York Times*, 7 May 2022, https://www.nytimes.com/2022/05/07/world/asia/north-korea-missile-submarine.html.

57 Juho Lee, 'South Korea Conducts Second SLBM Test from KSS-III Submarine', Naval News, 25 April 2022, https://www.navalnews.com/naval-news/2022/04/south-korea-conducts-second-slbm-test-from-kss-iii-submarine/.

58 Sakshi Tiwari, 'Irony or What? After "Dumping" Aircraft Carrier, South Korea Plans to Develop Naval Variant of F-21 Fighters', *EurAsian Times*, 26 September 2022, https://eurasiantimes.com/aircraft-carrier-in-sight-south-korea-kf-21-fighter-jet/.

59 For the context on South Korean security strategy, see Government of the Republic of Korea, 'Strategy for a Free, Peaceful and Prosperous Indo-Pacific Region', 28 December 2022, https://www.mofa.go.kr/viewer/skin/doc.html?fn=20221228060752073.pdf&rs=/viewer/result/202301.

60   Keoni Everington, 'Taiwan to Launch 1st Indigenous Submarine in September 2023', *Taiwan News*, 27 December 2022, https://www.taiwannews.com.tw/en/news/4763111.

61   Holmes Liao, 'Taiwan's Risky Submarine Aspiration', *Diplomat*, 10 September 2022, https://thediplomat.com/2022/09/taiwans-risky-submarine-aspiration/.

62   Thomas Newdick, 'Taiwan's New Amphibious Assault Ship Bristles with Anti-air Missiles', War Zone, 30 September 2022, https://www.thedrive.com/the-war-zone/taiwans-new-amphibious-assault-ship-bristles-with-anti-air-missiles; and David Axe, 'With Old and New Frigates, the Taiwanese Navy Could Be Sailing into a Big Mess', *Forbes*, 17 November 2021, https://www.forbes.com/sites/davidaxe/2021/11/17/with-old-and-new-frigates-the-taiwanese-navy-could-be-sailing-into-a-big-mess/?sh=22528ca54a78.

63   'TKMS Launches Singapore's Second and Third Type 218SG Submarines', Naval Technology, 14 December 2022, https://www.naval-technology.com/news/tkms-singapores-second-third-type218sg/.

64   Mike Yeo, 'New Report Forecasts Singapore's Defence Market Growth', *Australian Defence Magazine*, 4 November 2021, https://www.australiandefence.com.au/defence/general/new-report-forecasts-singapore-s-defence-market-growth.

65   Ristian Atriandi Supriyanto, 'Scrutinizing Indonesia's Naval Modernisation Plans', Asia Maritime Transparency Initiative, Center for Strategic and International Studies, 10 March 2022, https://amti.csis.org/scrutinizing-indonesias-naval-modernization-plans/.

66   Daehan Lee, 'Philippines Awards Contract to South Korean Shipbuilder for Six Offshore Patrol Vessels', *Defense News*, 30 June 2022, https://www.defensenews.com/naval/2022/06/30/philippines-awards-contract-to-south-korean-shipbuilder-for-six-offshore-patrol-vessels/.

67   Nick Childs and Douglas Barrie, 'India's Aircraft Carrier Arrival: The Limits of Ambition?', IISS Military Balance Blog, 30 September 2022, https://www.iiss.org/blogs/military-balance/2022/09/indias-aircraft-carrier-arrival-the-limits-of-ambition.

68   Xavier Vavasseur, 'Indian Navy Commissions Second Project 15B Destroyer', Naval News, 19 December 2022,https://www.navalnews.com/naval-news/2022/12/indian-navy-commissions-second-project-15b-destroyer.

69   Usman Ansari, 'Pakistan Receives New Chinese-made Frigate: How Will It Fare Against India's Navy?', *Defense News*, 9 November 2021, https://www.defensenews.com/naval/2021/11/09/pakistan-receives-new-chinese-made-frigate-how-would-it-fare-against-indias-navy/.

70   Mark Thiessen, 'Patrol Spots Chinese, Russian Naval Ships off Alaska Island', AP News, 27 September 2022, https://apnews.com/article/russia-ukraine-china-alaska-honolulu-coast-guard-54638cccc30d5a0f8879022f493a6302.

71   'Australia Accuses China of Shining Laser at Warplane', BBC News, 19 February 2022, https://www.bbc.co.uk/news/world-australia-60446928.

72   Euan Graham, 'Assessing the Solomon Islands' New Security Agreement with China', IISS Analysis, 5 May 2022, https://www.iiss.org/blogs/analysis/2022/05/china-solomon-islands.

73   Jack Detsch, 'US Looks to Check Chinese Advances at Cambodian Naval Base', *Foreign Policy*, 5 December 2022, https://foreignpolicy.com/2022/12/05/us-china-cambodia-ream-naval-base/.

74   Wataru Okada, 'China's Coast Guard Law Challenges Rule-based Order', *Diplomat*, 28 April 2021, https://thediplomat.com/2021/04/chinas-coast-guard-law-challenges-rule-based-order/.

75   Liu Xuanzun, 'China's "Most Powerful" Carrier Group Enters West Pacific for Drills Amid Japan's Breakaway from Defense-only Principle', *Global Times*, 17 December 2022, https://www.globaltimes.cn/page/202212/1282043.shtml.

76   Idrees Ali, 'US Warships Transit Taiwan Strait, First since Pelosi Visit', Reuters, 28 August 2022, https://www.reuters.com/world/asia-pacific/exclusive-us-warships-carrying-out-taiwan-strait-passage-first-since-pelosi-2022-08-28/.

77   US, Navy, Marine Corps, and Coast Guard, 'Advantage at Sea: Prevailing with All-domain Naval Power', Tri-Service Maritime Strategy 2020, 16 December 2020, pp. 9–14, https://media.defense.gov/2020/Dec/16/2002553074/-1/-1/0/TRISERVICESTRATEGY.PDF.

78   US, Department of Defense, '2022 National Defense Strategy', pp. 12–13.

79   Mallory Shelborne, 'US 3rd Fleet Expanding Operational Role in Indo-Pacific', USNI News, 3 August 2022, https://news.usni.org/2022/08/03/u-s-3rd-fleet-expanding-operational-role-in-indo-pacific.

80   Mallory Shelborne, 'Navy Expanding Attack Submarine on Guam as a Hedge Against

Growing Chinese Fleet', USNI News, 2 November 2022, https://news.usni.org/2022/11/02/navy-expanding-attack-submarine-presence-on-guam-as-a-hedge-against-growing-chinese-fleet.

81 US Navy, 'RIMPAC 2022 Concludes', 5 August 2022, https://www.navy.mil/Press-Office/News-Stories/Article/3118649/rimpac-2022-concludes/.

82 US Embassy and Consulates in India, 'Japan Hosts Australia, India, US in Malabar Naval Exercise 2022', 14 November 2022, https://in.usembassy.gov/japan-hosts-australia-india-u-s-in-naval-exercise-malabar-2022/.

83 See Australian Government, Defence, 'Indo-Pacific Endeavour Returns to Australia', 2 December 2022, https://www.defence.gov.au/news-events/releases/2022-12-02/indo-pacific-endeavour-returns-australia; and 'With Eye on China, Japan Deploys MSDF Flotilla to 11 Indo-Pacific Countries', Japan Times, 18 June 2022, https://www.japantimes.co.jp/news/2022/06/18/national/msdf-pacific-flotilla-china/.

84 Commander, Task Force (CTF) 71 Public Affairs, 'US Navy Support Australia's Indo-Pacific Deployment Alongside Canada, Japan in the South China Sea', US Navy, 17 October 2022, https://www.navy.mil/Press-Office/News-Stories/Article/3189914/us-navy-supports-australias-indo-pacific-deployment-alongside-canada-japan-in-t/.

85 Stephen Dziedzic and Andrew Greene, 'Australia No Longer Sending Navy to the Middle East, Shifts Focus to Asia-Pacific, China', ABC News, 23 October 2020, https://www.abc.net.au/news/2020-10-23/australia-will-stop-sending-navy-to-middle-east-to-shift-focus/12808118.

86 Maritime Security Challenges Conference 2022, November 2022, remarks by the Commander, Royal Canadian Navy, Vice-Admiral Angus Topshee, https://www.youtube.com/watch?v=xPNOYnWsFOY.

87 Demetri Sevastopulo, 'Canada to Send More Warships through Taiwan in Signal to China', Financial Times, 5 December 2022, https://www.ft.com/content/b19721e8-7bfc-44f2-9f72-971a63d2bfac.

88 US Indo-Pacific Command Public Affairs, 'US, Japan and Republic of Korea Conduct a Trilateral Ballistic Missile Defence Exercise', 6 October 2022, https://www.cpf.navy.mil/Newsroom/News/Article/3182274/us-japan-and-the-republic-of-korea-conduct-a-trilateral-ballistic-missile-defen/.

89 See Japan, Ministry of Foreign Affairs, 'Japan–Australia Reciprocal Access Agreement', 6 January 2022, https://www.mofa.go.jp/a_o/ocn/au/page4e_001195.html; Japan, Ministry of Foreign Affairs, 'Signing of Japan–UK Reciprocal Access Agreement', 11 January 2023, https://www.mofa.go.jp/erp/we/gb/page1e_000556.html; and Rene Acosta, 'US, Philippines Add Four More Sites to EDCA Military Basing Agreement', USNI News, 2 February 2023, https://news.usni.org/2023/02/02/u-s-philippines-add-four-more-sites-to-edca-military-basing-agreement.

90 Adam Stahl and Bradley A. Thayer, 'The Coast Guard Is Vital to Defending Taiwan against China', Hill, 31 October 2021, https://thehill.com/opinion/national-security/578615-the-coast-guard-is-vital-to-defending-taiwan-against-china/.

91 See, for example, Bryan Clark, 'Build a Fleet that Contests Every Inch', USNI Proceedings, July 2022, https://www.usni.org/magazines/proceedings/2022/july/build-fleet-contests-every-inch; and Captain Joshua Taylor, 'A Campaign Plan for the South China Sea', USN Proceedings, August 2022, https://www.usni.org/magazines/proceedings/2022/august/campaign-plan-south-china-sea.

92 Australian Government, Defence, 'Pacific Maritime Security Program', https://www.defence.gov.au/programs-initiatives/pacific-engagement/maritime-capability.

93 Geoffrey F. Gresh, 'The New Great Game at Sea', War on the Rocks, 8 December 2020, https://warontherocks.com/2020/12/the-new-great-game-at-sea/.

94 See UK Government, 'Global Britain in a Competitive Age: The Integrated Review of Security, Defence, Development and Foreign Policy', 16 March 2021, https://www.gov.uk/government/publications/global-britain-in-a-competitive-age-the-integrated-review-of-security-defence-development-and-foreign-policy; and UK, Ministry of Defence, 'Defence in a Competitive Age', 30 July 2021, https://www.gov.uk/government/publications/defence-in-a-competitive-age.

95 Harry Adams, 'CSG21: Japanese, UK and US Carriers Join Forces for Exercise', Forces.net, 4 October 2021, https://www.forces.net/news/csg21-japanese-us-and-uk-carriers-join-forces-exercise.

96 See UK, Ministry of Defence, 'Chief of the Defence Staff RUSI Lecture 2022', 14 December

2022, https://www.gov.uk/government/speeches/chief-of-the-defence-staff-rusi-lecture-2022. While the bulk of the CSG21 deployment was made up of UK naval assets, it also included a US Marine Corps F-35B *Lightning* II squadron as part of the carrier air group, a US Navy destroyer and a Dutch air-defence frigate.

97 See France, Ministry for Europe and Foreign Affairs, 'France's Indo-Pacific Strategy', February 2022, particularly pp. 9–10, https://www.diplomatie.gouv.fr/IMG/pdf/en_dcp_a4_indopacifique_022022_v1-4_web_cle878143.pdf.

98 Xavier Vavasseur, 'French Navy Plans Aircraft Carrier Mission to the Pacific in 2025', Naval News, 22 July 2022, https://www.navalnews.com/naval-news/2022/07/french-navy-aircraft-carrier-mission-pacific-in-2025/.

99 'French Rafales Conduct Navy's Longest Fighter Projection into Asia', Aviation Week, 20 January 2023, https://aviationweek.com/defense-space/budget-policy-operations/french-rafales-conduct-navys-longest-fighter-projection-asia.

100 Sébastian Seibt, 'France Wades into the South China Sea with Nuclear Attack Submarine', France24, 12 February 2021, https://www.france24.com/en/france/20210212-france-wades-into-the-south-china-sea-with-a-nuclear-attack-submarine.

101 IISS, 'IISS Shangri-La Dialogue 2022: Common Challenges for Asia-Pacific and European Defence'. See speech by Netherlands Minister of Defence Kajsa Ollongren, 12 June 2022, https://www.youtube.com/watch?v=aK3bRVsaFr8.

102 European Commission, High Representative of the Union for Foreign and Security Affairs, 'The EU Strategy for Cooperation in the Indo-Pacific', 16 September 2021, p. 13, https://www.eeas.europa.eu/sites/default/files/jointcommunication_2021_24_1_en.pdf.

103 For an English translation, see Anna Davis and Ryan Vest, 'Maritime Doctrine of the Russian Federation', US Naval War College, Russia Maritime Studies Institute, 31 July 2022, https://dnnlgwick.blob.core.windows.net/portals/0/NWCDepartments/Russia%20Maritime%20Studies%20Institute/20220731_ENG_RUS_Maritime_Doctrine_FINALtxt.pdf?sv=2017-04-17&sr=b&si=DNNFileManagerPolicy&sig=2zUFSaTUSPcOpQDBk%-2FuCtVnb%2FDoyo6Cbh0EI5tGpl2Y%3D.

104 Brendan Cole, 'China, Russia and Iran Team Up for Joint Naval Exercises', *Newsweek*, 18 January 2022, https://www.newsweek.com/russia-ukraine-vladimir-putin-kyiv-pacific-fleet-iran-china-1670278.

105 'Iranian Warships Tracked Passing through South Pacific', RNZ, 3 January 2023, https://www.rnz.co.nz/news/world/481838/iranian-warships-tracked-passing-through-south-pacific.

CHAPTER 4

CHINA'S BELT AND ROAD INITIATIVE A DECADE ON

MEIA NOUWENS

Senior Fellow for Chinese Security and Defence Policy, IISS

Dalian, Liaoning, China (Shunli Zhao/Getty Images)

China's Belt and Road Initiative (BRI) has served as an avenue for Chinese infrastructure development across the Asia-Pacific. However, not all countries there have received equal attention or embraced BRI membership. Following a 2018 peak, BRI investments have slowed, providing a window for Western alternatives. While concerns of 'debt-trap' diplomacy – due to indebtedness to China – may not have been borne out, Beijing seems to be moving towards promoting Chinese-centric norms of security, development and digital governance.

THE BRI IN THE ASIA-PACIFIC AND ITS EVOLVING THEMATIC FOCUS

The BRI's focus in the Asia-Pacific has shifted in line with Beijing's strategic interests, with most investment being directed towards Southeast Asia and South Asia. The BRI has also shifted from hard-infrastructure projects to digital-infrastructure projects. New diplomatic initiatives build on Chinese infrastructure and connectivity investments to promote Chinese narratives and norms.

BRI IMPLEMENTATION: CHINESE RHETORIC VS WESTERN APPREHENSIONS

Beijing has espoused the BRI as a project to increase connectivity and infrastructure. Western concerns have focused on China's intentions and the potential for debt-trap diplomacy. However, Beijing might find itself in a debt trap of its own making following the BRI's early years of unregulated investment and recipient countries' economic difficulties.

RIPOSTES TO THE BRI: INITIATIVES BY OTHER POWERS

Western actors have tried to offer alternatives to BRI infrastructure projects. And while even taken together such efforts do not equal the BRI's funding so far, their timing may be fortuitous: due to China's economic downturn, its spending on such projects is unlikely to increase in the near term.

THE BRI'S FUTURE AND ASIA-PACIFIC SECURITY

Beijing seeks to build on the BRI through new initiatives that promote Chinese concepts of security. Consequently, the Asia-Pacific will become a battleground for norms and values of relevance to the future of the international order. It will be important to observe the extent to which, and how, China manages to convert its BRI and digital investments into useful influence.

Sri Lankan labourers work along a
road in Colombo, 5 August 2018

The Belt and Road Initiative (BRI) has evolved significantly since its launch in 2013. Chinese President Xi Jinping announced the BRI in two speeches in 2013, outlining plans for a 'Silk Road Economic Belt' – involving overland routes for rail and road transportation – intended to deepen China's connectivity with Eurasia and boost trade between China, Eurasia and Europe; and a '21st Century Maritime Silk Road', expected to deepen maritime links between China, Southeast Asia, South Asia and Europe. The stated ambition was to build closer economic ties with China's neighbouring regions, ultimately linking it to the West, through five priority areas: coordinating policy, improving connectivity, reducing impediments to trade, integrating financial structures, and building people-to-people ties through exchanges and dialogues in various sectors. Over time, however, the BRI expanded in scope to become an umbrella term for any Chinese project in developing or emerging economies. The BRI also became a useful way for Beijing to expend its industrial overcapacity (through trade development) and promote its industrial strategy in new sectors (such as digital technology) beyond its national borders.

The BRI's geographical reach and thematic priorities have changed since its launch. So too has the scope of BRI projects. At first, the initiative concentrated on China's immediate neighbouring regions – Central Asia and Southeast Asia. Its focus has gradually extended westward, with projects linking China with Africa and South Asia and, ultimately, linking China to markets in Europe. Since 2018, the BRI has been used to deepen China's relations with Latin America and the South Pacific. However, within the Asia-Pacific, the initiative's scope and implementation have also been diverse. While Southeast Asia, Central Asia, South Asia and the South Pacific have all been foci for the BRI (see Figure 4.1), Beijing's prioritisation between and within these sub-regions has changed over time. For example, an initial focus on projects in Central Asia was quickly supplanted by greater emphasis on projects in South and Southeast Asia.

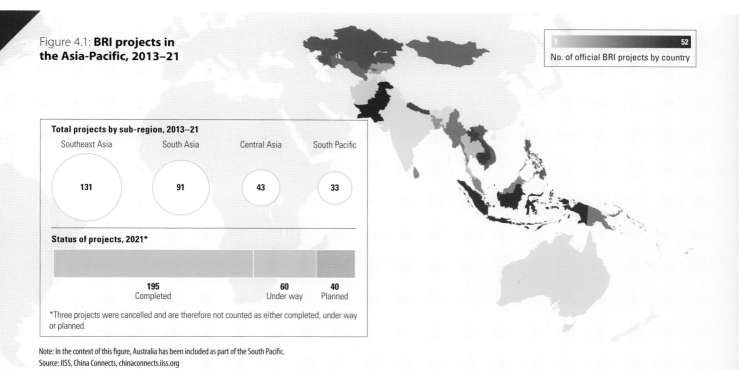

Figure 4.1: **BRI projects in the Asia-Pacific, 2013–21**

No. of official BRI projects by country

Total projects by sub-region, 2013–21

Southeast Asia	South Asia	Central Asia	South Pacific
131	91	43	33

Status of projects, 2021*

195 Completed	60 Under way	40 Planned

*Three projects were cancelled and are therefore not counted as either completed, under way or planned.

Note: In the context of this figure, Australia has been included as part of the South Pacific.
Source: IISS, China Connects, chinaconnects.iiss.org

In thematic terms, there was a boom in BRI physical-infrastructure projects around 2016, with Chinese companies building new rail, road and pipeline networks (or modernising existing networks) and investing in port infrastructure. Such investment raised concerns in the West, primarily because of China's alleged potential ability to exploit debt incurred from infrastructure-project loans in order to gain political influence in recipient countries. (Subsequent studies have indicated that the empirical evidence does not suggest this has been a widespread practice.) As a result of China's domestic economic downturn, Beijing has sought to exert greater central control over the initiative in recent years, and the number of new BRI infrastructure projects has slowed since 2019. While Beijing focuses on completing infrastructure projects that are already under way, the future of the BRI seems to lie in a related initiative: the Digital Silk Road (DSR). Initially branded as a subset of the BRI, the DSR has gained momentum since its launch in 2015 and differs from the BRI – not only in terms of its thematic focus but also its Chinese stakeholders, contract types and geographical reach. However, the roll-out of further Chinese digital investments abroad could be complicated by Beijing's desire for greater control over Chinese private-sector technology companies at home (to redirect business focus to the development of advanced components) and Washington's introduction of greater controls on the export of semiconductor and supercomputing technologies to China.

In 2021 and 2022, China launched several efforts to increase its influence along the BRI and DSR, announcing three new initiatives centred on Chinese values. While thin on detail, they outline the government's views on security (including data security) and development and are particularly focused on gaining influence in the Global South, building on Beijing's perception that the United States is a declining power and presenting a Chinese view of the rules-based international order.

While the US, its allies and other international partners have attempted to push back against China's global infrastructure and connectivity initiatives, alternatives to the BRI and DSR have not succeeded overall. Although countries are open to alternatives to the BRI and DSR, the US and its allies and partners have been unable thus far to provide infrastructure at the scale required to rival the BRI. Despite their changing nature, the BRI and the DSR remain important elements of China's foreign policy in the Asia-Pacific.

THE BRI IN THE ASIA-PACIFIC AND ITS EVOLVING THEMATIC FOCUS

The geographic and thematic foci of the BRI in the Asia-Pacific have shifted since 2013 in line with Beijing's strategic interests. While the initiative was launched in 2013 in Central Asia, over the last decade most BRI investment in the Asia-Pacific has been directed towards Southeast Asia and South Asia, with an uptick in investments in the South Pacific since 2018. Australia, India, Japan, South Korea and Taiwan have remained outside the BRI due to either bilateral political tensions with China or their alliance with the United States. The following assessment examines the geographical and sectoral emphases of the BRI in four Asia-Pacific sub-regions (Southeast Asia, South Asia, Central Asia and the South Pacific), presenting IISS data on officially branded BRI projects in each. It also assesses challenges to the BRI in each sub-region, as well as new Chinese initiatives that build on the BRI.

Southeast Asia

For trade, security and geopolitical reasons, Southeast Asia is likely to remain the Asia-Pacific sub-region that is most strategically important for Beijing. Many countries in Southeast Asia have strong trading relationships with China and play an important role in its supply chains. China has ranked as the Association of Southeast Asian Nations' (ASEAN) largest trading partner since 2009, while ASEAN has been China's largest trading partner since 2020. Additionally, vital maritime trade routes to China run through Southeast Asia; despite attempts to decrease reliance on maritime trade by expanding regional rail networks through the BRI, Chinese imports and exports remain dependent on shipping.[1] Moreover, Beijing seeks to foster the continuing non-alignment of Southeast Asian countries as a bulwark against greater regional alignment with the US, in what Beijing views as an era characterised by 'Cold War mentality' on the part of the US.[2]

In Southeast Asia, official BRI projects have been concentrated predominantly in Cambodia, Indonesia, Laos, the Philippines and Vietnam (see Figure 4.2). Chinese investment in Southeast Asia peaked in 2017, when nearly six times the number of projects were launched in the sub-region compared with 2013. Between 2013 and 2015, most BRI projects concerned transport and energy infrastructure. From 2016, they were diversified to include special economic zones and trade agreements with recipient countries. By 2020, the largest category of BRI investments in Southeast Asia focused on 'Health Silk Road' projects, which included the donation and sale of protective equipment and Chinese vaccines, as well as people-to-people connections through medical-expert visits and exchanges. Southeast Asia has also been a key destination for DSR investments, with Chinese firms playing a dominant role in telecommunications-infrastructure provision in poorer countries, including Cambodia, Laos and Myanmar. In more sophisticated markets

– Indonesia, Malaysia, the Philippines and Singapore – China's role has not been so dominant. While there has been much controversy in Western countries over the adoption of Chinese-owned next-generation network infrastructure, in Southeast Asia similar debate has often been absent. In Indonesia, for example, the government has prioritised bridging the 'two Indonesias' – that is, the highly connected part of the country centred on Java, and the less connected eastern part of the country – and has favoured Chinese investment because of its low cost and fast roll-out.[3] Aside from investments in physical infrastructure, Southeast Asia presents a growth market for Chinese digital platforms and services due to its large, growing and 'tech-savvy' population.[4]

Challenges to the BRI in Southeast Asia include concerns about economic dependencies on China (such as in the Philippines), ethnic tensions (in Indonesia, for example), and corporate social responsibility issues relating to the standards of projects (such as in Indonesia, Malaysia, Thailand and Vietnam).[5] These concerns have at times impacted governments, as protesters have claimed that their governments have become too favourably disposed towards China and placed maintaining favourable bilateral relations ahead of wider national interests. Ethnic tensions have at times been fuelled by the view that China-led BRI projects only benefit migrant workers from China. In Indonesia, for example, the number of Chinese guest workers residing in the country rose from 17,515 in 2015 to 30,000 in 2018, while domestic unemployment remained around 5% during that time.[6]

China's growing economic clout in Southeast Asia is reflected in public-opinion polls about economic influence in the region. According to the State of Southeast Asia 2023 Survey Report published by the Singapore-based ISEAS–Yusof Ishak Institute, over 59.9% of respondents considered China the most influential economic power in Southeast Asia (of this number, 64.5% were worried about China's economic influence), while 41.5% regarded China as the most influential political and strategic power in the region (of this number, 68.5% were worried about China's expanding influence in these areas).[7] The most indebted countries to China in Southeast Asia are Cambodia, Laos and Myanmar, which

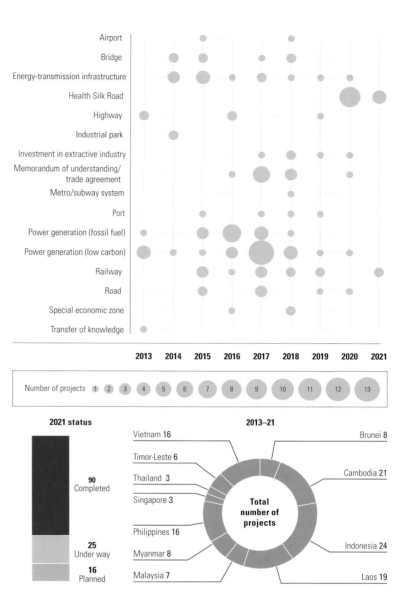

Figure 4.2: **BRI projects in Southeast Asia, 2013–21**

Source: IISS, China Connects, chinaconnects.iiss.org

are also three of the top five countries that have received the most BRI funding. Several countries in Southeast Asia, including Myanmar and Vietnam, have sought alternatives to BRI investment. For example, in 2018, Thailand proposed a regional effort to create alternatives to Chinese infrastructure funding through the establishment of an Ayeyawady-Chao Phraya-Mekong Economic Cooperation Strategy (ACMECS) fund worth US$500 million.[8] This was ultimately funded by Thailand, with contributions from Australia, Japan, South Korea and the US. In Vietnam, the EU Global Gateway initiative is

Protesters march towards the Chinese consulate in Metro Manila on the Philippines' Independence Day, 12 June 2019

(Jes Aznar/Getty Images)

funding the Tra Vinh nearshore wind farm.[9] Myanmar, in turn, has looked to India for infrastructure financing, such as in the India–Myanmar Border Area Development project, including for the construction of roads, bridges and schools in Chin State and the Naga Self-Administered Zone.[10] Alternatives to BRI funding have been successful in limited cases, although such endeavours have not yet been able to match the BRI's offer at scale.

Controversies pertaining to Chinese firms' alleged lack of corporate social responsibility when implementing BRI projects in Southeast Asia have led to disputes over land ownership, labour rights, corruption and environmental impact. Ethnic tensions have also arisen, with concerns sometimes voiced by local populations that Chinese workers on BRI projects have received higher pay. For example, a high-speed-railway project linking the Thailand–Laos border to the Thailand–Malaysia border faced pushback from Bangkok, with the government denying China's request for development rights on the land on either side of the railway. Thai policymakers also pushed back on the issue of whether Chinese engineers would be allowed to work in Thailand, though a compromise was ultimately reached.[11] This pushback should be seen within the context of the domestic criticism levelled at the Thai government at the time for its perceived close relationship with China and overreliance on Beijing for diplomatic and strategic support.[12]

South Asia

Of the countries in the South Asia sub-region, Pakistan has received the largest share of BRI investment, while smaller states there have attempted to use Chinese investment to hedge against India. Sri Lanka, under then-president Mahinda Rajapaksa, saw Chinese investment through the BRI as an economic opportunity but also as a ballast to its fractious relationship with India.[13] Similarly, Nepal and Maldives have alternated between prioritising China or India in their foreign relations, depending on the governments in power at the time. Chinese investments in the region have not necessarily created more favourable conditions for Beijing's influence. Chinese investment in South Asia has been one factor encouraging India to align more closely with the West, notably through the Quad (a grouping of Australia, India, Japan and the US); India has also agreed to the potential establishment of the US–India Gandhi–King Development Foundation, as well as to collaborate with the US to provide joint development finance where possible – including through a partnership between the US Agency for International Development and India's Development Partnership Administration, which seeks to expand development activity in third countries.[14]

More than half of official BRI projects in South Asia have been in Pakistan (see Figure 4.3). Almost one-quarter have been in Nepal. While also recipients of BRI investment, taken together Sri Lanka and Maldives accounted for less than one-seventh of BRI projects in the sub-region. Between 2013 and 2021, China invested in 18 different categories of BRI projects in South Asia.[15] These included energy, real estate, transport infrastructure, digital infrastructure and services, trade agreements, special economic zones and industrial parks. From 2013–16, Chinese BRI investment in South Asia focused primarily on energy and transport infrastructure. However, from 2016 it widened in scope to include special economic zones, industrial parks and new trade agreements.

The BRI in South Asia has achieved its intended goal of exporting Chinese industrial overcapacity abroad. From 2010–18, for example, the value of Chinese industrial-goods exports to Pakistan increased from US$3.1 billion to US$8.2bn.[16] Nevertheless, South Asian BRI projects have faced security, political, economic, geographical and governance

Figure 4.3: **BRI projects in South Asia, 2013–21**

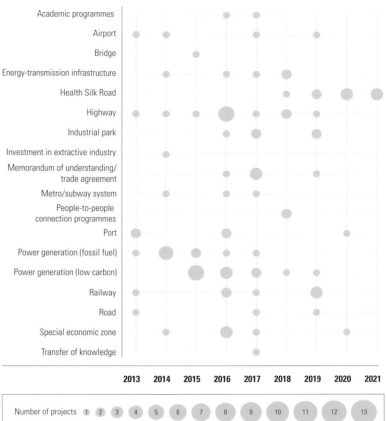

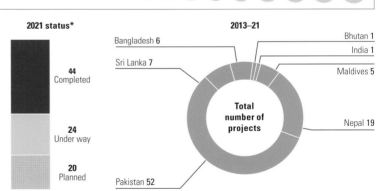

*Three projects were cancelled and are therefore not counted as either completed, under way or cancelled.

Source: IISS, China Connects, chinaconnects.iiss.org

challenges. Since 2018, the number of new BRI projects agreed to in South Asia has slowed due to worsening economic conditions in Maldives, Pakistan and Sri Lanka. In addition, some of the existing projects are located in geographically challenging locations, such as Pakistan's Himalayan interior, which is seeing construction of railway infrastructure and pipelines as part of the China–Pakistan Economic Corridor (CPEC) project. The costs of transporting via these infrastructure projects once finished would far exceed the cost of the maritime-shipping options to which they supposedly provide an alternative. According to one study, 'if a Chinese oil company chose to move 200,000 bpd [barrels per day] of crude [oil] through the Burma–China pipeline and 250,000 bpd through the Pakistan–China line, it could lose roughly a billion dollars a year compared to what it would have paid to move the oil by sea to eastern China'.[17] Other estimates claim that shipping oil from the Persian Gulf to the east coast of China would cost just US$2 per barrel, compared to potentially US$15 per barrel to move it overland from Pakistan to western China and then through further distribution centres to China's eastern region.[18] Bureaucratic and governance challenges also exist, as countries like Nepal do not have the bureaucratic capacity to get large-scale infrastructure projects off the ground. For example,

The Chinese-operated Gwadar Port in Balochistan, southwest Pakistan

(SM Rafiq Photography/Getty Images)

the Trans-Himalayan railway project has been on hold since 2014 as Nepal lacks the technical expertise and engineers to conduct a feasibility study of the project or review any study that would be carried out by China. Further stalling the project is the fact that neither Nepal nor China wishes to fund the feasibility study.[19] Meanwhile, in Pakistan the BRI has faced some of its most severe security challenges so far, with numerous terrorist attacks targeting infrastructure projects or Chinese personnel working on them. The CPEC runs through insecure parts of Pakistan, and Chinese nationals have been targeted by extremists in Quetta and Karachi.[20] In June 2017, the Islamic State (ISIS) claimed that it had killed two Chinese nationals who were abducted from Quetta.[21] In December 2017, Beijing warned Chinese nationals publicly that more attacks on Chinese nationals in Pakistan could be imminent. In 2018, gunmen opened fire on employees of Cosco Shipping Lines Pakistan, killing one Chinese national.[22] In September 2022, a Chinese-Pakistani national was killed at a dental clinic in Karachi, while in April that year three Chinese teachers were killed in Karachi by a suicide bomber.[23]

Central Asia

By the time the BRI was launched, bilateral relations between China and countries in Central Asia (Kazakhstan, Kyrgyzstan, Tajikistan, Turkmenistan and Uzbekistan) were already extensive. Beijing sought to strengthen economic ties with the region, particularly to help boost the economic development of China's less wealthy western provinces. Indeed, in 2013, China was the top trading partner of Turkmenistan and Uzbekistan and the second-largest trading partner for the other countries in the sub-region.[24] Central Asia has also played an important role in expanding China's access to energy imports from the region and Russia. Energy and transportation projects had already started prior to the launch of the BRI, as China became a net importer of oil in 1993 and turned to Russia and Central Asia for energy imports.[25] In the late 1990s, China National Petroleum Corporation acquired the rights to two major oilfields in Kazakhstan and constructed a Kazakhstan–China oil pipeline.[26] BRI energy-focused projects thus expanded on an existing network of oil and gas pipelines. Chinese investments were welcomed by Central Asian governments and have focused on energy, transport corridors and, since 2018, helping Central Asian countries to diversify their economic bases, notably through investments in digital infrastructure.

Large flagship BRI projects for Central Asia were announced soon after the BRI's launch, focused primarily on power-generation projects, extractive industries and railway networks to carry gas and oil to China while also facilitating the export of goods from China. In addition to signing numerous memoranda of understanding and trade agreements, Chinese-built and -operated special economic zones (such as those in Kazakhstan) were intended to facilitate trade with China. However, from 2017 onwards Chinese investment in the sub-region through the BRI diversified to include greater investment in roads and highways, as well as in low-carbon power-generation infrastructure through solar and wind parks and hydroelectric power plants. From 2020 onwards, new BRI projects focused almost entirely on health initiatives (see Figure 4.4) – in line with China's health diplomacy during the coronavirus pandemic. Though Chinese tech companies have been invested in Central Asia since the early 2000s, such firms have expanded into the sub-region more significantly since 2018, taking leading shares in national ICT network infrastructures and rolling out surveillance-related technologies, as well as 'smart city' projects.[27]

Figure 4.4: **BRI projects in Central Asia, 2013–21**

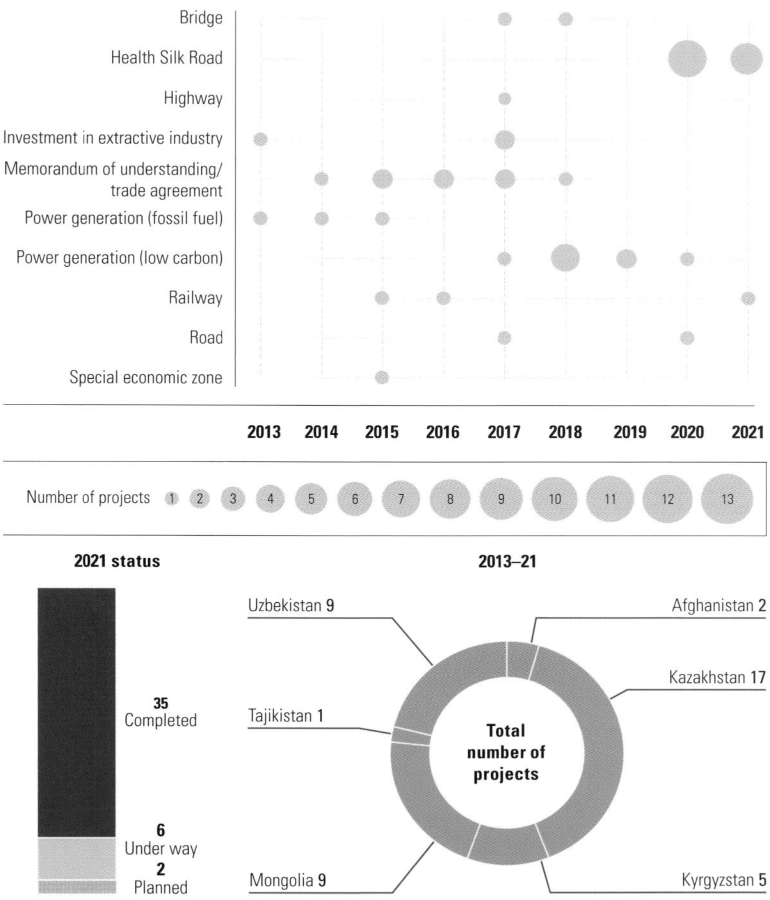

Source: IISS, China Connects, chinaconnects.iiss.org

New Chinese-built transport-connectivity infrastructure in the sub-region has increased rail traffic between Europe and Asia, particularly since the coronavirus pandemic. From 2016–21, the annual number of China–Europe freight trains increased from 1,702 to 15,183, with an increase of nearly 80% in the first quarter of 2021 compared to the same period in 2020.[28] However, the vast majority of trade between Europe and China is still carried out by shipping: in 2019, over 95% of trade in goods between Germany and China was transported by shipping.[29] Future investment in Central Asian rail networks connecting Europe and China is doubtful. In 2022, China–EU rail freight saw a 34% drop in volume via the 'Northern Corridor' due to the Russian war of aggression in Ukraine and as ocean freight costs fell back to pre-pandemic levels.[30] Even if the war in Ukraine were to end, the future of Europe–China freight transport would not look positive. Economic and political developments in Europe could lead to a drop in demand for freight from China, while the greater fragmentation of global supply chains that exclude China could continue to impact the demand for freight transport between China and Europe. Moreover, the BRI has not been spared in Central Asia from political concerns over undue Chinese influence, or from corruption scandals, which in some cases have led to the cancellation of Chinese projects.[31] In 2019, former prime minister of Kyrgyzstan Sapar Isakov was charged with corruption following his attempted lobbying for the interests of a Chinese company in a project to modernise the Bishkek Thermal Power Station.[32] In 2019, Kazakhstan decided to end infrastructure financing from China for a light-railway transit project, due to embezzlement of the funds.[33]

South Pacific

While Chinese agreements with certain countries in the Pacific Islands have raised concerns in some Western capitals since 2018 – a notable example being the 2022 China–Solomon Islands security agreement – the sub-region is only a minor destination for BRI investment.[34] Despite this, Western anxiety over the potential for greater Chinese influence has led to increased infrastructure funding from Western countries, notably Australia, New Zealand and the US.[35]

Then Chinese premier Li Keqiang and Solomon Islands Prime Minister Manasseh Sogavare inspect honour guards during a welcome ceremony in Beijing, 9 October 2019

(Wang Zhao/AFP via Getty Images)

Papua New Guinea, Solomon Islands, Vanuatu and the Federated States of Micronesia have received the largest shares of BRI projects in the South Pacific, with Papua New Guinea accounting for almost a quarter of the projects in the sub-region between 2013 and 2021 (see Figure 4.5). BRI investment was slow to gain momentum in the South Pacific; the number of projects agreed per year only picked up significantly in 2018. While early projects were focused on airport infrastructure and low-carbon power-generation infrastructure, in 2017 multiple trade agreements were signed. Additionally, BRI projects diversified to include investments in extractive industries, bridges, energy-transmission infrastructure and ports. In 2020, during the coronavirus pandemic, Health Silk Road projects were signed with eight Pacific Island states.[36]

Despite Chinese loans and grants to the sub-region, China and the BRI have made only a minimal impact in recipient Pacific Island states. There has not been any significant shift in Chinese investment or trade towards the sub-region, with the exception of Papua New Guinea. Exports from China to the South Pacific have increased twelvefold in value between 2000 and 2018, though the numbers for exports from Pacific Island countries to China have grown at a much less impressive rate.[37] Papua New Guinea, however, has continued to have significantly stronger trade ties with Australia than with China in both imports and exports.[38] In Australia, concerns of debt-trap diplomacy in the South Pacific have been prominent.[39] Such concerns have proved an obstacle for the BRI, despite these claims being largely unproven empirically. Of the South Pacific countries, Samoa, Tonga and Vanuatu are the most indebted to China, with Tonga owing roughly 25% of its total annual GDP to the Export–Import Bank of China (Eximbank).[40] This has prompted Pacific powers – including Australia, New Zealand and the US – to pay closer attention to the Pacific Island states and consider providing alternatives to the BRI by supporting socio-economic development projects. Further major Chinese investment in the form of large-scale physical-infrastructure projects is unlikely given the existing debt burdens and the lack of demand for Chinese loans. In 2021, Samoa scrapped a China-backed port-development project, while a road project with Papua New Guinea has been stalled since the contract for the project was signed in 2017. Only two countries signed up to new loans with China between 2017 and 2021: Solomon Islands, for the 2023 Pacific Games Stadium, and Kiribati, for agricultural and technology support.[41] Instead, the BRI is likely to focus on its existing connectivity projects in sub-regions closer to China and with greater economic potential.

New diplomatic initiatives

In addition to the BRI initiatives and DSR investment in these countries, in recent years China has launched three new initiatives directed at the Global South: the Global Initiative on Data Security – also referred to as the Global Data Security Initiative (GDSI) – the Global Development Initiative (GDI)

Figure 4.5: **BRI projects in the South Pacific, 2013–21**

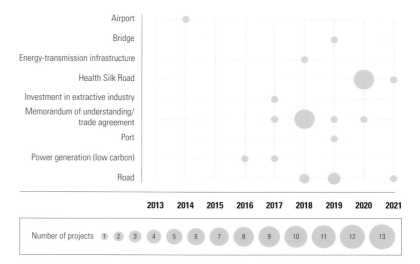

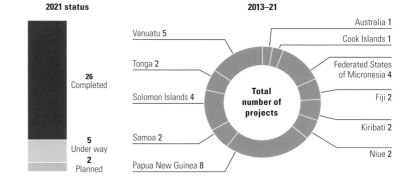

Note: In the context of this figure, Australia has been included as part of the South Pacific.

Source: IISS, China Connects, chinaconnects.iiss.org

and the Global Security Initiative (GSI). These initiatives, revealed in documents offering different levels of detail, appear to be intended to build on the past decade of Chinese infrastructure and connectivity investments to promote Chinese narratives and norms in line with Beijing's view of the international order and its national interests.

The GDSI was launched in 2020 and proposes a framework for data security, data storage and digital commerce (see Figure 4.6). It adds a normative layer to China's half-decade of global digital investment through the DSR. China organised a diplomatic roadshow across Central Asia, Africa and Europe to garner support for the initiative, through speeches by Xi and presentations by ministers and high-level officials from the Ministry of Foreign Affairs. While the relevant official document is light on detail, the GDSI has been viewed in the West as China's riposte to the US 'clean network initiative' (launched in 2020) and expounds principles of 'multilateralism', security development and 'fairness and justice'.[42] When mentioned by Chinese officials, the GDSI's emphasis oscillates between security and digital economy. For example, when the initiative was discussed at the China–Germany–EU leadership meeting in 2020, it was framed as a way to develop a global digital economy. However, when speaking at the Shanghai Cooperation Organisation summit two months later, Xi framed the GDSI through a lens of security and stability, presenting it as a way to build a more 'peaceful, secure, open, cooperative, and orderly' cyberspace.[43] The GDSI is

Figure 4.6: **China's Global Initiative on Data Security: eight tenets**

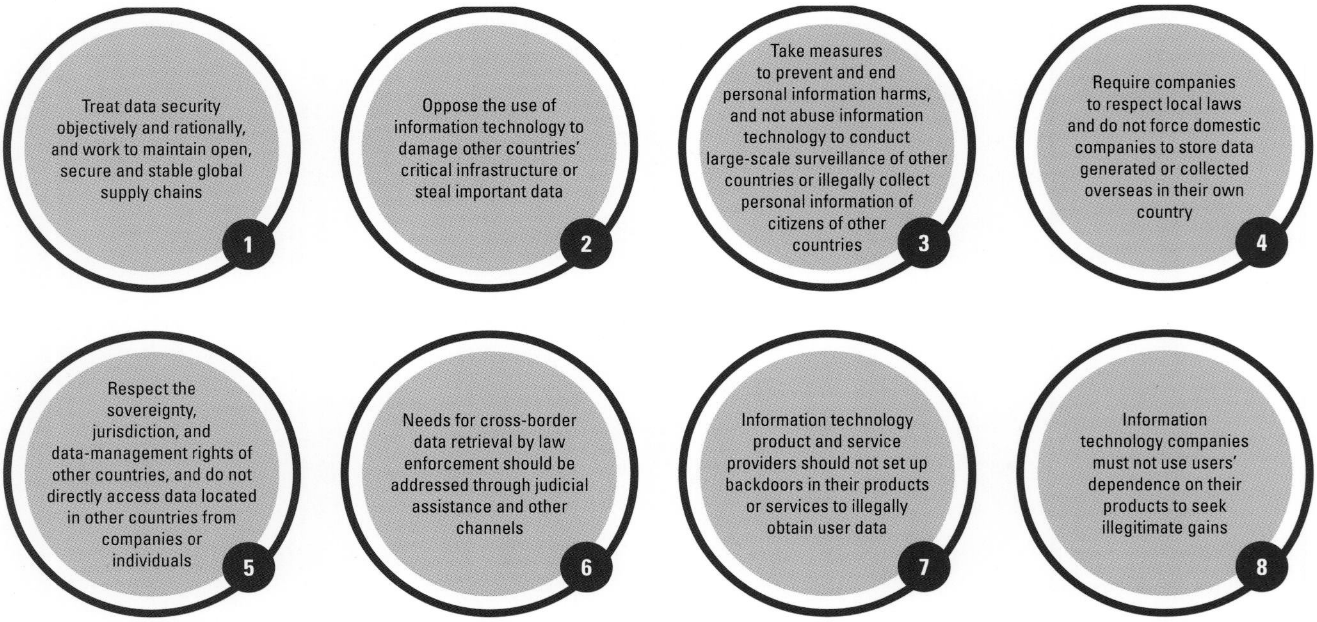

Treat data security objectively and rationally, and work to maintain open, secure and stable global supply chains **1**

Oppose the use of information technology to damage other countries' critical infrastructure or steal important data **2**

Take measures to prevent and end personal information harms, and not abuse information technology to conduct large-scale surveillance of other countries or illegally collect personal information of citizens of other countries **3**

Require companies to respect local laws and do not force domestic companies to store data generated or collected overseas in their own country **4**

Respect the sovereignty, jurisdiction, and data-management rights of other countries, and do not directly access data located in other countries from companies or individuals **5**

Needs for cross-border data retrieval by law enforcement should be addressed through judicial assistance and other channels **6**

Information technology product and service providers should not set up backdoors in their products or services to illegally obtain user data **7**

Information technology companies must not use users' dependence on their products to seek illegitimate gains **8**

Note: The eight tenets are as translated by DigiChina, from the original Chinese-language speech in 2020 by then-foreign minister Wang Yi.
Source: DigiChina, digichina.stanford.edu

seemingly promoted in different ways to different audiences, focusing on narratives that might garner the most support from different partners.

The GDI was launched by Xi in his speech to the United Nations General Assembly in September 2021. The initiative aims to represent China as a leader of the Global South, offer an alternative to the 'Western-led' international order, and build on Beijing's narrative that the US and the wider West are in decline. The GDI includes as priority areas 'poverty alleviation, food security, COVID-19 response and vaccine, development financing, climate change and green development, industrialization, digital economy and connectivity'.[44] Launched at a time when the global coronavirus pandemic was slowing down, the GDI was also framed as a way for China to help the Global South recover from the social and economic challenges caused by the pandemic. Despite a lack of detail on the initiative, over 50 countries have joined the 'UN Group of Friends of the Global Development Initiative', established by China less than four months after the GDI's launch. However, in addition to outlining support for socio-economic development, the GDI also seeks to promote Chinese views on human rights and the 'collective', in line with Beijing's efforts to reshape global rules and governance. With regard to the former, the GDI frames 'development' as a prerequisite for human rights. Effectively positing that human rights are a secondary matter runs counter to the UN Universal Declaration of Human Rights and suggests that human rights are voluntary, while also leaving vague the definition of 'development', the supposedly necessary precondition for respecting human rights. The GDI also makes numerous mentions of the 'collective' and the 'greater good', in line with Beijing's views that the preferences of the state should override individual rights.[45]

Initially proposed in April 2022, the GSI was formally launched with a concept paper on 21 February 2023. The document outlines core concepts and principles for global peace and security, offering some detail on China's plan for the initiative. The GSI lists China's commitment to six principles: 'common, comprehensive, cooperative and sustainable security … respecting the sovereignty and territorial integrity of all countries … abiding by the purposes and principles of the UN Charter … taking the legitimate security concerns of all countries seriously … peacefully resolving differences and disputes between countries

President Xi Jinping announces the Global Development Initiative in a virtual address to the UN General Assembly in New York City, US, 21 September 2021

(Mary Altaffer/POOL/AFP via Getty Images)

through dialogue and consultation … [and] maintaining security in both traditional and non-traditional domains'.[46] The GSI also offers broad plans for priority areas of cooperation. Listed first is putting forward a 'New Agenda for Peace' and other proposals in the UN. The initiative also outlines China's position on the need for peaceful coexistence between major countries, preventing nuclear war and avoiding arms races. Additionally, the initiative seeks to promote regional security solutions for and by regional states in Southeast Asia, the Middle East, Africa, Latin America and the Caribbean. It is likely that Beijing seeks to replicate its concept of 'Asia for Asians' in other regions, which could potentially weaken the existing world order as well as US capacity to help manage or resolve crises in other regions. In addition to listing existing and new platforms for cooperation and dialogue, the GSI also mentions detailed examples of Chinese programmes, such as China's offer to 'provide other developing countries with 5,000 training opportunities in the next five years to train professionals for addressing global security issues'.[47]

These three initiatives aim to promote Chinese-centric norms and values in the Global South. This ambition will be particularly relevant in developing and emerging economies where China has invested heavily in development aid or infrastructure projects through the BRI and DSR. It also allows Beijing to continue to shape the international system in its favour at a time when large-scale infrastructure projects are not feasible due to economic conditions in China and questions of demand (as outlined earlier in this chapter). Beijing has previously argued that the BRI is 'an economic cooperation initiative, not a geopolitical or military alliance'.[48] However, these three initiatives indicate that Beijing's engagement with the Global South is not just based on the provision of aid or helping to develop local economies; it is now expanding more formally to promote Chinese concepts of security, based closely on China's own concept of comprehensive national security, its 'golden prescription for global challenges' and development, and the storage, processing and transfer of data globally according to Chinese norms.[49]

BRI IMPLEMENTATION: CHINESE RHETORIC VS WESTERN APPREHENSIONS

Official Chinese and Western rhetoric on the BRI present similar interpretations of both the role of the Chinese government and the ambition behind the initiative. They differ, however, on China's intent. While Beijing has espoused the BRI as a project to increase connectivity and infrastructure, linking regions and benefiting recipient countries' economic growth, Western views of the BRI have tended to be more suspicious of China's intentions. Indeed, in 2017, then US secretary of defense James Mattis stated that 'no one nation should put itself in a position of dictating "one belt, one road"'.[50] In 2021, the G7 expressed concern about China's 'coercive' economic policies and 'debt-trap' diplomacy towards developing countries.[51] That same year, then US secretary of state Rex Tillerson criticised the BRI for burdening recipient countries with job losses for local populations – due to the import of Chinese labour to manage and work on BRI projects – and 'enormous levels of debt'.[52]

Judging BRI implementation: statecraft vs 'partycraft'

By 2021, over half (64%) of the BRI projects in Southeast Asia, the South Pacific and South Asia had been completed, while 22% were ongoing and 14% were still at the planning stage.[53] These statistics give the impression – at least, at first glance – that implementation of the BRI has been and continues to be largely successful.

However, judging implementation against these metrics risks overlooking both the fact that the last decade of BRI implementation has in some ways proved to be chaotic and also the question of recipient countries' agency. The BRI's roll-out in the last ten years has lacked central bureaucratic oversight and control and a coherent implementation strategy. It was originally advertised by Beijing as a systematic project intended to 'promote the connectivity of Asian, European and African continents and their adjacent seas, establish and strengthen partnerships among the countries along the Belt and Road, set up all-dimensional, multi-tiered and composite connectivity networks, and realize diversified, independent, balanced and sustainable development in these countries'.[54] However, the BRI's early years were marred by a lack of leadership and structure. Instead of being led by the Ministry of Foreign Affairs and Ministry of Commerce, as might have been expected for a major foreign-policy initiative focused on socio-economic development and connectivity, managing the BRI was instead delegated to the National Development and Reform Commission (NDRC), which sought to fold China's domestic economic planning agenda into the BRI. The initiative also lacked concrete policies that directed how, where and by whom projects would be implemented. Instead, the BRI has been run according to vague action plans issued by the Chinese Communist Party's (CCP) BRI Leading Small Group and the NDRC. Existing infrastructure projects were rebranded as BRI projects, while various Chinese stakeholders at different levels of government and industry used the initiative as a vehicle for pursuing their own interests – with the incentive of government financial support.

This apparent lack of coordination calls into question whether the BRI is the example of Chinese statecraft that both the Chinese government and Western commentators have claimed it to be: a strategic, coordinated, plan-driven and target-oriented action in pursuit of clear, long-term goals using the tools of the state and operated by a unitary actor through directed steps. The reality of the BRI is that 'propaganda exceeds implementation, activity overtakes purpose, and actors further down the hierarchy have much latitude in interpreting the terms of their involvement'.[55] Instead of being seen as effective tools of statecraft, the BRI and DSR should perhaps be viewed as tools of the CCP's 'partycraft': 'a campaign-style mobilization' that is able to 'create bursts of activity and overcome bureaucratic inertia, working simultaneously through state institutions, the party structure and popular participation'.[56] This would explain why the BRI has not had the large-scale effect anticipated by Western politicians and officials at the peak of BRI investments globally in 2016. Importantly, the idea of debt-trap diplomacy turned out to be unproven and China's investment in nearly 60 ports worldwide has not – contrary to the expressed fears of some commentators – provided it with immediate access to a global network of dual-use ports, let alone naval bases.[57]

Debt-trap diplomacy for whom?

Proponents of the theory that the BRI is a tool for China's debt-trap diplomacy (such as the former Trump administration in the US) often point to China's control over Hambantota Port in Sri Lanka.[58] Following unsuccessful efforts to gain investment from the US and India for the port project, in 2015 Chinese construction firm China Harbour Group Engineering Company and China Eximbank agreed to fund a contract to build, own, operate and transfer the port following heavy lobbying by the Chinese firms. While some commentators have attributed China Merchants Port Holdings Company and China Harbour's 99-year lease as proof that the Chinese project was a 'debt-for-equity' swap (as a result of Sri Lanka's deep indebtedness to China), research has shown the opposite. Colombo's need to refinance the port project came about due to complex and long-standing national economic and financial problems in the Sri Lankan economy – and there was never a default. Furthermore, rather than being used to pay off China Eximbank, the US$1.12bn cash infusion was used to strengthen Sri Lanka's foreign reserves.[59]

China is the world's largest private lender. However, the notion that Beijing can leverage global debt as a strategic means to gain access to any and all strategic equity is a myth. Rather, it could be asked whether, instead of trapping sovereign countries in Chinese debt for strategic value, Beijing has inadvertently been caught in a debt trap of its own making.

Nearly 60% of China's overseas loans are currently held by countries considered to be in financial distress, compared with just 5% in 2010.[60] This phenomenon has only been exacerbated by the coronavirus pandemic and the war in Ukraine, which have put China's overseas-lending portfolio at higher risk than ever before. Russia was China's largest foreign debtor, accounting for over 15% of BRI lending in the first five years of the initiative. Russia, Belarus and Ukraine together accounted for 20% of China's overseas lending over the last two decades.[61] Moreover, countries involved in the BRI

Workers welcome a port visit from China's space- and missile-tracking ship *Yuan Wang* 5 in Hambantota, Sri Lanka, 16 August 2022

(Ishara S. Kodikara/AFP via Getty Images)

are requesting debt restructuring from China. For example, in 2022 Pakistan sought to reschedule US$27bn of bilateral debt, mostly owed to China.[62]

China's lending boom has already largely ended, however, and the outbreak of full-scale war in Ukraine in 2022 added additional risk of contagion to its other loans. China is therefore likely to reduce significantly – or halt – lending in the near term and to be hesitant to renegotiate existing debts. It is also noteworthy that while China has in the past two decades focused on bilateral debt restructuring involving Chinese state-owned banks, in February 2023 it called on the G20 to multilateralise the debt burden that China faces, calling for 'joint action, fair burden' in debt settlement.[63]

The question of some countries' indebtedness to China – as a consequence of Beijing's BRI investments – has been linked to several Western governments' concerns that Beijing seeks to invest in ports funded under the BRI in order to build dual-use facilities that could be used to support its naval-expansion programme. So far, the Chinese navy has used the ports of Gwadar in Pakistan and Hambantota in Sri Lanka, while China is reportedly building a naval facility at Ream Naval Base in Cambodia. The US Department of Defense has suggested that in the Asia-Pacific, China 'has likely considered' Cambodia, Indonesia, Myanmar, Pakistan, Singapore, Sri Lanka and Thailand as potential locations for military-logistics facilities.[64] While at present the People's Liberation Army (PLA) has just one official overseas military base (in Djibouti), it is reasonable to assume that the PLA may consider expanding its access and potential ownership of military bases across the Asia-Pacific in the future in order to provide logistic support that could better enable its international projection of military power. However, speculation in the US, India and elsewhere from 2004 onwards that China seeks to develop a chain of naval bases across the Indian Ocean, sometimes referred to as the 'string of pearls', has so far not materialised in any clear-cut form.

Analysis of the BRI has tended to focus more on perceived Chinese intent than on recipient states' agency in decision-making on BRI projects. Countries that receive Chinese investment usually understand very well the geopolitical context in which they are situated and, as a result, are hesitant to make overt choices between strategic alignment with the US or with China. They understand that joining the BRI could be seen as acquiescing to Chinese geopolitical strategy. When counter-offers to the BRI have been available, Chinese influence has appeared to have had a limited impact in determining a recipient country's choice. For example, in 2018 the government of Papua New Guinea chose to uphold a deal with the Chinese company Huawei to build its internet infrastructure and submarine cables, calling an 11th-hour counter-offer by Australia, Japan and the US 'a bit patronising' as Huawei had already completed over half of the project.[65] Since then, Australia, Japan and the US have successfully won contracts for submarine-cable projects intended to connect Nauru, Palau, Papua New Guinea and Solomon Islands.[66]

RIPOSTES TO THE BRI: INITIATIVES BY OTHER POWERS

In the Asia-Pacific, a significant amount of funding is required to develop infrastructure. In 2017, the Asian Development Bank assessed that developing countries in Asia would require US$26 trillion in infrastructure between 2017 and 2030.[67] Since 2013, it is estimated that China has spent between US$1trn and US$2trn on the BRI.[68] China likely lacks the capacity to respond

Table 4.1: **China and the West: global-connectivity initiatives announced, 2013–22**

Year	Initiative	Countries/organisations
2013	Belt and Road Initiative	China
2015	Digital Silk Road	China
2018	Strategy for Connecting Europe and Asia	European Union
2018	Funding for Indo-Pacific infrastructure development	US
2019	Blue Dot Network	US, Japan, Australia
2020	Global Initiative on Data Security	China
2021	Build Back Better World	G7 (Canada, France, Germany, Italy, Japan, UK, US (+EU))
2022	Partnership for Global Infrastructure and Investment	G7 (including EU)
2022	Global Gateway	European Union
2022	Quad Joint Leaders' Statement, 24 May 2022 – US$50 billion of infrastructure assistance and investment in the Indo-Pacific over the next five years	Quad (India, Japan, Australia, US)
2022	Jointly Advancing the Global Development Initiative and Writing a New Chapter for Common Development	China
2022	Global Security Initiative concept paper	China

Source: IISS

comprehensively to the demand for new infrastructure across Asia. In principle then, Western and Japanese alternatives to the BRI may have useful and welcome roles to play.

Initially, Western countries (and countries with complicated relationships with China, such as India) were ambivalent about the BRI. However, in 2017, then US National Security Council senior director for East Asia Matt Pottinger led the US delegation to the first Belt and Road Forum.[69] Some Western views verged on the positive. While addressing the EU Parliament in 2018, EU High Representative for Foreign Affairs and Security Policy and European Commission Vice President Federica Mogherini stated: 'only if we engage together with China, we can make our interests, our goals and our vision on connectivity converge'.[70]

However, the European Union, Japan and the US have subsequently made multiple efforts to provide alternatives to Chinese infrastructure projects (see Table 4.1). Some of these initiatives have yet to result in a single successful project, while others have been too slow to get off the ground, or to expand geographically, to offer realistic options to recipient countries seeking infrastructure investments.[71]

In September 2018, the EU launched its Strategy for Connecting Europe and Asia (known as the EU–Asia Connectivity Strategy).[72] It focuses on transport, energy, digital-network and people-to-people projects, as well as promoting sustainable finance. The US was quick to follow, with Congress passing the Better Utilization of Investments Leading to Development (BUILD) Act in October 2018, which sought to restructure the Overseas Private Investment Corporation into a new agency – the US International Development Finance Corporation – with a doubled

G7 leaders meeting at their summit in Cornwall, United Kingdom, 11 June 2021

(Karwai Tang/Pool/Anadolu Agency via Getty Images)

investment cap of US$60bn.[73] The agency was authorised to invest equity in development projects instead of just providing loans through private-sector participation. In July 2018, the Trump administration announced that it would also make US$113m available for infrastructure-development programmes in the Asia-Pacific.[74] Even taken together, these funds stood in stark contrast to the estimated US$1trn that China had already spent on the BRI. The announcement of the Blue Dot Network in 2019, a joint agreement by Australia, Japan and the US (and, later, with Indian participation) to collaborate on the promotion of quality infrastructure investments, made the lack of Western financing in the face of Chinese spending even more obvious.[75] The agreement had no funding attached to it, instead seeking to compete with the BRI by acting as a certification process for infrastructure investment to assure projects were of high quality and sustainable and that their funding's origin was transparent. To date, these efforts have had little success in competing with the BRI's global reach across multiple sectors.

Perhaps having recognised that greater financing would be required to provide genuine alternatives to the BRI's offerings, the US and EU have both launched reformulated infrastructure initiatives. In June 2021, the US, together with other members of the G7, launched the Build Back Better World (B3W) initiative, intended to provide 'hundreds of billions of dollars of infrastructure for low- and middle-income countries in the coming years'.[76] Just over a year later, the G7 relaunched the B3W as the Partnership for Global Infrastructure and Investment (PGII), this time providing more details of what it entailed. The US planned to provide US$200bn through the PGII over the following five years – through grants, federal financing and private-sector investment.[77] The other G7 countries would provide an additional US$400bn by 2027.[78] Unlike in previous efforts, examples of pilot projects were provided at the launch of the partnership, such as a US$2bn solar project in four southern Angolan provinces, disbursing a US$3.3m technical grant for a multi-vaccine manufacturing facility in Senegal, building the Southeast Asia–Middle East–Western Europe 6 submarine telecommunications cable, and financial support to renovate or construct over 100 hospitals and clinics across Côte d'Ivoire, among others.[79]

In 2022, the EU also relaunched its previous connectivity strategy, this time through the EU Global Gateway. The previous connectivity initiative was focused predominantly on Asia; the Global Gateway expands this effort to other regions. Similar to the G7's PGII in its intentions and scope, the Global Gateway had by early 2023 allocated roughly US$10.8bn in sustainable connectivity, energy and green-transition projects in Southeast Asia. Far more (some US$162bn) has been allocated to Global Gateway activity in Africa, where the EU seeks to finance projects in green transition, digital transition, sustainable growth, health systems, education and training, energy and agri-food systems.[80]

Even taken together, the EU and G7 initiatives will not equal the funding that has been spent so far by China on the BRI. Their timing may be fortuitous, however: Chinese spending on global infrastructure projects peaked in 2018 and, as a result of China's economic downturn, is unlikely to pick up again anytime soon.[81] Furthermore, China's unwillingness (and perhaps inability) to renegotiate existing BRI debt in developing countries may provide other countries with the opportunity to boost their soft power if they are able to help mediate low- and middle-income countries' negotiations with China, or to provide financing where Beijing cannot.[82]

THE BRI'S FUTURE AND ASIA-PACIFIC SECURITY

Viewed in its entirety, over the past decade the BRI has had some impact in the Asia-Pacific, though the levels of activity and challenges vary at the sub-regional and national levels. Domestic and regional political contexts in recipient countries have been important factors influencing how the BRI has evolved. Fears that the BRI was a systematic plan by which China would increase its influence on governments and control of strategic infrastructure across Asia arose from overestimations of China's capacity – and an underestimation of the importance of national and regional political contexts. While some countries, such as Pakistan, have turned to Beijing for large-scale infrastructure projects through the BRI and for economic, political and military support, others, such as Australia, India and Japan, have opted not to join the BRI at all. Most countries in the region find themselves in between these two poles, as members of the BRI (and recipients of Chinese investment and loans) that are – in the context of US–China competition – unwilling to make geopolitical choices in favour of China.

Over the past decade, the BRI has slowed down. The focus on hard-infrastructure projects apparent in its early years is unlikely to return. Instead, greater focus is being placed on digital-infrastructure projects, as well as the expansion of Chinese ICT platforms and services across the Asia-Pacific, as countries in the region seek either to increase their digital connectivity through roll-outs of next-generation ICT networks or to expand their digital economies. While in the West China's digital expansion has faltered due to concerns about data security, surveillance and intelligence-gathering risks, similar concerns are not as widespread in the Asia-Pacific, where Chinese internet companies still find strong market demand. However, the state of China's domestic economy and its restricted access to the core advanced components needed for infrastructure roll-out (due to US export controls on semiconductors) could complicate China's appetite for lending to high-risk countries and its ability to supply advanced technologies.

Finally, although the BRI's expansion has slowed, Beijing is seeking to build on the BRI and DSR through the promotion of new initiatives that promote Chinese norms and values. Consequently, the Asia-Pacific, and particularly countries in the region that have to date hedged between the US and China, will become a battleground for ideas, norms and values of relevance to the future of the international order. As a result, it will be important in the coming years to observe the extent to which, and how, China manages to convert its BRI and digital investments into useful influence.

NOTES

1   Bao Jiang, Jian Li and Chunxia Gong, 'Maritime Shipping and Export Trade on "Maritime Silk Road"', *Asian Journal of Shipping and Logistics*, vol. 34, no. 2, 2018, pp. 83–90, https://www.sciencedirect.com/science/article/pii/S2092521218300233.

2   'China Urges US to Drop "Cold War" Mentality', Reuters, 7 October 2020, https://www.reuters.com/article/usa-asia-pompeo-china-idUSKBN26S0KU.

3   Meia Nouwens et al., 'China's Digital Silk Road: Integration into National IT Infrastructure and Wider Implications for Western Defence Industries', IISS Research Paper, 11 February 2021, pp. 14–20, https://www.iiss.org/blogs/research-paper/2021/02/china-digital-silk-road-implications-for-defence-industry.

4   *Ibid.*

5   'Asia-Pacific Nations View Chinese Investment with Suspicion', Pew Research Center, 4 December 2019, https://www.pewresearch.org/global/2019/12/05/chinas-economic-growth-mostly-welcomed-in-emerging-markets-but-neighbors-wary-of-its-influence/pg_2019-12-05_balance-of-power_2-07/. See also 'Indonesia to Propose Projects Worth US$91 Billion for China's Belt and Road', *Straits Times*, 20 March 2019, https://www.straitstimes.com/asia/se-asia/indonesia-to-propose-projects-worth-us91-bilion-for-chinas-belt-and-road; Wilda Asmarini and Maikel Jerfiando, 'Indonesia Asks China for Special Fund Under Belt and Road: Minister', Reuters, 3 July 2019, https://www.reuters.com/article/us-indonesia-china-beltandroad-idUSKCN1TY1DU; 'PM Values Efforts to Promote International Connectivity at Belt and Road Forum', Vietnam Investment Review, 30 April 2019, https://vir.com.vn/pm-values-efforts-to-promote-international-connectivity-at-belt-and-road-forum-67444.html; Yukako Ono, 'China's High-speed Train Plans in Southeast Asia Stumble', Nikkei Asia, 28 December 2017, https://asia.nikkei.com/Economy/China-s-high-speed-train-plans-in-Southeast-Asia-stumble; and Stefania Palma, 'Malaysia Cancels China-backed Pipeline Projects', *Financial Times*, 9 September 2018, https://www.ft.com/content/06a71510-b24a-11e8-99ca-68cf89602132.

6   Angus Lam, 'Domestic Politics in Southeast Asia and Local Backlash Against the Belt and Road Initiative', Foreign Policy Research Institute, 15 October 2020, https://www.fpri.org/article/2020/10/domestic-politics-in-southeast-asia-and-local-backlash-against-the-belt-and-road-initiative/.

7   ASEAN Studies Centre, ISEAS–Yusof Ishak Institute, 'The State of Southeast Asia: 2023 Survey Report', 9 February 2023, p. 3, https://www.iseas.edu.sg/wp-content/uploads/2025/07/The-State-of-SEA-2023-Final-Digital-V4-09-Feb-2023.pdf.

8   '$200m Contribution Set for ACMECS Fund', *Nation*, 18 June 2019, https://www.nationthailand.com/business/30371316.

9   European Commission, 'Global Gateway in the Middle East, Asia and the Pacific', https://international-partnerships.ec.europa.eu/policies/global-gateway/initiatives-region/initiatives-middle-east-asia-and-pacific_en.

10 Sreeparna Banerjee, 'India's Connectivity Projects with Myanmar, Post-coup: A Stocktaking', Observer Research Foundation (ORF)*, ORF Issue Brief,* no. 617, February 2023, https://www.orfonline.org/research/indias-connectivity-projects-with-myanmar-post-coup/.

11 Benjamin Zawacki, 'Of Questionable Connectivity: China's BRI and Thai Civil Society', Council on Foreign Relations, 7 June 2014, https://www.cfr.org/blog/questionable-connectivity-chinas-bri-and-thai-civil-society.

12 Shawn W. Crispin, 'China–Thailand Railway Project Gets Untracked', *Diplomat*, 1 April 2016, https://thediplomat.com/2016/04/china-thailand-railway-project-gets-untracked/.

13 Anubhav Shankar Goswami, 'Sri Lanka's Discarded Balancing Act Between India and China Explained', *Journal of Indo-Pacific Affairs*, Air University, 7 October 2021, https://www.airuniversity.af.edu/JIPA/Display/Article/2803695/sri-lankas-discarded-balancing-act-between-india-and-china-explained/.

14 US, Department of State, 'Fourth Annual US–India 2+2 Ministerial Dialogue', 11 April 2022, https://www.state.gov/fourth-annual-u-s-india-22-ministerial-dialogue/.

15 IISS, 'China Connects', 2022, https://chinaconnects.iiss.org/.

16 World Integrated Trade Solution, https://wits.worldbank.org/about_wits.html. Data

accessed: Chinese Machinery and Electronics, raw materials and chemicals exports to Pakistan 2010–2018.

17 Andrew S. Erickson and Gabriel B. Collins, 'China's Oil Security Pipe Dream – The Reality, and Strategic Consequences, of Seaborne Imports', *Naval War College Review*, vol. 63, no. 2, 2010, p. 13, https://digital-commons.usnwc.edu/cgi/viewcontent.cgi?article=1599&context=nwc-review.

18 Rahul Jaybhay, 'China's Pipeline Dream in Pakistan', *Interpreter*, 30 June 2020, https://www.lowyinstitute.org/the-interpreter/china-s-pipeline-dream-pakistan.

19 Ramesh Bhushal, 'Nepal and China to Study Trans-Himalayan Railway', *Nepali Times*, 18 September 2022, https://www.nepalitimes.com/news/nepal-and-china-to-study-trans-himalayan-railway.

20 Meia Nouwens and Helena Legarda, 'Guardians of the Belt and Road', IISS Research Paper, 17 August 2018, https://www.iiss.org/blogs/research-paper/2018/08/guardians-belt-and-road.

21 'Islamic State Claims It Killed Two Chinese in Pakistan', BBC News, 9 June 2017, https://www.bbc.co.uk/news/world-asia-40211431.

22 'Chinese Shipping Employee Killed in Karachi', Gandhara (Radio Free Europe/Radio Liberty), 5 February 2018, https://gandhara.rferl.org/a/pakistan-chinese-engineer/29021102.html.

23 'Pakistan Attack: Chinese National Shot Dead at Karachi Dental Clinic', BBC News, 28 September 2022, https://www.bbc.co.uk/news/world-asia-63066745; and Ali Siddiqi, 'Attack on Chinese Workers in Pakistan Challenges New Government', VOA News, 28 April 2022, https://www.voanews.com/a/attack-on-chinese-workers-in-pakistan-challenges-new-government/6547926.html.

24 IMF, 'Direction of Trade Statistics', https://data.imf.org/regular.aspx?key=61013712. Analysis based on trade statistics for each country's exports to and imports from China in 2013.

25 Sergei Troush, 'China's Changing Oil Strategy and Its Foreign Policy Implications', Brookings Institution, 1 September 1999, https://www.brookings.edu/articles/chinas-changing-oil-strategy-and-its-foreign-policy-implications/.

26 César B. Martínez Álvarez, 'China-Kazakhstan Energy Relations Between 1997 and 2012', *Journal of International Affairs*, 1 January 2016, https://jia.sipa.columbia.edu/china-kazakhstan-energy-relations-1997-2012.

27 IISS, 'China Connects'.

28 'China–Europe Freight Trains Reaching 12,000 in 2020, up 50%', *Global Times*, 19 January 2021, https://www.globaltimes.cn/page/202101/1213258.shtml; 'China's Railway Freight Volume Up 12 Pct in Q1', Xinhua, 10 April 2021, http://www.xinhuanet.com/english/2021-04/10/c_139871263.htm; and Yin Yeping and Tao Mingyang, 'China–Europe Freight Train a Pillar in Global Trade', *Global Times*, 16 June 2022, https://www.globaltimes.cn/page/202206/1268338.shtml.

29 Sebastian Korporal, 'Trade China–Europe: Sea Freight', KPMG, 16 July 2021, https://kpmg.com/de/en/blogs/home/posts/2021/07/trade-china-europe-sea-freight.html.

30 Ganyi Zhang, 'China–EU Rail Freight: A Highly Sensitive Market', Upply, 21 February 2023, https://market-insights.upply.com/en/china-eu-rail-freight-a-highly-sensitive-market.

31 'Two Former Kyrgyz Prime Ministers Receive Prison Terms', Radio Free Europe/Radio Liberty, 6 December 2019, https://www.rferl.org/a/two-former-kyrgyz-prime-ministers-receive-prison-terms-/30311583.html.

32 *Ibid*.

33 Darkhan Umirbekov, 'Kazakhstan: Anti-graft Agents Spring into Action over LRT Scandal', Eurasianet, 11 October 2019, https://eurasianet.org/kazakhstan-anti-graft-agents-spring-into-action-over-lrt-scandal.

34 China, Ministry of Foreign Affairs, 'Wang Yi on China–Solomon Islands Bilateral Security Cooperation', 3 June 2022, https://www.fmprc.gov.cn/eng/zxxx_662805/202206/t20220603_10698478.html.

35 Agence France-Presse, 'Solomon Islands Drops Chinese Tech Giant Huawei for Billion-dollar Undersea Cable, Signs Australia', *South China Morning Post*, 13 June 2018, https://www.scmp.com/news/asia/diplomacy/article/2150616/solomon-islands-drops-chinese-tech-giant-huawei-billion-dollar.

36 IISS, 'China Connects'.

37 Matthew Dornan and Sachini Muller, 'The China Shift in Pacific Trade', Devpolicy Blog, 15 November 2018, https://devpolicy.org/china-in-the-pacific-australias-trade-challenge-20181115/.

38 'Papua New Guinea Trade', World Integrated Trade Solution, https://wits.worldbank.org/CountrySnapshot/en/PNG.

39 Julia Hollingsworth, 'Why China Is Challenging

Australia for Influence over the Pacific Islands',
CNN, 22 July 2019, https://edition.cnn.
com/2019/07/22/asia/china-australia-pacific-
investment-intl-hnk/index.html.

40 Nick Perry, 'China's Largesse in Tonga
Threatens Future of Pacific Nation', AP News,
11 July 2019, https://apnews.com/article/
asia-pacific-business-ap-top-news-china-beijing-
eee7979adb6c470396306c9e4a5d5f7e.

41 Jonathan Barrett, 'Samoa to Scrap China-backed
Port Project Under New Leader', Reuters, 20 May
2021, https://www.reuters.com/world/asia-pacific/
samoa-shelve-china-backed-port-project-under-
new-leader-2021-05-20/; 'China to Build Papua
New Guinea's First National Road System',
Global Construction Review, 24 November 2017,
https://www.globalconstructionreview.com/
china-build-papua-new-guineas-first-national-
road/; and Alexandre Dayant et al., 'Chinese Aid
to the Pacific: Decreasing, but Not Disappearing',
Interpreter, 25 January 2023, https://www.
lowyinstitute.org/the-interpreter/chinese-aid-
pacific-decreasing-not-disappearing.

42 China, Ministry of Foreign Affairs,
'Implementing the Global Security Initiative
to Solve the Security Challenges Facing
Humanity', Speech by Minister of Foreign
Affairs Qin Gang, 22 February 2023, https://
www.fmprc.gov.cn/mfa_eng/wjdt_665385/
zyjh_665391/202302/t20230222_11029589.html.

43 Chaeri Park, 'Knowledge Base: China's "Global
Data Security Initiative" 全球数据安全倡议',
DigiChina, 31 March 2022, https://digichina.
stanford.edu/work/knowledge-base-chi-
nas-global-data-security-initiative/.

44 China, Ministry of Foreign Affairs, 'Position
Paper of the People's Republic of China
for the 77th Session of the United Nations
General Assembly', 17 September 2022, https://
www.fmprc.gov.cn/mfa_eng/wjdt_665385/
wjzcs/202209/t20220917_10767412.html.

45 Mercedes Page, 'Unpacking China's Global
Development Initiative', Interpreter, 1
August 2022, https://www.lowyinstitute.org/
the-interpreter/unpacking-china-s-global-
development-initiative.

46 China, Ministry of Foreign Affairs, 'The Global
Security Initiative Concept Paper', 21 February
2023, https://www.fmprc.gov.cn/mfa_eng/
wjbxw/202302/t20230221_11028348.html.

47 Ibid.

48 Tom Mitchell, 'Beijing Insists BRI Is No Marshall
Plan', Financial Times, 25 September 2018, https://
www.ft.com/content/48f21df8-9c9b-11e8-88de-
49c908b1f264.

49 'China's Global Development Initiative
Is Not as Innocent as It Sounds', The
Economist, 9 June 2022, https://www.
economist.com/china/2022/06/09/
chinas-global-development-initiative-is-not-as-
innocent-as-it-sounds?utm_medium=cpc.
adword.pd&utm_source=google&ppc
campaignID=18156330227&ppcadID=&utm_
campaign=a.22brand_pmax&utm_content=
conversion.direct-response.anonymous&gclid=
EAIaIQobChMI64Dz_5_e_QIVkJftCh2W9
wioEAAYASAAEgKl_fD_BwE&gclsrc=aw.ds.

50 Nectar Gan and Robert Delaney, 'United States
Under Donald Trump Is Veering Away from
China's Belt and Road', South China Morning
Post, 25 April 2019, https://www.scmp.com/
news/china/article/3007504/united-states-under-
trump-veering-away-chinas-belt-and-road.

51 Keita Nakamura, 'G-7 Concerned About
China's "Coercive" Economic Policies:
Statement', Kyodo News, 13 December 2021,
https://english.kyodonews.net/news/2021/12/
da0a4f87c4f9-update1-g-7-concerned-about-
chinas-coercive-economic-policies-uk.
html; Thomas P. Cavanna, 'What Does
China's Belt and Road Initiative Mean for
US Grand Strategy?', Diplomat, 5 June
2018, https://thediplomat.com/2018/06/
what-does-chinas-belt-and-road-initiative-
mean-for-us-grand-strategy/; AFP, 'China's
Xi Seeks to Rewrite Global Trade Rules as US
Retreats', INQUIRER.net, 16 May 2017, https://
newsinfo.inquirer.net/897003/chinas-xi-seeks-
to-rewrite-global-trade-rules-as-us-retreats; and
Michael Schuman, 'The US Can't Make Allies
Take Sides over China', Atlantic, 25 April 2019,
https://www.theatlantic.com/international/
archive/2019/04/us-allies-washington-chi-
na-belt-road/587902/.

52 Gan and Delaney, 'United States Under
Donald Trump Is Veering Away from China's
Belt and Road'.

53 IISS, 'China Connects'.

54 China, Ministry of Foreign Affairs, 'Vision and
Actions on Jointly Building Silk Road Economic
Belt and 21st-Century Maritime Silk Road', 28
March 2015, https://www.fmprc.gov.cn/eng/
topics_665678/2015zt/xjpcxbayzlt2015nnh/
201503/t20150328_705553.html.

55 Todd H. Hall and Alanna Krolikowski, 'Making Sense of China's Belt and Road Initiative: A Review Essay', *International Studies Review*, vol. 24, no. 3, September 2022, https://academic.oup.com/isr/article/24/3/viac023/6654852.

56 *Ibid.*

57 IISS, 'China Connects'.

58 Anthony Rowley, 'China's Belt and Road: "Sour Grapes" Claims of Debt-trap Diplomacy Are Not Supported by Evidence', *South China Morning Post*, 2 November 2020, https://www.scmp.com/comment/opinion/article/3107835/chinas-belt-and-road-sour-grapes-claims-debt-trap-diplomacy-are-not.

59 Deborah Brautigam and Meg Rithmire, 'The Chinese "Debt Trap" Is a Myth', *Atlantic*, 6 February 2021, https://www.theatlantic.com/international/archive/2021/02/china-debt-trap-diplomacy/617953/.

60 Tom Hancock and Matthew Hill, 'Debt Defaults Are a Stress Test for China's Soft Power Strategy', Bloomberg, 26 September 2022, https://www.bloomberg.com/news/articles/2022-09-26/debt-crisis-puts-scrutiny-on-china-soft-power.

61 Sebastian Horn, Carmen M. Reinhart and Christophe Trebesch, 'China's Overseas Lending and the War in Ukraine', VOXEU/ Centre for Economic Policy Research, 11 April 2022, https://cepr.org/voxeu/columns/chinas-overseas-lending-and-war-ukraine.

62 David Lawder and Jorgelina Do Rosario, 'Pakistan Seeks Rescheduling of $27 Billion in Bilateral Debt', Reuters, 15 October 2022, https://www.reuters.com/markets/asia/pakistan-seeks-rescheduling-27-bln-bilateral-debt-finance-minister-2022-10-15/.

63 Joe Cash, 'China Calls for "Joint Action" in Debt Settlements at G20', ZAWYA, 24 February 2023, https://www.zawya.com/en/projects/bri/china-calls-for-joint-action-in-debt-settlements-at-g20-dnvcysri.

64 US, Office of the Secretary of Defense, 'Military and Security Developments Involving the People's Republic of China', 29 November 2022, p. 144, https://media.defense.gov/2022/Nov/29/2003122279/-1/-1/1/2022-MILITARY-AND-SECURITY-DEVELOPMENTS-INVOLVING-THE-PEOPLES-REPUBLIC-OF-CHINA.PDF.

65 Tom Westbrook, 'PNG Upholds Deal with Huawei to Lay Internet Cable, Derides Counter-offer', Reuters, 26 November 2018, https://www.reuters.com/article/us-papua-huawei-tech-id USKCN1NV0DR.

66 Anthony Bergin and Samuel Bashfield, 'Australia Must Do More to Secure the Cables that Connect the Indo-Pacific', *Strategist*, Australian Strategic Policy Institute, 2 August 2022, https://www.aspistrategist.org.au/australia-must-do-more-to-secure-the-cables-that-connect-the-indo-pacific/.

67 Asian Development Bank, 'Meeting Asia's Infrastructure Needs', February 2017, https://www.adb.org/publications/asia-infrastructure-needs.

68 Jonathan E. Hillman, 'How Big Is China's Belt and Road?', Center for Strategic and International Studies, 3 April 2018, https://www.csis.org/analysis/how-big-chinas-belt-and-road.

69 'US to Send Delegation to China's Belt and Road Summit', Reuters, 12 May 2017, https://www.reuters.com/article/us-china-silkroad-usa-idUSKBN18816Q.

70 European Union, External Action Service, 'Speech by HR/VP Mogherini at the Plenary Session of the European Parliament on the State of the EU–China Relations', 11 September 2018, https://www.eeas.europa.eu/node/50337_en.

71 Asian Development Bank, 'Developing Asia Needs to Invest More Than 5% of GDP Over Next Decade for Infrastructure', 29 October 2019, https://www.adb.org/news/developing-asia-needs-invest-more-5-gdp-over-next-decade-infrastructure.

72 European Commission, 'EU Steps Up Its Strategy for Connecting Europe and Asia', 19 September 2018, https://ec.europa.eu/commission/presscorner/detail/en/IP_18_5803.

73 Gan and Delaney, 'United States Under Donald Trump Is Veering Away from China's Belt and Road'.

74 'US Secretary of State Mike Pompeo to Visit Singapore This Week, Plans S$154m Worth of Investments in Indo-Pacific', *Straits Times*, 31 July 2018, https://www.straitstimes.com/world/united-states/us-plans-s154-million-worth-of-investments-in-indo-pacific-pompeo.

75 Jerre V. Hansbrough, 'From the Blue Dot Network to the Blue Dot Marketplace: A Way to Cooperate in Strategic Competition', in Alexander L. Vuving (ed.), *Hindsight, Insight, Foresight: Thinking About Security in the Indo-Pacific* (Honolulu, HI: Daniel K. Inouye Asia-Pacific Center for Security Studies, 2020).

76 White House, 'FACT SHEET: President Biden and G7 Leaders Launch Build Back Better

World (B3W) Partnership', 12 June 2021, https://www.whitehouse.gov/briefing-room/statements-releases/2021/06/12/fact-sheet-president-biden-and-g7-leaders-launch-build-back-better-world-b3w-partnership/.

77 White House, 'FACT SHEET: President Biden and G7 Leaders Formally Launch the Partnership for Global Infrastructure and Investment', 26 June 2022, https://www.whitehouse.gov/briefing-room/statements-releases/2022/06/26/fact-sheet-president-biden-and-g7-leaders-formally-launch-the-partnership-for-global-infrastructure-and-investment/.

78 *Ibid*.

79 White House, 'Additional PGII Projects', https://www.whitehouse.gov/wp-content/uploads/2022/06/Other-PGII-projects.pdf.

80 European Commission, 'EU–Africa: Global Gateway Investment Package', https://commission.europa.eu/strategy-and-policy/priorities-2019-2024/stronger-europe-world/global-gateway/eu-africa-global-gateway-investment-package_en.

81 Christina Lu, 'China's Belt and Road to Nowhere', *Foreign Policy*, 13 February 2023, https://foreignpolicy.com/2023/02/13/china-belt-and-road-initiative-infrastructure-development-geopolitics/.

82 Shivangi Acharya and David Lawder, 'US, China to Hold Deputy-level Bilateral Talks on Debt – Sources', Reuters, 24 February 2023, https://www.reuters.com/business/us-china-hold-deputy-level-bilateral-talks-debt-sources-2023-02-24/.

CHAPTER 5

JAPAN STEPS UP: SECURITY AND DEFENCE POLICY UNDER KISHIDA

ROBERT WARD

IISS Japan Chair; Director of
Geo-economics and Strategy

YUKA KOSHINO

Research Fellow for Security
and Technology Policy, IISS

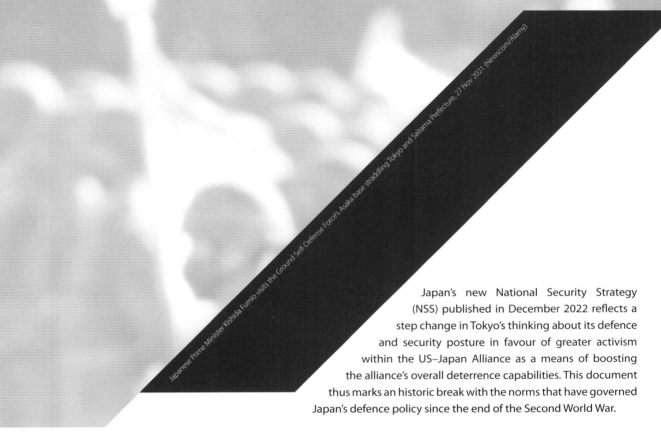
Japanese Prime Minister Kishida Fumio visits the Ground Self-Defense Force's Asaka base straddling Tokyo and Saitama Prefecture, 27 Nov 2021 (Newscom/Alamy)

Japan's new National Security Strategy (NSS) published in December 2022 reflects a step change in Tokyo's thinking about its defence and security posture in favour of greater activism within the US–Japan Alliance as a means of boosting the alliance's overall deterrence capabilities. This document thus marks an historic break with the norms that have governed Japan's defence policy since the end of the Second World War.

JAPAN'S DETERIORATING STRATEGIC ENVIRONMENT

Tokyo's updated NSS paints a bleak picture of Japan's strategic environment, which it describes as being the most 'severe and complex' it has been since 1945. Russia's invasion of Ukraine has aggravated Japan's concerns about threats to the Indo-Pacific status quo, particularly with regard to China's intentions towards Taiwan. The recent chill in Japan's relations with Russia, the evolving China–Russia strategic relationship and North Korea's accelerating development of weapons of mass destruction have added to Tokyo's concerns.

JAPAN'S RESPONSE

Key changes posited by the new NSS include a doubling of the defence budget in the next five years; acquisition of counterstrike capabilities; enhancing capabilities in new domains, such as space; the establishment of a Permanent Joint Headquarters to unify command over the armed services; a strategic focus on the islands in Japan's southwest, which would be most immediately threatened by a Taiwan contingency; and boosting Japan's war-fighting sustainability and resilience.

CHALLENGES FOR IMPLEMENTATION

Notwithstanding the ambition of the new NSS, Japan faces a number of implementation challenges, including capacity shortages in terms of human resources and defence-technological capabilities, and the question of how to pay for the defence-budget increase.

Viewed from Tokyo, 2022 brought a marked deterioration in the security environment around Japan that has widened the geopolitical fault lines in its immediate neighbourhood and beyond. The Japanese government's bleak assessment of the strategic environment was evident in the historic new National Security Strategy (NSS) and two related documents, the National Defense Strategy (NDS) and the Defense Buildup Program (DBP), which were all published on 16 December 2022.[1] Replacing the 2013 NSS – Japan's first such document – the 2022 NSS speaks of 'historical changes in

A shipwreck on a beach in the Russia-occupied southern Kuril Islands, claimed by Japan as the Northern Territories, 16 March 2022

(Natalia Zakharova/Anadolu Agency via Getty Images)

power balances, particularly in the Indo-Pacific region' that are 'defining an era', recognising that Japan's security environment is 'as severe and complex as it has ever been since the end of World War II'.[2] This assessment contrasts with the previous NSS, which, while for example flagging concerns about threats to the global commons from unilateral attempts to change the status quo, took a relatively benign view of Japan's strategic challenges.[3]

JAPAN'S DETERIORATING STRATEGIC ENVIRONMENT

Deteriorating relations with Russia

An important trigger for Japan's rising alarm was Russia's invasion of Ukraine in February 2022. Japan's alignment with the other members of the G7 in terms of condemning and imposing economic sanctions in response to Russia's war of aggression, together with financial and material support for Ukraine, chilled already tepid Japan–Russia relations.[4] The immediate impact was to stall bilateral negotiations over the four disputed islands north of Hokkaido (the southern Kuril Islands, annexed by Soviet forces in 1945 and claimed by Japan as the Northern Territories) and for Russia to suspend related talks with Japan on a bilateral peace treaty.[5] Consequently, Tokyo's position regarding the islands has also hardened, signalling the end of the more emollient Russia policy pursued under the late Abe Shinzo's second premiership from 2012–20. In March 2022, Tokyo reverted to its description of the islands as 'inherent territories of Japan' that are 'under illegal occupation', replacing a formulation describing them as 'islands over which Japan has sovereignty'.[6]

Abe's engagement strategy towards Russia was premised in part on Japan's strategic need to prevent cooperation between Russia and China. However, securing significant concessions from Moscow always appeared an optimistic ambition, particularly given Russia's strategic need to retain the islands and the changes to its constitution in July 2020, which, inter alia, prohibited the 'alienation' of Russian territories.[7] Notwithstanding China's concerns over Russia's prosecution of its war against Ukraine and, notably, Moscow's threats to use nuclear weapons, the rapid evolution of Sino-Russian strategic relations is adding more fuel to Tokyo's strategic concerns. Examples of the operationalisation of these relations around Japan include the Sino-Russian aerial patrols over the Sea of Japan (East Sea) and the East China Sea in November 2022 – in which Russian bombers

Map 5.1: **China and Russia: selected joint patrols and exercises, 2019–22**

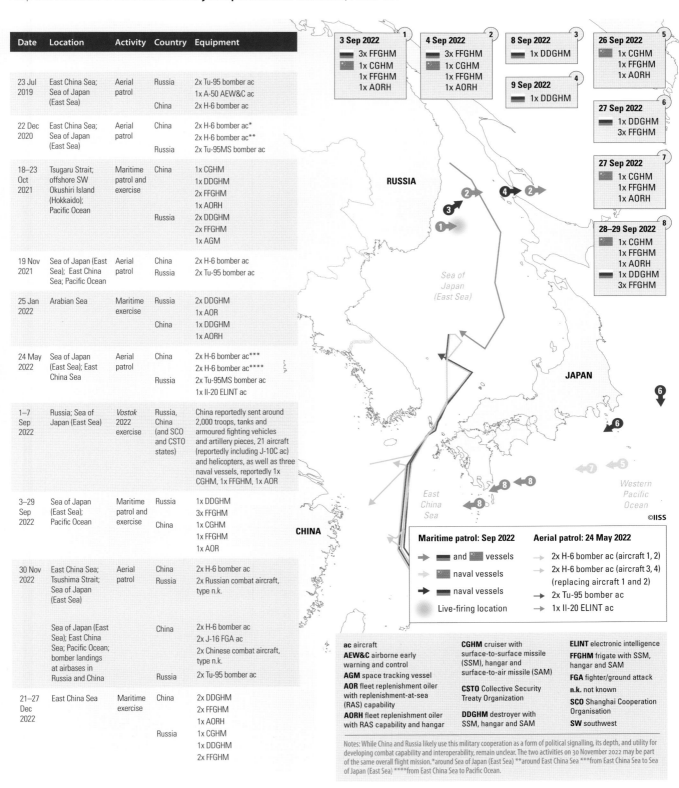

landed in China for the first time and Chinese aircraft then flew to Russia – and a joint maritime patrol in October 2021 that cruised around Japan's Honshu, Shikoku and Kyushu islands en route to the East China Sea (see Map 5.1).[8]

Sources: IISS; Japan, Ministry of Defense, www.mod.go.jp

Map 5.2: **Chinese and North Korean ballistic-missile launches into or over Japan's exclusive economic zone (EEZ), 2019–Feb 2023**

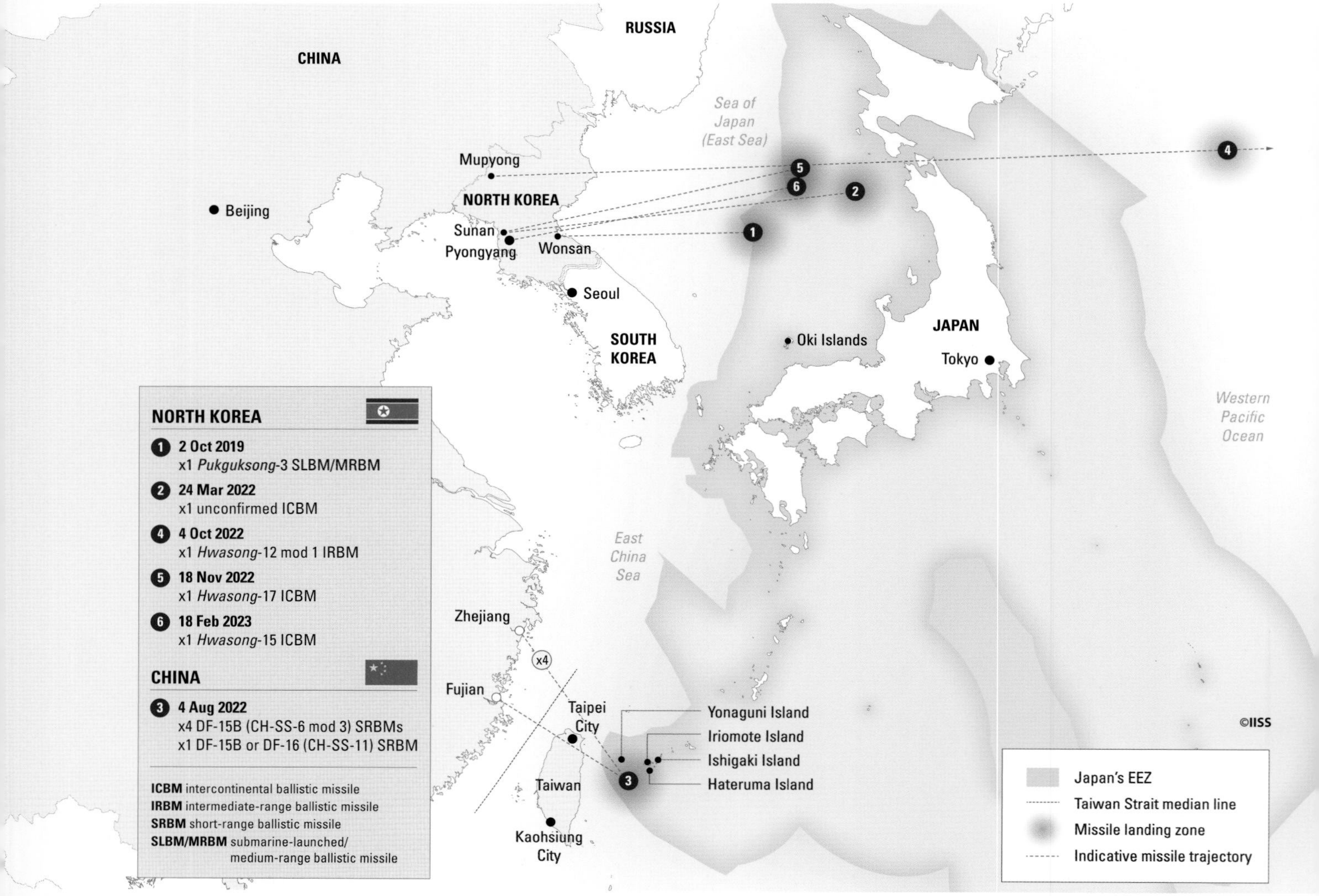
RUSSIA
CHINA
Sea of Japan (East Sea)
Mupyong
NORTH KOREA
Beijing
Sunan
Pyongyang
Wonsan
Seoul
SOUTH KOREA
Oki Islands
JAPAN
Tokyo
Western Pacific Ocean
East China Sea
Zhejiang
Fujian
x4
Taipei City
Taiwan
Kaohsiung City
Yonaguni Island
Iriomote Island
Ishigaki Island
Hateruma Island
©IISS
NORTH KOREA
1 2 Oct 2019
x1 *Pukguksong*-3 SLBM/MRBM
2 24 Mar 2022
x1 unconfirmed ICBM
4 4 Oct 2022
x1 *Hwasong*-12 mod 1 IRBM
5 18 Nov 2022
x1 *Hwasong*-17 ICBM
6 18 Feb 2023
x1 *Hwasong*-15 ICBM
CHINA
3 4 Aug 2022
x4 DF-15B (CH-SS-6 mod 3) SRBMs
x1 DF-15B or DF-16 (CH-SS-11) SRBM
ICBM intercontinental ballistic missile
IRBM intermediate-range ballistic missile
SRBM short-range ballistic missile
SLBM/MRBM submarine-launched/ medium-range ballistic missile
Japan's EEZ
Taiwan Strait median line
Missile landing zone
Indicative missile trajectory

Note: North Korea also launched a modified KN-23 SRBM on 25 March 2021, which Japan initially assessed not to have landed in its EEZ – however, South Korea's reassessment indicates that it may have.

Sources: Japan, Ministry of Defense, mod.go.jp; IISS

Rising tensions around Taiwan

Particularly since the 2020–21 administration of prime minister Suga Yoshihide, Japan has been more willing to articulate its concerns about Taiwan's security. A joint statement following a summit between Suga and US President Joe Biden in April 2021 included a reference to the 'importance of peace and stability across the Taiwan Strait'. It was the first time that Taiwan had been mentioned in a US–Japan leaders' statement since the 1969 summit between then US president Richard Nixon and then Japanese prime minister Sato Eisaku.[9] It was followed in July 2021 by the first mention in a Japanese defence white paper of the importance of the stability of the 'situation surrounding Taiwan' for Japan's security.[10] Concurrently, Japan has sought to strengthen its international partners' interest in participating in efforts to preserve Taiwan's security. Thus, in his keynote address to the June 2022 Shangri-La Dialogue, Japanese Prime Minister Kishida Fumio linked European and East Asian security, asserting that 'Ukraine today may be East Asia tomorrow'.[11] Kishida's subsequent attendance at a NATO summit – becoming the first Japanese prime minister to do so – in Madrid in June further underscored his linking of European and Asian security.

Triggers for Japan's greater willingness to voice its concerns about the stability of its southern flank include the increasingly strong rhetoric from Chinese President Xi Jinping regarding Beijing's intent to absorb Taiwan into the People's Republic of China; China's intense territorial needling around the Senkaku/Diaoyu islands, which Japan controls and China claims; and the rapid rise in China's military spending, which is now estimated to be some five times larger than that of Japan.[12] Moreover, in a belligerent response to then-speaker of the US House of Representatives Nancy Pelosi's visit to Taiwan in August 2022, China conducted its largest-ever live-fire military exercises around the island, firing five ballistic missiles into Japan's exclusive economic zone (EEZ) (See Map 5.2).[13] This crisis focused Japanese attention on both the vulnerability of the Senkaku/Diaoyu islands, which lie just 170 kilometres east of Taiwan, and the strategic importance of the Nansei Islands, which lie close to the disputed territory and would be a key staging post for any joint response by the United States and Japan to a Chinese attack on Taiwan.

Intensification of North Korean missile launches

In 2022, there was also a ratcheting up of the threat to Japanese security posed by North Korea. Pyongyang fired around 90 cruise and ballistic missiles, notching up a record for the number of missiles fired in one year. Indeed, one assessment indicated that 2022 accounted for some one-quarter of the 270 missiles fired and nuclear devices tested by North Korea since 1984.[14] Pyongyang's activities included the resumption of intercontinental ballistic missile (ICBM) tests for the first time since 2017. Of particular concern to Japan were the launch of an ICBM on 24 March (Pyongyang claimed this was a *Hwasong*-17, which would allow it to strike the US mainland with a large payload); the launch of an intermediate-range ballistic missile (IRBM) over Japan on 4 October – the first anniversary of Kishida's becoming prime minister – marking the first time since 2017 that a North Korean missile had overflown Japanese territory; a *Hwasong*-17 launch on 18 November (the missile landed in Japan's EEZ some 200 km off the west coast of Hokkaido); and the launch on 18 December (shortly after Japan's release of its new NSS) of two ballistic missiles capable of reaching Japan, which landed in the Sea of Japan (East Sea) outside Japan's EEZ.

As of February 2023, North Korea had not yet resumed testing nuclear devices despite scrapping in March 2022 a self-imposed moratorium on such tests in effect since November 2017. However, the intensity of Pyongyang's ballistic-missile tests in 2022 and early 2023 (a *Hwasong*-15 ICBM launch took place on 18 February, landing in Japan's EEZ off the west coast of Hokkaido) suggests that it continues to prioritise development of asymmetric capabilities. US intelligence reports in late 2022 suggesting that North Korea was supplying Russia with materiel for its war against Ukraine added further to Tokyo's perception of the vulnerability of Japan's western flank.[15]

JAPAN'S RESPONSE

Against this background, the 2022 NSS represents an historic break with the norms that have governed Japan's defence policy since 1945. One important initiative mentioned in the document is that Japan will develop 'comprehensive national power', which includes diplomatic, defence, economic, technological and intelligence capabilities and reflects the 'comprehensive' nature of the security challenge from China.[16] The articulation of these capabilities is in itself a major advancement from the 2013 NSS, which attempted to take a cross-governmental approach to national security for the first time but remained primarily focused on diplomatic and defence capabilities. The most transformative element of the 2022 NSS, however, was the government's commitment to bolster its national defence capabilities to an unprecedented level to take 'primary responsibility' to defend itself in the event that Japan is

Japan Ground Self-Defense Force troops at Camp Asaka in Tokyo, 27 November 2021

(KIYOSHI OTA/POOL/AFP via Getty Images)

invaded.[17] This is a step change from Japan's previous defence and security policy, which relied on US security guarantees, and has broader implications for Japan's role in the US–Japan Alliance as well as in regional security more generally in the event of conflict, for example over Taiwan.

Shift in approach, unprecedented spending increases

Although the second Abe administration laid out much of the groundwork for this shift to occur, Kishida's administration deserves credit for revamping Japan's defence and security posture in two ways. Firstly, it has developed Japan's first post-war NDS, positing ends, means and ways to deter aggression and to disrupt and repel an invasion of Japan in the next decade. The NDS, modelled after the US National Security Strategy, was a structural break from previous recommendations made through the National Defense Program Guidelines (NDPG), which were first introduced in 1976 amid the Cold War detente between the Soviet Union and the US and were updated most recently in 2018. The purpose of the NDPG was to define the size of the Japan Self-Defense Forces (JSDF, Japan's de facto armed forces) and to inform the five-year procurement plan – the Mid-Term Defense Program – needed to meet the 'minimum necessary' capability standard suggested by Article 9 of the Japanese constitution, which renounces 'war as a sovereign right' and prohibits the country from possessing land, sea and air forces.[18] Therefore, the NDPG was not based on a war-fighting strategy per se. Indeed, the first NDPG in 1976 recommended building a 'Basic Defence Force' sufficient to prevent a power vacuum from emerging in East Asia; therefore, the force structure it described was not meant to counter particular threats. In contrast, the NDS seeks to respond to an 'opponent's capabilities and new ways of warfare' to inform the five-year DBP.[19]

Secondly, the Kishida administration has committed Tokyo to doubling defence-related spending to 2% of GDP and to invest ¥43 trillion (US$325 billion) to cover Japan's 'fundamentally reinforced defense capabilities' in fiscal years 2023/24 to 2027/28.[20] For Japan, the unparalleled size and speed of this defence-spending increase is an historic departure from the ceiling (1% of GDP) adopted by the Miki Takeo government in 1976 and continued even under the second Abe administration, which pursued robust security reforms to respond to growing security challenges from North Korea and China.[21] If realised, this increase will make Japan's defence budget the third largest globally after the US and China.

Important influences on the planned increase in defence spending were the Japanese government's threat assessments and simulations, which revealed that the JSDF would not be ready to deter aggression and respond to the threats potentially posed to Japan by 2027/28.[22] Referring to Russia's full-scale invasion of Ukraine, the NDS claimed that unilateral changes to the status quo by force could also happen in the Indo-Pacific and that intentions of aggression are difficult to assess.[23] It may not be a coincidence that the NSS's target coincides with former commander of US Indo-Pacific Command (INDOPACOM) Admiral Philip Davidson's assessment – conveyed in March 2021 – that China could invade Taiwan as early as 2027.[24]

The government's effort to implement step changes in JSDF capabilities focuses on seven key areas (see Figure 5.1 for more detail):

▸ stand-off defence capabilities
▸ integrated air and missile defence (IAMD)
▸ uncrewed defence capabilities
▸ cross-domain operational capabilities
▸ mobile deployment capabilities and protection of civilians
▸ command and control (C2) and intelligence-related capabilities
▸ the sustainability and resiliency of JSDF operations during wartime[25]

Implications for JSDF posture and operations

Drawing lessons from the war in Ukraine, these capabilities are expected to enhance Japan's defence and security posture in the three areas most relevant to potential contingencies around Japan. The first

Figure 5.1: **Japan's Defense Buildup Program, 2022**

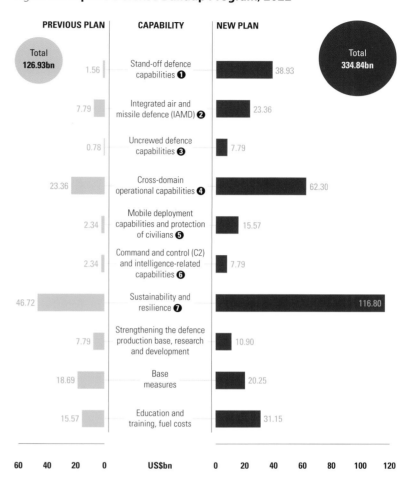

Source: Japan, Ministry of Defense, mod.go.jp

is Japan's response to the diverse missile threats posed by China and North Korea. The 2022 NSS established the ambition for the JSDF to possess the capability to 'mount effective counterstrikes against the opponent to prevent further attacks' in the case of attacks against Japan or a third country.[26] The documents are vague regarding the specific targets (and whether to include the opponent's C2 structure) and they are expected to be decided on a case-by-case basis.[27] This is a major shift from Japan's existing missile-defence architecture, which relies on intercepting missiles through ballistic missile

A Type-12 anti-ship missile on display during a symposium at Kisarazu Air Field in Chiba Prefecture, Japan, 16 June 2022

(David Mareuil/Anadolu Agency via Getty Images)

defence (BMD) systems rather than possessing a counterstrike capability.[28] The debate over acquiring counterstrike capability is not new – the constitutionality of the capability was first stated by then-prime minister Hatoyama Ichiro as early as 1956.[29] However, political, budgetary and technical challenges prevented successive governments from acquiring the capability, despite growing public support for this since 2017, when North Korea increased its missile launches.[30]

To develop this counterstrike capability, Tokyo seeks to deploy indigenous stand-off missiles that are currently under development. It is also consulting with the US over the purchase of *Tomahawk* land-attack missiles for earlier deployment in 2026.[31] First outlined in the 2018 NDPG, stand-off defence is defined by the government as 'capabilities to deal with ships and landing forces attempting to invade Japan including remote islands from the outside of their threat envelopes'.[32] Three types of indigenous missiles are under development: upgraded Type-12 anti-ship missiles with their range extended from 200 km to 900 km and with a new capacity to attack mobile targets; Block 1 hyper-velocity gliding projectiles; and hypersonic cruise missiles.

Developing a counterstrike capability to pursue a US-like 'integrated air and missile defence' (IAMD) would strengthen Japan's deterrence against the emerging missile challenges posed by highly manoeuvrable Chinese hypersonic-weapons systems, as well as saturation attacks from both China and North Korea. Rapid development and mass production of diverse stand-off missiles could also help reduce the growing discrepancy in IRBM numbers between China on the one hand and the US and Japan on the other, adding credibility to deterrence.[33]

The second area of enhancement is cross-domain operational capability, including the relatively new domains of space, cyber and the electromagnetic spectrum. Under the 2018 NDPG, Japan established several new units to enhance capabilities in these domains, such as Space Domain Mission Units for space situational awareness; a Cyber Defense Command to enhance the defence of JSDF networks across its branches; and electronic-warfare units within the Japan Ground Self-Defense Force (JGSDF, Japan's de facto army) to monitor radar and other emissions from potential adversaries. However, the NDS goes further by recognising these domains as 'vitally important' for carrying out cross-domain operations in response to the complex threats facing Japan.[34] In particular, it underscores the importance of the role of space in information gathering, communications and positioning functions in support of Japan's new counterstrike capability.[35] It also calls for a major expansion of the number of personnel working in the cyber-related units – such as the JSDF Cyber Defense Command – from 800 to about 4,000 by 2027, to enhance protection of its critical networks. The total number of defence-ministry and JSDF personnel engaging in cyber is expected to grow to 20,000 by the end of fiscal year 2027.[36]

A Japan Air Self-Defense Force C-130 plane departs from Iruma Air Base in Saitama Prefecture to evacuate Japanese nationals from Afghanistan, 24 August 2021

(STR/JIJI PRESS/AFP via Getty Images)

The 2022 NSS emphasised the need to strengthen Japan's cyber security through a whole-of-government approach. Among the most innovative measures in this regard was the introduction of an 'active cyber defence', which allows the relevant government authority, including the JSDF, to use a limited offensive capability to 'penetrate and neutralize attacker's servers' in advance of potential attacks against Japan's networks.[37] This makes strategic sense for Japan, given that the current porosity of its cyber defences and the weakness of its security-clearance frameworks are barriers to closer security cooperation with the US and like-minded partners. The NSS also calls for a restructuring of the National Center of Incident Readiness and Strategy for Cybersecurity (known as NISC), which, inter alia, coordinates intra-government cyber-policy formation, to create a new centralised organisation to implement these cyber-security policies.[38]

Highly significantly for cross-domain operations is the establishment of the Permanent Joint Headquarters (PJH) headed by a joint-service commander, which will unify the command of the JGSDF, the Japan Maritime Self-Defense Force (JMSDF, Japan's de facto navy) and the Japan Air Self-Defense Force (JASDF, Japan's de facto air force) to conduct joint operations in times of conflict as well as in peacetime.[39] This is a breakthrough from organisational and operational standpoints. Under the existing Japan Self-Defense Forces Law, the JSDF can form joint task forces (JTFs) temporarily to conduct specific missions, such as BMD. However, in practice JTFs have not operated comprehensively across domains despite being joint units (formed by units from two or three branches of the JSDF). Moreover, JTFs have been led by senior commanding officers from different branches of the JSDF. As a result, the chain of command has been complex – undermining efforts to develop a unified approach for cross-domain operations.[40] The new PJH and its commander will be indispensable as Japan seeks to operationalise the envisaged counterstrike capabilities, given that the relevant missile systems are expected to be deployed across the three JSDF branches.[41]

The third area of enhancement is the defence of the southwestern region, where Japan's Ryukyu Islands are located, to prepare for a potential contingency in the Senkaku/Diaoyu islands or the Taiwan Strait. Since 2016, Japan has been rapidly expanding JSDF units in the Ryukyu Islands – as well as deploying new units there – to enhance its capabilities to defend this relatively remote territory.[42] In light of growing tensions in the Taiwan Strait and increased naval activities by China in the Senkaku/Diaoyu islands and the Western Pacific, which China accessed through the Ryukyu Islands, the three documents take further steps to ensure that, from peacetime to contingency, preparations for a potential conflict in the southwest region of Japan are informed by a whole-of-government approach. For example, the JSDF, the Japan Coast Guard (JCG) and the police will conduct training and exercises to practise responses to potential 'grey-zone' and wartime challenges, including the protection of critical infrastructure, such as nuclear-power plants.[43] The JSDF and the JCG will further enhance coordination by establishing an information-sharing mechanism and by developing new procedures so that the Ministry of Defense may exercise operational control over the JCG in the event of an armed attack against Japan.[44]

The document also calls for Japan to increase investment in transport capabilities and to conduct a major military reorganisation in order to facilitate the mobile and rapid deployment of JSDF and civil-protection capabilities. To help achieve this aspiration, Tokyo seeks to expand the use and functions of existing airports and seaports as well as civilian aircraft and vessels.[45] In addition, major procurement for the JSDF under the DBP includes eight transport ships, six C-2 transport aircraft and 13 KC-46A aerial refuelling/transport aircraft.[46] To make JSDF units more mobile across the Japanese archipelago, the DBP calls for the reorganisation of 14 ground divisions and brigades based outside Okinawa into deployable mobile units.[47]

The government has also earmarked one-third (approximately US$112bn) of the total new investment in defence for war-fighting sustainability and resilience, such as procurement of ammunition stocks and fuel, development of storage facilities, and improvement of the operational availability of defence equipment in Japan's southwestern region.[48] It also seeks to enhance the hardening of JSDF bases and to expand the functions and capacity of JSDF hospitals in the region.[49]

Developing other elements of 'comprehensive national power', such as economic and intelligence capabilities, will also be important for Japan as it seeks to implement its defence goals and shape a favourable security environment. For example, the NSS outlines an 'all-of-economy' response to threats of economic coercion that includes promoting the rules-based economic order under the Comprehensive and Progressive Agreement for Trans-Pacific Partnership and enhancing economic security through supply-chain resilience and dual-use-technology protection and promotion. These steps serve to continue the efforts made by the Japanese government to enhance inter-agency coordination of economic-security policy under the 2022 Economic Security Promotion Act.

IMPLICATIONS FOR THE US AND LIKE-MINDED PARTNERS

Through these defence reforms, Tokyo seeks to play a greater role – in conjunction with the US and other like-minded partners – in responding to the spectrum of security threats, ranging from peacetime and grey-zone challenges to outright conflict. In relation to the US–Japan Alliance, the new strategic documents emphasise their alignment with the national-security and -defence strategies released by the Biden administration in 2022 and call for the alliance to enhance 'joint deterrence capabilities of both countries in an integrated manner'.[50] The NDS states that Japan will play a larger role in regional security and that the government's approach is supported by the Japanese public.[51] The US administration welcomed Japan's new security-policy documents immediately after their release and held a series of high-level meetings – such as the Biden–Kishida summit and the US–Japan Security Consultative Committee (also known as the Foreign and Defense Ministers' Meeting, or '2+2') – within a month of their publication to deepen cooperation.[52]

Japanese Prime Minister Kishida Fumio and US President Joe Biden shake hands during their summit in Washington DC, 13 January 2023

(MANDEL NGAN/AFP via Getty Images)

There are several areas of opportunity for enhancing joint deterrence and response capability under the new Japanese posture. One is counterstrike capability. The NDS states that Japan will gain support from the US in the realm of information gathering to make Japan's counterstrike capability more effective.[53] Japan's development of a US-style IAMD – a concept that seeks to respond to airborne threats through 'unified and optimized operation of various sensors and shooters through networks' – leaves room for Japan to become integrated into the US IAMD if the two forces develop a joint C2 structure like that of NATO.[54] The JSDF's new PJH commander is expected to serve as a direct counterpart to the INDOPACOM commander, enabling enhanced operational coordination and bilateral planning for a potential regional conflict.[55] An increase in joint and shared use of Japanese and US military facilities is expected to further enhance readiness for such a contingency.

Beyond cooperation under the US–Japan Alliance, the NSS further states ambitions to 'build a multilayered network' among US regional alliances and like-minded countries in pursuit of both Japan's Free and Open Indo-Pacific (FOIP) framework and enhanced deterrence.[56] In particular, the NSS calls for increased military-to-military engagement; intelligence exchanges through signing information-protection agreements; acquisition and cross-servicing agreements; reciprocal access agreements (RAAs); joint development and transfer of defence equipment and technology; provision of capacity-building support; cooperation and coordination of strategic communication; and the expansion and deepening of joint Flexible Deterrent Options with Japan's partners through diplomatic, intelligence and economic means.[57] The signing of regional RAAs with Australia in 2021 and the United Kingdom in 2022, the second and third countries, respectively, with which Japan has such agreements (after the US), were historically significant and further demonstrated Tokyo's willingness to intensify security cooperation with like-minded partners. Following the first Japan–Philippines Foreign and Defense Ministerial Meeting in 2022, Tokyo is also deepening military exchanges with the Philippines, both bilaterally

(David Wa/Alamy Stock Photo)

Japan Ground Self-Defense Force soldiers make an amphibious landing and distribute aid as part of the KAMANDAG exercise in the Philippines, 6 October 2018

and trilaterally with the US (see Figure 5.2).[58] Due to the Philippines' geographical location, this cooperation has strategic importance in the context of preparations for potential regional contingencies.

The promotion of defence-equipment and -technology transfer is another area where Tokyo seeks to make progress in cooperation with like-minded countries. As of February 2022, Japan had signed defence-equipment and -technology transfer agreements with 12 countries.[59] However, the only major agreement on the transfer of equipment to another country's armed forces (rather than to coastguards or other paramilitary forces) so far has been a 2020 contract to sell three fixed long-range radar systems and one mobile air-surveillance radar system to the Philippines for deployment in the Bashi Channel.[60] Tokyo sees its collaboration with the UK and Italy on joint next-generation fighter development – through the Global Combat Air Programme (GCAP) – as a major opportunity to integrate its defence businesses into global defence-industrial supply chains and to develop Japan's advanced defence-industrial base and increase its opportunities for international sales. The GCAP intends to produce a replacement for Japan's F-2 combat aircraft by 2035.

CHALLENGES FOR IMPLEMENTATION

Japan, however, faces a number of challenges in implementing its defence- and security-reform agenda. One challenge will be whether Japan can overcome its shortages of funding, manpower and defence-technological capabilities. The Kishida administration is seeking to increase taxes to support the defence-budget increase. However, there is no political consensus on such measures. While Japanese public opinion seems broadly supportive of the need to bolster national defence, polls suggest some 60–80% of the public wants Kishida to hold a snap general election before any defence-budget tax increases are implemented.[61] JSDF capacity will also face

Figure 5.2: **Japan: selected joint combat and non-combat exercises with partner countries, 2012–21**

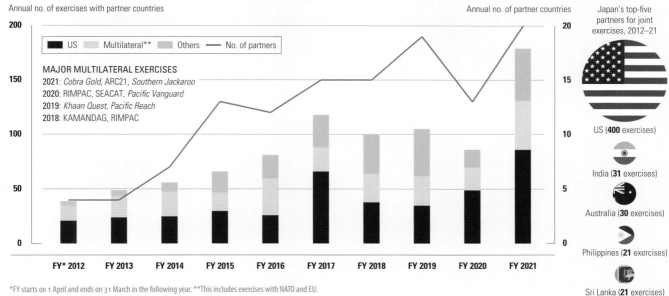

*FY starts on 1 April and ends on 31 March in the following year. **This includes exercises with NATO and EU.

Source: Japan, Ministry of Defense, *Defense of Japan* (volumes 2014–22), www.mod.go.jp

constraints as the government does not plan to increase the number of JSDF personnel in order to implement new initiatives, such as counterstrike capability and cyber defence. Tokyo seeks to accelerate investments to develop and use uncrewed naval, aerial and ground systems to mitigate personnel shortages. However, this approach will still require skilled personnel capable of developing and operating the new systems. Former senior JSDF personnel have claimed that Tokyo has to increase JSDF personnel numbers to 300,000 – from the current 247,000 – but the JSDF continues to face serious recruitment challenges.[62] The challenge is exacerbated by the rapid ageing of Japanese society and the country's declining population.[63]

Japan's defence-industrial and -technological base may also struggle to meet the JSDF's requirements. Major Japanese defence businesses are generally only small parts of much larger conglomerates, contributing an average of just 4% of total group revenue and with only a single customer, Japan's Ministry of Defense.[64] According to Japan's Ministry of Finance, the operating profit margin for defence equipment was 7.7% in the 2020/21 financial year, compared with 10% in major Western defence industries.[65] Although Tokyo eased its arms-export restrictions in 2014, overseas sales have remained minimal due to the costly procedures of going through multiple approval processes across governments and the unpredictability of the government's decision-making process.[66] The lack of overseas sales reflects Japan's dearth of experience in selling defence equipment abroad, one leading example of which was its unsuccessful bid in 2016 to sell *Soryu*-class submarines to Australia.[67] Tokyo is preparing to introduce a series of new measures, including new legislation by mid-2023 to reinforce its defence industry through cash injections; support for cyber-security protection to prevent technology outflow; and further revisions to the arms-export guidelines to facilitate third-country transfers of defence equipment. Government and public efforts to improve the predictability of sales opportunities abroad will be a vital factor in maintaining and expanding the domestic production and technology base.[68]

Another set of challenges is the administration's need to overcome sectionalism across government as it attempts to meet its comprehensive national power development targets. The new defence and security documents call for close cooperation between the Ministry of Defense, the JSDF and civilian agencies – such as the police, JCG and local governments – to enhance Japan's national security (such as through closer coordination across government to ensure the security of the Ryukyu Islands), cyber security and intelligence activities. It will not be an easy task to overcome cultural and organisational differences to improve the stove-piped nature of communications between them. Enduring sectionalism within the JSDF is a good example, and may be an obstacle to effective and timely implementation of the daunting list of goals included in the NDS and DBP. A report has suggested that the JGSDF, the JMSDF and the JASDF are struggling to reach agreement on the location of the PJH, leading its establishment to be postponed to 2024 or 2025.[69] A delay could have major implications for Tokyo's push to improve cross-domain operations and for US–Japan defence cooperation.

The new documents also call for close coordination with civilian research institutions and commercial technology firms to facilitate the JSDF's adoption of advanced dual-use technologies in the realms of space and cyber. Interactions between the civilian sector and defence agencies have improved following, for example, new government initiatives to better coordinate strategy-making for dual-use-technology protection and promotion. These include sending defence-ministry officials to the Cabinet Office to offer expertise for inward-direct-investment screening and information management, and the government's ¥500bn (almost US$3.73bn) investment fund for advanced technologies, such as artificial intelligence and quantum technologies.[70] However, there remains a significant gap between defence and civilian research and development and there is room for improvement in non-military agencies' understanding of future war-fighting trends and techniques – a shortcoming that threatens to undermine Japan's potential in defence-relevant advanced technology.

The last set of challenges for implementation concerns Japan's ability to manage relations with and control the expectations of domestic and external stakeholders and partners. High public support for a defence build-up and for deepening Japan's role within the US–Japan Alliance – demonstrated in poll surveys – signals strong support for Japan to play a greater role in maintaining regional stability, including in the event of conflict. However, the sustainability of this support is still in question. While the government seeks to enhance ammunition stockpiles and facilities for wartime resiliency and sustainability in the Ryukyu Islands, the plan risks resistance from local governments, as in the case of Tokyo's failure to deploy surface-to-ship and surface-to-air missiles on Miyako Island after establishing a new base there in 2019.[71] Experts from the US and Japan have speculated about a possible nuclear threat from China, for example, as a scenario that could constrain Japan's course of action in the event of regional conflict.[72] Thus, discussions with local stakeholders and US counterparts will be critical to foster greater understanding of and support for Tokyo's policies among local stakeholders and to manage the expectations of the US regarding a realistic role for Japan in a potential Taiwan contingency.

Tokyo will further need to be attentive to extra-regional partners' capacity and political will to engage in Indo-Pacific security. Since 2018, for example, several European countries have launched Indo-Pacific policy documents – which echo elements of Japan's FOIP – to demonstrate their interest in preserving the rules-based order and stability in Asia. These include France (2018), Germany (2020) and the United Kingdom (2021). The EU also published such a document in 2021. These actors have also been increasing their military engagement in the region to help deter any

Japanese Prime Minister Kishida Fumio and his British counterpart Rishi Sunak sign the Japan–UK Reciprocal Access Agreement in London, 11 January 2023

(Carl Court/Getty Images)

coercive attempts to challenge the status quo. However, Russia's war on Ukraine and the robust military assistance from Europe to help Ukraine defend itself are raising questions about their ability to continue their engagement, especially given post-coronavirus-pandemic budget constraints and economic pressures.[73] The signing of an RAA with the UK in January 2023 was significant for Tokyo. However, whether the two countries' militaries can significantly enhance practical defence cooperation will depend on the UK's political and financial capacity to commit a larger persistent presence to the region or, at least, to undertake a major military deployment to the region on the scale of the 2021 Carrier Strike Group. Active diplomacy may therefore be required from Tokyo to encourage its European partners to maintain the momentum of deeper defence and security involvement in its region.

CONCLUSION

The security policies of the Kishida administration represent a structural break in Japan's security posture. In effect, they put an end to the so-called Yoshida Doctrine, under which Japan relied on the US for its defence, maintained a 'low posture' in international affairs and pursued an economy-first domestic-policy stance, and which dominated Japan's security discourse for most of the post-war period.[74] If successful, the reforms outlined in the new NSS will increase significantly Japan's role in its security alliance with the US and thereby reinforce Tokyo's deterrence capabilities in terms of lethality and range. Moreover, Tokyo's efforts to build and reinforce friendly coalitions and networks in the region are designed to further amplify Japan's influence there. The discussions in February 2023 between Japan and the Philippines on deepening their bilateral security cooperation are yet another example of this.[75] By extension, Tokyo hopes that these reforms will provide a credible security underpinning for the foreign-policy activism that gathered pace under the second Abe administration, with an emphasis on deployment of Japanese geo-economic power.

Japanese public opinion is largely supportive of the planned changes. This support is all the more striking given the intensity of the negative public reaction to the legislation the Diet passed in 2015 to enable 'collective self-defence' in situations in which Japan's survival was threatened. The Liberal Democratic Party's policy platform for the July 2022 upper-house election, which led on foreign and security policy, was another sign of how much the public debate in Japan has changed with regard to security issues.[76] The focus in the new NSS on 'reinforcing the social base' suggests the government is aware that it will have to continue to proselytise on the need for further security reforms.[77] However, rising public concern about China's intentions in the region suggests that a return to the Yoshida Doctrine is now highly unlikely. Notwithstanding political differences over how to pay for the expansion of Japan's security role, the coming decade is likely to bring with it further profound changes in Japan's security posture that will be transformative both for Japan and for the broader Indo-Pacific.

NOTES

1   Japan, Cabinet Secretariat, 'National Security Strategy of Japan', December 2022, https://www.cas.go.jp/jp/siryou/221216anzenho-shou/nss-e.pdf; Japan, Ministry of Defense, 'National Defense Strategy', 16 December 2022, https://www.mod.go.jp/j/approach/agenda/guideline/strategy/pdf/strategy_en.pdf; and Japan, Ministry of Defense, 'Defense Buildup Program', 16 December 2023, https://www.mod.go.jp/j/approach/agenda/guideline/plan/pdf/program_en.pdf.

2   Japan, Cabinet Secretariat, 'National Security Strategy of Japan', December 2022, pp. 1–2.

3   Japan, Cabinet Secretariat, 'National Security Strategy of Japan', 17 December 2013, https://www.cas.go.jp/jp/siryou/131217anzenhoshou/nss-e.pdf.

4   Japan, Ministry of Foreign Affairs, 'Response to the Situation in Ukraine', 10 March 2023, https://www.mofa.go.jp/erp/c_see/ua/page3e_001171.html.

5   Kamata Tomoko, 'Japan–Russia Peace Treaty Talks Suspended', NHK World-Japan, 5 April 2022, https://www3.nhk.or.jp/nhkworld/en/news/backstories/1958/.

6   Miki Okuyama, 'After Ukraine, Japan Reverts to Old Line on Russian-controlled Islands', Nikkei Asia, 10 March 2022, https://asia.nikkei.com/Politics/International-relations/After-Ukraine-Japan-reverts-to-old-line-on-Russian-controlled-islands.

7   Anna Zotéeva, 'From the Russian Constitution to Putin's Constitution: Legal and Political Implications of the 2020 Constitutional Reform', UI Brief no. 5, Swedish Institute of International Affairs, December 2020, p. 5, https://www.ui.se/globalassets/ui.se-eng/publications/ui-publications/2020/ui-brief-no.-5-2020.pdf.

8   Dzirhan Mahadzir, 'Japanese, Korean Fighters Scrambled in Response to Joint Russia–China Bomber Patrol', USNI News, 30 November 2022, https://news.usni.org/2022/11/30/japanese-korean-fighters-scrambled-in-response-to-joint-russia-china-bomber-patrol; and Hatano Tsukasa and Kuwamoto Futoshi, `Chū Ro ga Hatsu no Gōdō Junshi Katsudō, Nihon Rettō wo Shūkai' [China and Russia conduct their first joint patrol, circle Japanese archipelago], Nihon Keizai Shimbun, 23 October 2021, https://www.nikkei.com/article/DGXZQOGM233DF0T21C21A0000000/. See also Kentaro Shiozaki, 'China, Russia Military Activity Near Japan Up 2.5 Times Since Ukraine', Nikkei Asia, 14 July 2022, https://asia.nikkei.com/Politics/International-relations/China-Russia-military-activity-near-Japan-up-2.5-times-since-Ukraine.

9   White House, 'US–Japan Joint Leaders' Statement: "US–Japan Global Partnership for a New Era"', 16 April 2021, https://www.whitehouse.gov/briefing-room/statements-releases/2021/04/16/u-s-japan-joint-leaders-statement-u-s-japan-global-partnership-for-a-new-era/; and 'Joint Statement Following Discussions with Prime Minister Sato of Japan', 21 November 1969, The American Presidency Project, https://www.presidency.ucsb.edu/documents/joint-statement-following-discussions-with-prime-minister-sato-japan.

10   Japan, Ministry of Defense, 'Defense of Japan

Pamphlet', 2021, p. 19, https://www.mod.
go.jp/en/publ/w_paper/wp2021/DOJ2021_
Digest_EN.pdf. See also '"Taiwan Jōsei no
Antei Juyō" Bōei Hakusho ni Hatsu Meiki'
[Defence white paper refers for the first time to
the importance of the stability of the situation
surrounding Taiwan], *Nihon Keizai Shimbun*,
13 July 2021, https://www.nikkei.com/article/
DGXZQOUA093K00Z00C21A7000000/.

11 Japan, Ministry of Foreign Affairs, 'Keynote
Address, Friday 10 June 2022, Fumio Kishida,
Prime Minister of Japan', Keynote Address
at the IISS Shangri-La Dialogue 2022, 10
June 2022, p. 7, https://www.mofa.go.jp/
files/100356160.pdf.

12 Japan, Ministry of Foreign Affairs, 'Trends in
China Coast Guard and Other Vessels in the
Waters Surrounding the Senkaku Islands, and
Japan's Response', 9 September 2022, https://
www.mofa.go.jp/region/page23e_000021.html.
In 2022, Japan's defence budget was US$48.1bn,
compared with US$242bn for China. See IISS,
The Military Balance 2023 (Abingdon: Routledge
for the IISS), pp. 237, 257.

13 'China Sends Missiles Flying over Taiwan',
The Economist, 4 August 2022, https://www.
economist.com/china/2022/08/04/china-
sends-missiles-flying-over-taiwan; and
Ryo Nemoto and Rieko Miki, '5 Chinese
Missiles Land in Japan's EEZ: Defense Chief',
Nikkei Asia, 4 August 2022, https://asia.
nikkei.com/Politics/International-relations/
Taiwan-tensions/5-Chinese-missiles-land-in-
Japan-s-EEZ-defense-chief.

14 Carlotta Dotto, Brad Lendon and Jessie Yeung,
'North Korea's Record Year of Missile Testing Is
Putting the World on Edge', CNN, 26 December
2022, https://edition.cnn.com/2022/12/26/asia/
north-korea-missile-testing-year-end-intl-hnk/
index.html. See also Choe Sang-hun, 'Tracking
North Korea's Missile Launches', *New York
Times*, 9 March 2023, https://www.nytimes.com/
article/north-korea-missile-launches.html.

15 Julian E. Barnes, 'Russia Is Buying North
Korean Artillery, According to US Intelligence',
New York Times, 5 September 2022, https://
www.nytimes.com/2022/09/05/us/politics/
russia-north-korea-artillery.html.

16 Japan, Cabinet Secretariat, 'National Security
Strategy of Japan', December 2022, p. 3.

17 *Ibid.*, p. 4; and Japan, Ministry of Defense,
'National Defense Strategy', p. 10.

18 Japan, Ministry of Defense, 'Other Basic
Policies', https://www.mod.go.jp/en/d_policy/
basis/others/index.html; and Japan, Prime
Minister of Japan and His Cabinet, 'The
Constitution of Japan', 3 November 1946, https://
japan.kantei.go.jp/constitution_and_govern-
ment_of_japan/constitution_e.htm.

19 Yuka Koshino, 'Japan's Transformational
National-security Documents', IISS Analysis,
21 December 2022, https://www.iiss.org/blogs/
analysis/2022/12/japans-transformational-na-
tional-security-documents.

20 Japan, Prime Minister's Office, 'Press Conference
by Prime Minister Kishida', 16 December 2022,
https://japan.kantei.go.jp/101_kishida/state-
ment/202212/_00006.html. The Japanese fiscal
year starts on 1 April and ends on 31 March.

21 'Japan's Defense Budget and the 1% Limit',
Nippon.com, 18 May 2018, https://www.nippon.
com/en/features/h00196/.

22 'Kishida Naikaku Sōri Daijin Kisha Kaiken'
[Prime Minister Kishida press conference],
Prime Minister's Office of Japan, 16 December
2022, https://www.kantei.go.jp/jp/101_kishida/
statement/2022/1216kaiken.html.

23 Japan, Ministry of Defense, 'National Defense
Strategy', p. 8.

24 Mikio Sugeno and Tsuyoshi Nagasawa, 'Xi's
Potential 2027 Transition Poses Threat to
Taiwan: Davidson', Nikkei Asia, 18 September
2021, https://asia.nikkei.com/Editor-s-Picks/
Interview/Xi-s-potential-2027-transition-poses-
threat-to-Taiwan-Davidson.

25 Japan, Ministry of Defense, 'National Defense
Strategy', p. 12.

26 Japan, Cabinet Secretariat, 'National Security
Strategy of Japan', December 2022, p. 19.

27 'Japan Ruling Bloc Agrees on Acquiring
"Counterstrike Capability"', Kyodo News, 2
December 2022, https://english.kyodonews.net/
news/2022/12/3054d5b15ef4-japan-ruling-bloc-to-
agree-on-acquiring-counterstrike-capability.html.

28 Japan, Ministry of Defense, 'Missile Defense',
https://www.mod.go.jp/en/d_architecture/
missile_defense/index.html.

29 Japan, Cabinet Secretariat, 'National Security
Strategy of Japan', December 2022, p. 19.

30 James L. Schoff and David Song, 'Five Things
to Know About Japan's Possible Acquisition
of Strike Capability', Carnegie Endowment
for International Peace, 14 August 2017,
https://carnegieendowment.org/2017/08/14/

five-things-to-know-about-japan-s-possible-ac-
quisition-of-strike-capability-pub-72710.

31 'Kishida, Biden Vow to Boost Japan Defense
Capabilities, Eyeing Taiwan', Kyodo News,
14 January 2023, https://english.kyodonews.
net/news/2023/01/ac73810d2f43-japan-us-lead-
ers-to-confirm-importance-of-taiwan-peace.
html?phrase=Tomahawk%20&words=Tomahawk.

32 Yuka Koshino, 'Japan to Accelerate
Its Acquisition of Stand-off Defence
Capabilities', IISS Analysis, 27 September
2022, https://www.iiss.org/blogs/
analysis/2022/09/japan-to-accelerate-its-acquisi-
tion-of-stand-off-defence-capabilities.

33 For further details on missile gaps, see, for
example, David Lague, 'Special Report: US
Rearms to Nullify China's Missile Supremacy',
Reuters, 6 May 2020, https://www.reuters.
com/article/us-usa-china-missiles-specialre-
port-us-idUSKBN22I1EQ. For examples of
opinion polls, see 'Over 60 Pct Say Japan Needs
Counterstrike Capabilities: Jiji Poll', Nippon.
com, 16 June 2022, https://www.nippon.com/en/
news/yjj2022061600753/.

34 Japan, Ministry of Defense, 'National Defence
Strategy', p. 16.

35 Ibid., p. 5.

36 Japan, Ministry of Defense, 'Defense Buildup
Program', pp. 11–12.

37 Japan, Cabinet Secretariat, 'National Security
Strategy of Japan', December 2022, p. 24; and
Japan, Ministry of Defense, 'National Defense
Strategy', p. 26.

38 Japan, Cabinet Secretariat, 'National Security
Strategy of Japan', December 2022, p. 24.

39 Japan, Ministry of Defense, 'National Defense
Strategy', p. 30.

40 Ogi Hiroto,'Jieitai "Jōsetsu Tōgō Shireibu"
Wa "Okujō Oku Ka" (Jō) Sutando Ofu Bōei
Nōryoku No Tōgō Unyō Kara Kangaeru' [Is
the Japanese Self-Defense Force's "Permanent
Joint Headquarters" necessary? Part 1: Thinking
from the perspective of integrated operation
of stand-off defence capabilities], Foresight,
12 January 2022, https://www.fsight.jp/arti-
cles/-/49473.

41 Ibid.

42 See, for example, Japan, Ministry of Defense,
'Defense of Japan 2022', August 2022, p. 249,
https://www.mod.go.jp/en/publ/w_paper/
wp2022/DOJ2022_EN_Full_02.pdf.

43 Japan, Ministry of Defense, 'National Defense
Strategy', p. 17.

44 Japan, Ministry of Defense, 'Defense Buildup
Program', p. 30.

45 Ibid., p. 16.

46 Ibid., pp. 15–16.

47 Ibid., p. 19.

48 For budget breakdown, see Japan, Ministry of
Defense, 'Bōei Seibi Keikaku ni tsuite' [About
the Defense Buildup Program], p. 3, https://
www.mod.go.jp/j/policy/agenda/guideline/plan/
pdf/plan_outline.pdf.

49 Japan, Ministry of Defense, 'Defense Buildup
Program', pp. 45–46.

50 Japan, Ministry of Defense, 'National Defense
Strategy', p. 19.

51 Miki Okuyama, 'More Japanese Want Bigger
Role in US Security Alliance: Poll', Nikkei Asia,
25 January 2023, https://asia.nikkei.com/Politics/
Defense/More-Japanese-want-bigger-role-in-
U.S.-security-alliance-poll.

52 White House, 'Statement by National Security
Advisor Jake Sullivan on Japan's Historic
National Security Strategy', 16 December 2022,
https://www.whitehouse.gov/briefing-room/
statements-releases/2022/12/16/statement-by-na-
tional-security-advisor-jake-sullivan-on-ja-
pans-historic-national-security-strategy/;
US Department of Defense, 'Joint Statement
of the 2023 US–Japan Security Consultative
Committee ("2+2")', 11 January 2023, https://
www.defense.gov/News/Releases/Release/
Article/3265559/joint-statement-of-the-2023-us-
japan-security-consultative-committee-22/;
and White House, 'Joint Statement of the
United States and Japan', 13 January 2023,
https://www.whitehouse.gov/briefing-room/
statements-releases/2023/01/13/joint-statement-
of-the-united-states-and-japan/.

53 Japan, Ministry of Defense, 'National Defense
Strategy', p. 19.

54 Ibid., p. 24. For US IAMD, see, for example, Col
Lynn 'Riddler' Savage, 'US INDOPACOM's
Integrated Air and Missile Defense Vision
2028: Integrated Deterrence Toward a Free
and Open Indo-Pacific', Air University,
28 January 2022, https://www.airuniver-
sity.af.edu/JIPA/Display/Article/2915508/
us-indopacoms-integrated-air-and-missile-de-
fense-vision-2028-integrated-deterre/.

55 Rieko Miki, 'Japan to Establish Self-Defense
Forces "Joint Command" in 2024', Nikkei Asia,
29 October 2022, https://asia.nikkei.com/Politics/

Japan-to-establish-Self-Defense-Forces-joint-command-in-2024.

56 Japan, Cabinet Secretariat, 'National Security Strategy of Japan', December 2022, p. 13.

57 *Ibid.*

58 Japan, Ministry of Foreign Affairs, 'First Japan–Philippines Foreign and Defense Ministerial Meeting (2+2)', 9 April 2022, https://www.mofa.go.jp/press/release/press4e_003111.html.

59 Japan signed the agreement with Australia, France, Germany, Indonesia, India, Italy, Malaysia, the Philippines, Thailand, the UK, US and Vietnam. See Japan, Ministry of Defense, 'Rēwa Yonen Ban Bōei Hakusho' [Defense of Japan 2022], August 2022, p. 463, https://www.mod.go.jp/j/press/wp/wp2022/pdf/wp2022_JP_Full_01.pdf.

60 Daishi Abe, 'Philippines Radar Deal Marks Japan's First Arms Export', Nikkei Asia, 29 August 2020, https://asia.nikkei.com/Business/Aerospace-Defense-Industries/Philippines-radar-deal-marks-Japan-s-first-arms-export.

61 Eric Johnston, 'Parliament Begins Budget Talks amid Focus on Kishida's Tax Plans', *Japan Times*, 30 January 2023, https://www.japantimes.co.jp/news/2023/01/30/national/budget-debates-kishida-polls/.

62 Kaneko Kaori and Tim Kelly, 'Japan's Manpower-light Defence Strategy Is a Flawed "Paper Plan", Officers Say', Reuters, 20 December 2022, https://www.reuters.com/world/asia-pacific/japans-manpower-light-defence-strategy-is-flawed-paper-plan-officers-say-2022-12-20/.

63 'Japan's Aging Population Poses Urgent Risk to Society, Says PM', *Guardian*, 23 January 2023, https://www.theguardian.com/world/2023/jan/23/japans-ageing-population-poses-urgent-risk-to-society-says-pm.

64 'Bōeisangyō, "Bōei" Uriage wa 4%, Shijō Kibo Chiisaku: Bōeihakusho wo Yomu (12)' [Defence industry, sales of 'defence' are 4%, small market size], Nikkei Shimbun, 14 September 2022, https://www.nikkei.com/article/DGXZQOUA3075M0Q2A830C2000000/.

65 Takahashi Kosuke, 'Japan Ups Profits for Its Defense Industry', *Diplomat*, 31 January 2023, https://thediplomat.com/2023/01/japan-ups-profits-for-its-defense-industry/.

66 Mori Eisuke, 'Matsukawa Rui ni Kiku "Bōeisangyō no Iji wa Anzenhoshōseisaku Sonomono Da"' [Asking Matsukawa Rui,

'maintaining defence industry is security policy itself'], Nikkei Business, 29 November, 2021, https://business.nikkei.com/atcl/gen/19/00179/112500082/?P=2.

67 IISS, *Arms Sales and Regional Stability: An Assessment* (Abingdon: Routledge for the IISS, 2022), December 2022, p. 142, https://www.iiss.org/publications/strategic-dossiers/strategic-dossier-arms-sales-and-regional-stability.

68 'LDP OKs Bill to Nationalize Defense Equipment Factories', *Jiji Press*, 5 February 2023, https://japannews.yomiuri.co.jp/politics/defense-security/20230205-89015/.

69 '<Dokuji> Tōgō Shireibu, Rainendo Sōsetsu Miokuri, Basho Meguri Tairitsu mo' [Exclusive: Permanent Joint Headquarters will not be established in the next fiscal year due to competition over location], *Sankei News*, 29 December 2022, https://www.sankei.com/article/20221229-4XIS73AZQVPONKLMKNXZCH2CSQ/.

70 Japan, Ministry of Defense, 'Defense of Japan 2022', p. 481.

71 'Miyako-jima e no Danyaku Hanyū ni "Beigun Shien no Misairu Iranai" Shushō Kantei Mae de Shimin ga Demo' ['We do not need missiles supported by the US', residents protest in front of the Prime Minister's Office regarding ammunition deployment on Miyako Island], *Tokyo Shimbun*, 11 November 2021, https://www.tokyo-np.co.jp/article/142242.

72 'Japan's Defence and Security Roles in a Taiwan Contingency with Satoru Mori and Zack Cooper', *Japan Memo* podcast, season 2 episode 11, IISS, 13 December 2022, https://www.iiss.org/blogs/podcast/2022/12/japan-s-defence-and-security-roles-in-a-taiwan-contingency.

73 Alice Billon-Galland and Hans Kundnani, 'How Ukraine Will Change Europe's Indo-Pacific Ambitions', Chatham House, 25 April 2022, https://www.chathamhouse.org/2022/04/how-ukraine-will-change-europes-indo-pacific-ambitions.

74 For further details on the Yoshida Doctrine, see Yuka Koshino and Robert Ward, *Japan's Effectiveness as a Geo-economic Actor: Navigating Great-power Competition*, Adelphi 481–483 (Abingdon: Routledge for the IISS, 2022), p. 19.

75 'Philippines' Marcos Open to a Troop Pact with Japan', Reuters, 13 February 2023, https://www.reuters.com/world/asia-pacific/philippines-marcos-open-troop-pact-with-japan-2023-02-13/.

76 Robert Ward (@RobertAlanWard),
    tweet, 17 June 2022, https://twitter.com/
    search?q=robertalanward%20kishida%20plat-
    form&src=typed_query&f=top.

77 Japan, Cabinet Secretariat, 'National Security
    Strategy of Japan', December 2022, p. 34.

CHAPTER 6

CONFLICT IN MYANMAR AND THE INTERNATIONAL RESPONSE

AARON CONNELLY

Senior Fellow for Southeast Asian
Politics and Foreign Policy, IISS

DR SHONA LOONG

Associate Fellow, IISS

Protesters in Yangon, Myanmar take part in a demonstration against the 1 February military coup, 9 February 2021 (Sai Aung Main/AFP via Getty Images)

In February 2021, the Myanmar Armed Forces launched a *coup d'état* that deposed the elected government, inciting a countrywide conflict between the military and a range of resistance actors. While ASEAN and the UN Security Council have taken consensus steps to penalise the junta, the latter's plan to hold elections (currently slated for the second half of 2023) could split the international community.

THE JUNTA AND ITS FORCES

The military has not been able to suppress the uprising. Although it has an advantage in arms, it is fighting on numerous fronts, sustaining significant casualties and struggling to recruit new cadets.

DIVERSE GROUPS FIGHTING THE JUNTA

Those fighting the military – including new groups formed after the 2021 coup and decades-old ethnic armed organisations (EAOs) – have forged new alliances that are challenging the junta's authority. While some EAOs have aligned with the National Unity Government (NUG), formed by elected members of parliament and their allies among ethnic-minority groups, others have prioritised their survival over supporting the NUG or the junta.

CONFLICT THEATRES IN POST-COUP MYANMAR

Myanmar's seven conflict theatres can be grouped into three categories. Borderland resistance strongholds, where EAOs and anti-junta forces coordinate closely; central contested areas, where ethnic Bamar majority areas – untouched by conflict in recent decades – have experienced high-intensity conflict post-coup, and where anti-junta forces have been fighting with relatively little support from EAOs; and non-aligned areas, where local EAOs focus on their own goals and challenge the junta without coordinating with the NUG.

THE INTERNATIONAL RESPONSE

The junta's April 2021 agreement to ASEAN's Five-Point Consensus has become the basis for international diplomacy regarding the conflict. However, disagreements remain both inside and outside ASEAN over whether to engage the junta or further isolate it.

In the early hours of 1 February 2021, the Myanmar Armed Forces launched a *coup d'état* that deposed the elected government and prevented legislators elected in November 2020 from taking office. Over the following weeks, opponents staged demonstrations against the coup. When those protests were suppressed by force – resulting in the deaths of more than 600 people in two months – many survivors took up arms against the junta.[1] Thousands pledged allegiance to the National Unity Government (NUG) formed by elected members of parliament (living in hiding or abroad) and their allies among ethnic-minority groups. In September 2021, the NUG declared it would wage a 'people's defensive war' against the State Administration Council (SAC), as the junta is known. Since the coup, 310 of the country's 330 townships have experienced one or more instances of armed violence.[2] Although Myanmar has experienced persistent clashes in ethnic-minority areas since the country gained independence from the United Kingdom in 1948, the scale of the current conflict is unprecedented. The resultant humanitarian crisis has led to displacement of people and humanitarian need on a scale greater than has been seen in Southeast Asia since the Cold War.

The nature and intensity of the conflict in Myanmar varies across seven theatres (see Map 6.1), which may be grouped into three broad categories. In the borderland resistance strongholds of southeast Myanmar, Kachin State and northwest Myanmar – ethnic-minority areas where established ethnic armed organisations (EAOs) have worked in concert with forces formed to challenge military rule since the 2021 coup – the resistance has successfully confronted junta forces and expanded the territory under its administration. In contested areas in the centre of the country with a Buddhist-Bamar majority, including the Dry Zone and lower Myanmar, these newer resistance forces have fought with less EAO support in some of the most brutal engagements since the coup. In non-aligned areas in Shan State and Rakhine, EAOs hold sway over large areas of the countryside, opposing rule from the centre but standing aloof from the broader resistance to the coup.

The international response to the conflict has centred on the Association of Southeast Asian Nations (ASEAN), which has taken a harder line towards the SAC than it did towards Myanmar's previous military governments. A 'Five-Point Consensus', agreed in April 2021 between ASEAN leaders and Senior General Min Aung Hlaing, the leader of the junta, has become the basis for international diplomacy to address the crisis. Min Aung Hlaing's refusal to meet the terms of the consensus, combined with questions over the legitimacy of his government, prompted ASEAN to exclude his regime from the bloc's summits and some ministerial meetings. Only Russia has offered unreserved support for the military government. Yet even Moscow chose not to veto a December 2022 United Nations Security Council (UNSC) resolution (UNSC Resolution 2669) expressing 'deep concern' at the 'limited progress on the implementation of ASEAN's Five Point Consensus' and calling for its full implementation.[3]

The junta has announced plans to hold elections in the second half of 2023. If these go ahead, they are unlikely to be competitive and will probably not be held in the large parts of the country affected by conflict. Election infrastructure, including polling places, may come under attack from opponents of the military regime, making them flashpoints for greater violence.[4] Yet even unsuccessful elections could split ASEAN and the broader international community between those prepared to maintain a hard line towards the junta on the one hand and those that are wary of leaving the Myanmar Armed Forces isolated for too long – for fear of losing what limited influence they have over the military – on the other. If they occur, elections are therefore likely to determine the course of both the conflict and the international response to it during 2023 and into 2024.

ORIGINS OF THE UPRISING

Non-violent demonstrations against the coup began days after the SAC seized power. At their peak in mid-February 2021, tens of thousands of people came onto the streets in cities and towns across the country. Shortly thereafter, the military began to fire rubber bullets and live rounds at protesters.[5] On 14 March, 80 people were killed in Yangon – 50 of them at a demonstration in the light-industrial estate of Hlaing Tharyar, which had become a centre of working-class resistance to the coup. In late March, the first armed clash between protesters and the SAC occurred in Kalay town, Sagaing Region, with protesters using homemade weapons to fend off an attack on a protest camp. They held off SAC forces for ten days, although 12 protesters were killed in the process.[6] On 9 April, demonstrators in the city of Bago, 90 kilometres northeast of Yangon, defended barricades with slingshots, fireworks and homemade airguns against an assault by soldiers from the 77 Light Infantry Division; 82 protesters were killed.[7] By mid-2021, skirmishes between the SAC and its opponents had developed into a bloody conflict encompassing areas of the country untouched by armed clashes for decades. Former protesters organised into local cells, which have attacked urban targets and waged guerrilla warfare in more remote areas. Many – but not all – of these cells are allied with the NUG, which was established two months after the coup by ousted lawmakers, representatives of ethnic-based political parties and armed groups, protest leaders, and democracy activists.[8] More than 95,000 civilians are estimated to have joined armed-resistance cells formed after the coup, of which 65,000 troops operate under the

Map 6.1: **Conflict theatres in post-coup Myanmar**

—	Country borders
▦	Township borders
▤	State/region borders

No. of violent events reported by conflict theatre, Feb 2021–Jan 2023

443	Rakhine
1,310	Kachin
1,421	Shan
2,709	Lower Myanmar
3,247	Northwest
3,578	Southeast
7,112	Dry Zone

Source: IISS

NUG's command.[9] The proportion of troops controlled by the NUG has generally risen over the past two years.[10]

EAOs, which have controlled territory and operated paramilitary forces in Myanmar's peripheries for decades, are also pivotal to the ongoing conflict. However, the EAOs vary significantly in terms of their military capacity and capability, their relationship with neighbouring countries, and their positioning vis-à-vis the wider anti-coup resistance. On one hand, some EAOs – particularly those close to Myanmar's borders with Thailand and India – are vocal supporters of the NUG. These EAOs have provided military training to former protesters and launched joint attacks against SAC targets. The NUG and its EAO allies have also formed joint command structures to coordinate their military operations, which are becoming increasingly cohesive as a result.[11] Other EAOs, located near the Myanmar–Bangladesh and Myanmar–China borders, are more equivocal towards the NUG, although they largely oppose the coup. Because EAOs oversee minority populations and local economies adjacent to Myanmar's international borders, their stances towards the SAC have been a significant factor in determining how Myanmar's neighbours have approached the conflict.

Myanmar's conflict is not a monolith. While the military is opposed by a range of actors, these actors' strategies and ultimate goals differ. NUG-allied EAOs see their participation in the wider anti-coup movement as a means of achieving their ethno-national goals within a future federal union. This differentiates them from the mostly ethnic-Bamar armed groups formed after the coup, whose primary goal – at least initially – was to oust the SAC and restore a civilian government to power. These latter groups could not have sustained their resistance to the coup, however, without the support of sympathetic EAOs. To account for these complexities, Myanmar's civil war is best understood by disaggregating conflict dynamics into seven interrelated theatres: the Dry Zone, Rakhine, Shan State, Kachin State, southeast Myanmar, northwest Myanmar and lower Myanmar.[12] In each theatre, combatants wage war in distinct configurations, although military outcomes in each shape the conflict's overarching dynamics.

THE JUNTA AND ITS FORCES

Myanmar is no stranger to military rule. The armed forces first assumed civil power in 1958, at the invitation of then-prime minister U Nu, in response to factionalism within the elected government. The then-commander of the army, General Ne Win, relinquished power after 18 months but overthrew the elected government again in 1962, this time without its consent.[13] For the next 49 years, Burma (renamed Myanmar in 1989) was ruled by successive juntas. In the years before the 2021 coup, Myanmar experienced a reprieve from military rule: following the 2010 general elections, it was governed first by the military-linked Union Solidarity and Development Party (USDP, 2011–16) and then by Aung San Suu Kyi's National League for Democracy (NLD, 2016–21). However, the military never gave up its involvement in politics. Myanmar's putative 'transition' to civilian rule occurred within the bounds of the junta-drafted 2008 constitution, which reserved one-quarter of parliamentary seats for the military. This gave the Myanmar Armed Forces a veto over constitutional change.

The day after the 2021 coup, Min Aung Hlaing established the SAC. The SAC initially consisted of 11 members – eight military officials and three civilians. The senior general appointed six more civilians to the SAC thereafter but it continues to be dominated by the military.[14] The majority of the SAC's military members have led regional military commands and directed counter-insurgency campaigns against EAOs.[15] Its military members are also all Bamar and Buddhist – reflecting the Myanmar Armed Forces' overall ethnic and religious makeup.

By numbers, the Myanmar Armed Forces remains the strongest fighting force in the country. Estimates of its personnel strength vary widely, though reports of recruitment shortfalls and regular understaffing suggest that there are unlikely to be more than 120,000 infantry troops.[16] It has a clear edge over other armed groups in terms of equipment and firepower, evidenced by its airstrikes using both attack helicopters and fixed-wing combat aircraft throughout 2022.[17] It operates equipment sourced – almost entirely before the coup – from China, Israel, Russia, Singapore, South Korea and Ukraine, as well as from a domestic defence industry run by the military itself.[18] However, it is fighting on an unprecedented number of fronts – including in central Myanmar's Dry Zone, where there had been minimal armed violence prior to the coup and where the military's supply lines were underdeveloped – and sustaining significant casualties in each.[19] In addition, there have been reports of thousands of defections.[20] As the war wears on, the military is likely to suffer from further attrition. Its inability to recruit new cadets has resulted in forced recruitment drives in some areas.[21]

The SAC is also able to deploy the Myanmar Police Force and pro-military militias against the opposition. The police force, which even before the coup was under the indirect control of the military's commander-in-chief rather than the civilian government, was deployed to crack down on protests immediately after the coup. In central Myanmar, the SAC has also hastily recruited and trained local militias ('Pyusawhti').[22] Undertrained and under-resourced, the Pyusawhti have not made a significant impact on conflict dynamics writ large. However, it has contributed to an overall climate of fear as its members abduct and attack civilians suspected of siding with the resistance. Moreover, plain-clothed Pyusawhti provide the military with intelligence in areas in which it is not accustomed to fighting – predominantly the Dry Zone.[23]

Senior General Min Aung Hlaing attends a ceremony in Naypyidaw marking the 75th anniversary of Myanmar's independence, 4 January 2023

(STR/AFP via Getty Images)

DIVERSE GROUPS FIGHTING THE JUNTA

Two types of armed organisations have opposed the SAC: anti-SAC groups, formed specifically to oppose the military rule established following the 2021 coup; and EAOs, which existed before the coup and which justify their existence in defence of ethno-national goals. New, post-coup alliances have formed between anti-SAC groups and EAOs, with these alliances helping both types of armed organisations to undermine the SAC's authority, particularly in rural and ethnic-minority areas.

Members of a People's Defence Force unit training in Kayin State, 24 November 2021

(Kaung Zaw Hein/SOPA Images/LightRocket via Getty Images)

In May 2021, the NUG coined the term 'People's Defence Force' (PDF) to refer to NUG-allied groups using arms to protect protesters.[24] In 2023, the term is often used by observers to refer to three types of anti-SAC groups, all of which formed after the coup: PDFs, which are larger units formed or recognised by the NUG; People's Defence Teams (PDTs), which are smaller units formed by the NUG to provide security at the village or neighbourhood level; and Local Defence Forces (LDFs), which are smaller units that fight the SAC but are not allied with the NUG.[25]

Estimates suggest that there are at least 95,000 PDF troops in total, consisting of approximately 65,000 PDF fighters allied with the NUG, 30,000 LDF fighters operating independently and an unknown number of PDT members.[26] These numbers are also fluid – 25% of LDF fighters converted to NUG-allied forces in the second half of 2022.[27] The general trend is towards the consolidation of anti-SAC forces under the NUG, even if the NUG is unlikely to ever bring them all under its command.

Anti-SAC forces have exhibited remarkable resilience. At the start of the conflict they were inexperienced, disorganised and under-resourced. For the most part, their fighters had not experienced war before the coup; they were mostly civil servants, civil-society workers, students and teachers responding to the SAC's crackdown on non-violent protests. However, whereas the military has continued to employ old strategies in use against dissidents for decades, anti-SAC forces' battlefield tactics have evolved. At first, anti-SAC forces often launched one-off attacks against SAC targets before disbanding.[28] They assassinated people suspected of links to the junta or destroyed junta-linked infrastructure, such as police stations and electricity offices, using improvised explosives, sometimes claiming the attacks on social media shortly after.[29] However, clashes between the SAC and anti-SAC forces lasting hours have become more common. In February 2023, a PDF in Sagaing Region reportedly held off SAC attacks for three days before retreating across the Chindwin River.[30]

Anti-SAC forces – and the NUG – have successfully raised funds for weapons. The latter claims to have raised more than US$100 million through the sale of 'Spring Revolution Special Treasury Bonds', the auction of military-linked properties, donations and voluntary taxes.[31] Anti-SAC troops have collected donations and taxes (the line between the two can be blurred) from supporters, businesses, landowners and road users.[32] Doing so has allowed many anti-SAC units to sustain themselves autonomously. Nonetheless, while the anti-SAC opposition has been able to support itself financially, it has not been able to raise enough money to procure the weapons that would give it a decisive military edge over the junta. Indeed, it faces significant challenges: funds from the diaspora and local populations could deplete as the war continues; the SAC seeks to stem funds flowing to the resistance, for example by shutting down the internet in opposition strongholds; and distributing funds raised can be difficult in contested areas.[33]

Kachin Independence Army recruits take part in field exercises in Laiza, Kachin State, 7 July 2014

(Taylor Weidman/LightRocket via Getty Images)

Moreover, anti-SAC forces have sustained themselves through increasingly formalised alliances with select EAOs. There are two command structures that are jointly led by the NUG and EAOs: the Central Command and Coordination Committee (C3C), and the Joint Command and Coordination (J2C). Formed in October 2021, the C3C brings the NUG and three EAOs – in the northwest, the Chin National Front (CNF); in the northeast, the Kachin Independence Organisation (KIO); and in the southeast, the Karenni Army (KA) – under a joint command structure.[34] The J2C is a bilateral structure that coordinates between the NUG and the Karen National Union (KNU), the largest southeastern EAO, which oversees eight 'columns'. Each of the columns is led by a KNU commander and a PDF deputy commander.[35] Military cooperation between anti-SAC forces and battle-hardened EAOs compensates for the former's relative inexperience in combat.

Not all EAOs, however, are aligned with the NUG. Some EAOs reject both the SAC's and NUG's claims to authority. The Arakan Army (AA), which currently controls large stretches of Rakhine, is one example. The AA sees its goals as distinct from those of the SAC and the NUG and it remains sceptical of the latter as a result of the NLD's repression of Rakhine nationalism during its term in government.[36] The AA was the Myanmar military's most belligerent opponent from 2018 to late 2020, when it agreed to an informal ceasefire three months before the coup. After nearly 18 months of a tense truce – during which the AA extended its influence throughout the Rakhine countryside, taking advantage of the pressure on the Myanmar Armed Forces in other parts of the country – fighting resumed in August 2022. Another informal ceasefire was agreed in late 2022.[37]

There are also EAOs that prioritise their own survival – which hinges on their control of local economies and relations with neighbouring countries' governments – over the nationwide goals articulated by the anti-SAC resistance. This group chiefly comprises Shan State EAOs, among them the United Wa State Army (UWSA), the Ta'ang National Liberation Army (TNLA) and the Shan State Progress Party (SSPP). Beijing fears that closer alignment between these EAOs and the NUG might result in greater Western influence on its border with Myanmar (as well as bring the fighting to this area). As a result, it has discouraged these groups from participating in the wider anti-coup resistance. However, Beijing has also sought to use its influence over these EAOs as leverage in its relationship with the junta. Should that relationship suffer, then Beijing might offer tacit approval for these groups to attack the SAC, though not as part of the broader anti-coup resistance.[38]

Finally, a small number of EAOs have engaged directly with the SAC, though these actors have had little impact on the overall conflict so far. Most prominent among these has been the UWSA, which sent an official without any significant decision-making power to talks in mid-2022, after which it released a statement saying that it would remain outside the ongoing conflict.[39] However, most EAOs that accepted invitations to such talks did not hold significant – if any – territories and could only muster a combined force of several hundred troops.[40] The SAC's pursuit of peace talks reflects a long-standing conflict-management strategy practised by successive military rulers in Myanmar. In the past, by pursuing ceasefires with some opponents, the military has been able to undermine solidarity among ethnic-minority groups and reduce the number of fronts on which it has had to fight.[41] This strategy has not achieved political stability; rather, it has engendered successive waves of ceasefires and conflict in ethnic-minority areas. The current conflict is a turning point not only because some of the junta's strongest opponents – namely the KIO and KNU – are fighting the military at the same time but also because they are coordinating their attacks with one another via the NUG and the anti-SAC forces allied with it.

CONFLICT THEATRES IN POST-COUP MYANMAR

Due to the range and configurations of actors in Myanmar, the conflict is best understood as the sum total of the dynamics in seven theatres, which can be grouped into three categories:

▸ Borderland resistance strongholds (southeast Myanmar, Kachin State and northwest Myanmar)

▸ Central contested areas (the Dry Zone and lower Myanmar)

▸ Non-aligned areas (Shan State and Rakhine).

Borderland resistance strongholds

Southeast Myanmar, Kachin State and northwest Myanmar – which border Thailand, China and India, respectively – see the closest coordination between EAOs and anti-SAC forces (see Map 6.2). The main EAOs in these theatres – the CNF, KIO, KNU and Karenni National Progressive Party (KNPP) – have been among the NUG's most vocal EAO allies. These actors have not only sent their own forces to fight the junta but have also trained former protesters willing to join the armed resistance. Joint operations between these EAOs and anti-SAC forces have allowed the combined resistance movement to launch assaults on military bases, particularly in Kayin State.[42] There have been near daily clashes in all three theatres.

Local populations have often paid a heavy price for their opposition to the SAC. Since the coup, Hpapun in southeast Myanmar – a KNU stronghold – has endured the most airstrikes out of all Myanmar's 330 townships.[43] There were 365 airstrikes and drone strikes throughout Myanmar between 1 February 2021 and 31 August 2022 – 29 of which took place in Hpapun.[44] Airstrikes have also wracked other parts of the southeast; together with ground offensives by the Myanmar Armed Forces, they have displaced approximately 296,000 people in the region.[45] A significant proportion of those displaced are believed to have crossed the border with Thailand, joining 91,000 refugees already living in camps in Thailand who were displaced by clashes between the KNU and Myanmar's military that took place before the coup.[46] In October 2022, Kachin State endured the single deadliest air attack since the coup: the military bombed a concert organised by the KIO, killing at least 50 people.[47]

In northwest Myanmar, as well as in the neighbouring Dry Zone, local populations have been subject to scorched-earth campaigns. In September 2021, the northwest drew international attention when shelling by the Myanmar Armed Forces displaced nearly all 12,000 residents of Thantlang town, which was set on fire and looted.[48] Over 50,000 people have crossed into India from the northwest and approximately 40,000 have been internally displaced.[49]

Nonetheless, EAOs in these theatres continue to stand behind the anti-coup resistance. The two main EAOs in the southeast – the KNU and KNPP – had been at war with Myanmar's military for more than six decades by the time of the 2021 coup. Both signed ceasefires in the decade before the coup, with these deals becoming increasingly unpopular with local populations as peace negotiations stalled. Seeing negotiations as a dead end and riding the wider resistance movement's appetite for federalism, the KNU and KNPP joined forces with the NUG and anti-SAC forces in their armed uprising. Even so, there are subtle differences between the KNU's and KNPP's approaches to anti-SAC forces. The KNU, the stronger of the two, subsumes anti-SAC forces under its control through the J2C, whereas the KNPP coordinates its attacks with anti-SAC forces via the C3C. The two EAOs have expanded their administrative systems in territories they have wrested from the SAC, which they use to provide humanitarian assistance, healthcare, and law and order.[50] In so doing, they seek to demonstrate the viability of EAO-led governance systems that exclude the SAC.

From its strongholds in Kachin State in northeast Myanmar, since early 2021 the KIO has pushed southwards into northern parts of the Dry Zone with the assistance of anti-SAC forces.[51] Formed in 1961 to advance Kachin ethno-nationalism, the KIO quickly became one of the Myanmar government's

Map 6.2: **Borderland resistance strongholds in post-coup Myanmar**

No. of violent events reported monthly by conflict theatre, Feb 2021–Jan 2023

Source: IISS

most formidable opponents. Over the following two decades, it gained control of and began to administer territory in Kachin and northern Shan states, which both border China. After a 17-year ceasefire (1994–2011) the KIO returned to combat re-energised by a new generation of leaders less willing to compromise with the central government.[52] After the coup, the KIO was one of the first EAOs to intensify offensives against the military, by seizing camps and outposts in March 2021.[53] The KIO now appears to have full command over PDFs in Kachin State and coordinates its attacks with the NUG and its allies as a member of the C3C.[54]

The main EAO in the northwest, the CNF, has fought for Chin self-determination since 1988. However, unlike the KNU, KNPP and KIO, it was relatively insignificant before the coup because it had not actively fought since the mid-2000s.[55] The CNF's recent inactivity has been partly attributed to the difficulties encountered in trying to unite the Chin polity, due to northwest Myanmar's sparse population and rugged, mountainous terrain; the lack of a common language; and poor roads and telecommunications infrastructure in rural areas.[56] A common enemy – the SAC – re-energised the CNF and stimulated interest in a unified front against the military regime. Camp Victoria – the CNF headquarters – became an epicentre for resistance activities. It is where thousands of former protesters have undergone military training – by the CNF – before being deployed elsewhere in northwest Myanmar and even central Myanmar.[57] The camp, located only a few kilometres from the Indian border, was the target of SAC airstrikes in January 2023. As with southeast Myanmar and Kachin State, resistance actors – comprising the CNF, ousted lawmakers, members of civil-society groups and protest leaders – have cooperated to establish governance systems in areas they control.[58] They claim, for example, to have reopened schools, allowing 2,800 primary students to return to the classroom.[59]

Central contested areas

The Dry Zone and lower Myanmar (see Map 6.3) are atypical insofar as they are the only two theatres that did not see armed violence in the decades before the 2021 coup. Due to their predominantly Buddhist-Bamar populations, these areas had been relatively untouched by the conflicts between EAOs and the Myanmar Armed Forces. Yet the Dry Zone on the border with Chin State and the commercial centre and former capital Yangon in lower Myanmar have become central to the post-coup conflict. In the absence of EAOs, the conflict here is driven by anti-SAC forces – both those allied with the NUG and those working independently.

In the first year of the conflict, PDFs deployed three main battlefield tactics: the use of improvised explosive devices, assassinations and ambushes. Their targets were not only SAC soldiers and police officers but also junta-linked assets, such as businesses owned by SAC members[60] and people associated with the junta, such as suspected informants.[61] However, the SAC is better equipped to crack down on its opponents in large towns and cities, making urban warfare costly for the resistance.[62] Consequently, anti-SAC forces rely on remote attacks rather than armed clashes and, particularly in lower Myanmar (including Yangon), have used remotely triggered explosive devices.[63] Nonetheless, in both theatres, anti-SAC forces have grown more organised and their weapons more advanced.

Due to their distance from cross-border black markets, many have begun to produce their own light weapons, including sub-machine guns.[64] Still, in comparison with forces in southeast and northwest Myanmar, anti-SAC forces in the Dry Zone and lower Myanmar struggle to hold pockets of territory.

Whereas it has invited EAOs to peace talks, the SAC regards anti-SAC forces as 'terrorists' undeserving of dialogue and negotiation.[65] Instead, it has dealt with them using counter-insurgency tactics that it had previously reserved for the most belligerent EAOs. Six of the ten townships with the highest incidence of infrastructure destruction – primarily houses and buildings burned down by the SAC – are in the Dry Zone. The other four are in northwest Myanmar.[66] Within the Dry Zone's Sagaing Region alone, in the two years following the coup, 684,300 people were internally displaced as a result.[67] In Yangon, suspected resistance fighters are subject to raids, abductions and arrests. In July 2022, the junta executed four anti-regime activists accused of abetting the armed resistance, having charged them under counter-terrorism laws. These were the first executions in Myanmar in more than three decades.[68] In late 2022, the SAC also deployed heavily armed soldiers to evict an estimated 60,000 residents from their homes in Yangon and reissued these lands to regime loyalists.[69]

Although the resistance has been less successful in these theatres, the military's behaviour in its historic strongholds may have lasting effects on Myanmar's politics. The home villages of tens of thousands of anti-SAC fighters have been destroyed. For them, the fight against the SAC will now be an existential matter. In the event of a SAC victory, these fighters are likely to remain deeply resentful towards Myanmar's military commanders.[70] Furthermore, the conflict has caused the Myanmar Armed Forces to turn against part of its traditional support base. Since Myanmar's independence, the military has declared that its *raison d'être* is to protect the Buddhist-Bamar population; since the coup, such rhetoric has rung hollow with anti-SAC forces and their supporters.[71]

Map 6.3: **Central contested areas in post-coup Myanmar**

No. of violent events reported monthly by conflict theatre, Feb 2021–Jan 2023

Source: IISS

Non-aligned areas

Finally, there are two theatres in which local actors are more ambivalent towards the NUG-led resistance: Rakhine on the border with Bangladesh, and those parts of Shan State bordering China (see Map 6.4). Most EAOs in both theatres have denounced the coup and have clashed with the military but are not coordinating their activities with anti-SAC forces, instead focusing on achieving their own goals.

The Brotherhood Alliance, consisting of the Rakhine-based AA together with the Shan-based TNLA and the Myanmar National Democratic Alliance Army (MNDAA), has denounced the coup and clashed with the SAC but insists on pursuing its constituent elements' shared causes.[72] There are three possible reasons why these groups have distanced themselves from the NUG. Firstly, they associate the NUG with ousted NLD lawmakers, whom they mistrust. The AA has been especially sceptical of the NLD as it led the suppression of Rakhine nationalists, which sparked the conflict there between the Myanmar Armed Forces and the AA in 2018.[73] As for the TNLA and the MNDAA, there had been no lasting reprieve to fighting in the northeast during the NLD's term in office. Secondly, more than in any other theatre in Myanmar, conflict in Shan State has been shaped by illicit economies, profiteering and factionalisation. This context has led local EAOs to prioritise survival and territorial autonomy over countrywide reforms.[74] Thirdly, China looms large in these groups' strategic calculations. Beijing has strategic interests in both Shan State, where it is involved in resource-extraction projects and where it seeks to secure its border, and Rakhine, where it had planned to build a deep-sea port and a special economic zone.[75] Furthermore, these EAOs access Chinese-made weapons through the UWSA, whose partnership with China has allowed it to develop into the strongest armed force of any EAO in Myanmar.[76]

These non-aligned areas are potential flashpoints in the conflict. Tensions persist between the SAC

Map 6.4: **Non-aligned areas in post-coup Myanmar**

No. of violent events reported monthly by conflict theatre, Feb 2021–Jan 2023

Source: IISS

and all members of the Brotherhood Alliance as well as other, smaller EAOs in Shan State. The situation in Rakhine is perhaps the most volatile, as in the past three years the AA has twice oscillated between signing ceasefires with the military and intense conflict. The AA used previous ceasefires as opportunities to expand its administration, acquiring influence over two-thirds of Rakhine and triggering retaliation from the Myanmar Armed Forces.[77] The Brotherhood Alliance EAOs are likely to remain aloof from resistance movements in the rest of Myanmar. However, if these groups were to change tack and challenge the SAC, in response to new SAC offensives or tacit approval from China, their combined strength could stretch the military in unprecedented ways.

Members of a People's Defence Force unit near Demoso, Kayah State, assemble homemade guns to be used in fighting against security forces, 4 June 2021

(STR/AFP via Getty Images)

THE INTERNATIONAL RESPONSE

The international community is often characterised as being divided over the question of how it should respond to the overthrow of Myanmar's elected government as a result of the 2021 *coup d'état*. However, there is broad consensus on several key points. On the day of the coup, condemnation was nearly universal: nine ASEAN foreign ministers quickly reached consensus on a statement calling for a 'return to normalcy', which was issued the same day by the then-chair of the organisation, Brunei.[78] In the weeks that followed, the foreign ministers of the G7 group and the Quad (Australia, India, Japan and the United States) issued statements condemning the coup, while the UN Human Rights Council adopted without a vote a resolution 'deploring' the coup and calling for an end to the state of emergency – the legal instrument that allowed Min Aung Hlaing to seize power.[79]

ASEAN's Five-Point Consensus

As violence in Myanmar escalated, the broader international community looked to ASEAN, as the relevant regional organisation, to determine a way out of the crisis. In April 2022, the nine leaders of the other ASEAN member states agreed to hold an extraordinary meeting with Min Aung Hlaing at the ASEAN Secretariat in Jakarta. Protesters in Myanmar criticised ASEAN leaders for inviting the senior general to join them, and burnt ASEAN flags.[80] While some leaders took pains to stress that they were merely meeting with Min Aung Hlaing and not including him among their number as a fellow leader, the junta repeatedly ran the footage of the meeting on state television in an attempt to convey the impression that Min Aung Hlaing had been accepted as Myanmar's leader by the international community.

(Indonesian Presidential Secreteriat/Anadolu Agency via Getty Images)

Leaders of ASEAN member states meet Senior General Min Aung Hlaing to discuss the Myanmar crisis at the ASEAN Secretariat in Jakarta, 24 April 2021

At the meeting on 22 April, the Five-Point Consensus was agreed between the nine ASEAN leaders and Min Aung Hlaing (see Figure 6.1). Though governments around the world voiced support for the Five-Point Consensus, Min Aung Hlaing quickly reneged on his commitments, indicating that he regarded them as merely advisory. Over the following two years, Myanmar accepted a small amount of humanitarian aid through the AHA Centre. After much negotiation, the special envoys of the ASEAN chairs Brunei (2021) and Cambodia (2022) have made visits to Myanmar (although they have not been allowed to meet with NLD leaders). Otherwise, the lack of meaningful progress on the Five-Point Consensus has led many to criticise it as a failed approach.

Although the Five-Point Consensus has not been successful in pushing the junta to cease violence or engage in dialogue with its opponents, it has played an important role in bridging divisions between the remaining nine member states. The maritime states of Brunei, Indonesia, Malaysia, the Philippines and Singapore have favoured isolating the junta, while the mainland states led by Thailand and including Cambodia, Laos and Vietnam argue for greater engagement with the junta. In October 2021, these divisions came to a head in two meetings between ASEAN foreign ministers over whether to invite Min Aung Hlaing to the ASEAN summit at the end of the month. Brunei, acting on its authority as the chair, opted not to issue an invitation to Min Aung Hlaing. Although Thailand objected to the decision, it found it difficult to make a case for the inclusion of Min Aung Hlaing given that he had failed to fulfil any of the terms of the Five-Point Consensus. Bangkok ultimately chose not to insist on his inclusion.

Over the following year, ministers from Myanmar were also excluded from ASEAN foreign and defence ministers' meetings. Moreover, the ASEAN Secretariat, acting as the depositary for the Regional Comprehensive Economic Partnership free-trade agreement,

Figure 6.1: **ASEAN's Five-Point Consensus on the situation in Myanmar, April 2021**

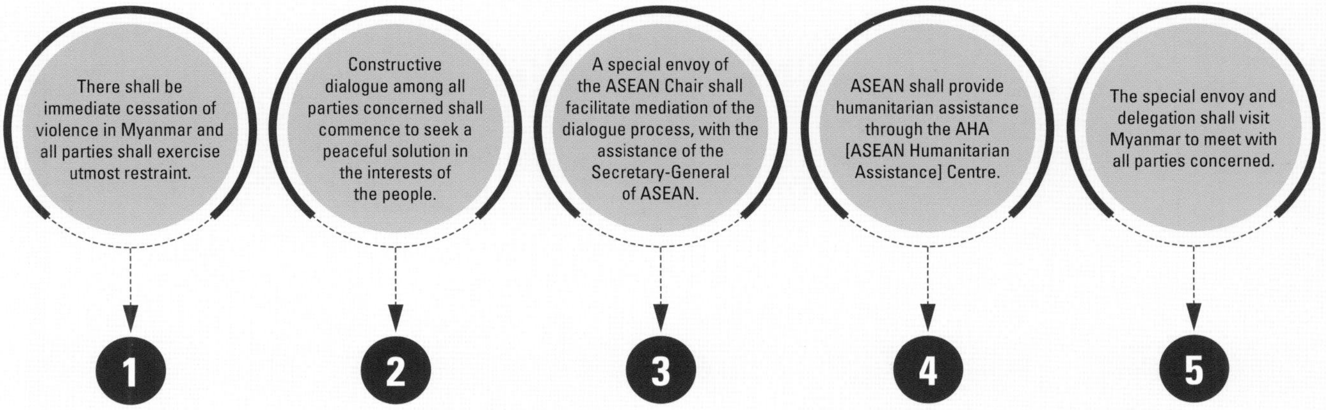

There shall be immediate cessation of violence in Myanmar and all parties shall exercise utmost restraint.

Constructive dialogue among all parties concerned shall commence to seek a peaceful solution in the interests of the people.

A special envoy of the ASEAN Chair shall facilitate mediation of the dialogue process, with the assistance of the Secretary-General of ASEAN.

ASEAN shall provide humanitarian assistance through the AHA [ASEAN Humanitarian Assistance] Centre.

The special envoy and delegation shall visit Myanmar to meet with all parties concerned.

1   **2**   **3**   **4**   **5**

Source: ASEAN, asean.org

has refused to accept the junta's instrument of accession. Though the junta's officials still participate in the work of ASEAN at a lower level, these steps amount to a de facto suspension of Myanmar from ASEAN at the bloc's most important meetings and with regard to its most important functions. While exclusion from ASEAN summits may not be Min Aung Hlaing's greatest challenge, it has deprived him of the opportunity to convey images to Myanmar's population that would suggest he has been accepted by the international community as the country's leader.

Neighbours offer limited engagement

Thailand is not the only neighbour of Myanmar that has sought to engage rather than isolate the junta. Bangladesh, China and India have all sought quiet ways to build bridges to the SAC despite joining in early statements condemning the coup. For each, concerns over a porous border lined with autonomous armed groups is the top priority in their relations with Myanmar. Officials from the three countries say that they must engage the junta if they are to manage the border and the challenges that emanate from it – particularly with regard to migrants and criminal activity. However, China, India and Thailand have also sought to hedge their bets on the outcome of the conflict by establishing discreet lines of communication with the NUG.

Despite allegations emerging in the weeks immediately following the coup that China had backed the military's seizure of civil power, no evidence has emerged to support such claims.[81] Indeed, the coup ran contrary to China's interests: Beijing had enjoyed good relations with the NLD government. Min Aung Hlaing, by contrast, had criticised Beijing's relationship with the AA and was thought to favour closer relations with India. Beijing has nevertheless sought to engage the new regime to secure its interests in infrastructure projects in Myanmar and security along the border. However, it has been disappointed by the junta's escalatory approach to the conflict.

For its part, New Delhi had become concerned over the course of Aung San Suu Kyi's first term that the NLD government was becoming too close to China. Given Min Aung Hlaing's stated antipathy towards China, Indian officials have seen the coup as an opportunity to beat back Chinese influence in Myanmar and make inroads of their own. Naval cooperation between India and Myanmar is a particularly bright spot for the junta. In October 2020, before the coup, India donated a *Kilo*-class submarine to Myanmar. Since the coup, regular talks between naval commanders from India and Myanmar in the Bay of Bengal have continued, while India invited Myanmar to participate in its *Milan* biennial regional naval exercise in February 2022.[82]

Further afield, few friends

Beyond Myanmar's immediate region, Russia has been the junta's only significant supporter. It has become the leading arms supplier to the military regime; its substantial training programmes for Myanmar Armed Forces personnel have continued despite the coup; and it included Myanmar in the *Vostok* military exercise in Russia's Far East in September 2022. A deal on the sale of Russian petrol to Myanmar has sought to provide a new market for Russian energy while lowering oil prices in Myanmar. In August 2022, Min Aung Hlaing travelled to Vladivostok for a meeting with Russian President Vladimir Putin – the senior general's most significant diplomatic engagement since the coup. However, even the close relationship between Russia and the junta was not enough to secure a Russian veto of UNSC Resolution 2669 in December 2022 – the first UNSC resolution on Myanmar since the country was admitted to the UN as Burma in 1949.

European and North American governments have followed through on their early condemnations of the coup by downgrading their diplomatic representation in Yangon, meeting with NUG officials and levying economic sanctions against the regime. Most of these governments have chosen not to replace their outgoing ambassadors to Myanmar, rather than have a new ambassador present their credentials to Min Aung Hlaing as chairman of the SAC.[83] Canada, the European Union, the United Kingdom and the US have sought to coordinate their implementation of sanctions to increase their effectiveness. Yet these sanctions appear to have had little effect on Myanmar's economy, particularly compared to the damage inflicted by the nationwide

Senior General Min Aung Hlaing meets Russian President Vladimir Putin on the sidelines of the Eastern Economic Forum in Vladivostok, Russia, 7 September 2022

(Valery Sharifulin/SPUTNIK/AFP via Getty Images)

strike known as the 'Civil Disobedience Movement' – which gripped the economy for months following the coup – or the military regime's macroeconomic mismanagement. It is possible that the sanctions' effectiveness could have been greater if they had been implemented more quickly; the relatively slow escalation ladder used by the administration of US President Joe Biden afforded the junta and its supporters time to adjust to the prospect of renewed economic isolation.

Three important middle powers in the Asia-Pacific – Australia, Japan and South Korea – have condemned the coup but remain reluctant to completely isolate the junta. Only Canberra has levied sanctions, although these came two years after the coup and were limited to basic financial sanctions and travel bans on high-ranking SAC officials. The relationship with Japan is particularly important for Myanmar, which has benefitted from substantial Japanese investment. Tokyo's approach is framed by an interest in protecting these investments and – like India – blocking deeper Chinese engagement in the country. Of the three middle powers, Australia and South Korea have chosen not to replace outgoing ambassadors, while Japan's ambassador, Maruyama Ichiro, has remained in place since the coup.[84]

Elections could split the international community

Though there is broad international agreement that the conflict in Myanmar should be resolved through negotiations and that any stable settlement must include some element of democratic participation, the junta's announced intention to hold an election in the second half of 2023 has proved divisive. The NLD would probably boycott the polls if given the opportunity, although regulations issued by the junta in January 2023 suggest that it will not be given the chance to do so. The polls are likely to be cancelled in much of the country where the conflict makes voting impossible and, even in other areas, polling stations could still come under attack from opponents of the military regime.

ASEAN and the broader international community are split between those prepared to maintain a hard line towards the junta and those that are wary of leaving the military isolated for too long. An election designed to supplant the results of the freely conducted 2020 election – which the Myanmar Armed Forces' proxy party lost – and marred by violence could be seen by governments in favour of isolating the military regime as a trigger for stronger sanctions. At the same time, some in China, India, Japan and Thailand might see the election as an opportunity to turn the page on the preceding two years in the hope that a new political equation in Myanmar will open up opportunities for progress in resolving the country's internal conflict and make engagement with the regime appear less objectionable. The resulting disagreement would bring into sharp relief disagreements within the Quad between the US and Australia on one side and India and Japan on the other. By contrast, ASEAN member states are likely to continue to find creative ways to bridge their differences, as any split in the bloc would threaten the organisation's convening role at the centre of the regional diplomatic architecture and thereby jeopardise its influence over major-power diplomacy in the region. Once lost, this influence would be difficult to regain.

NOTES

1   Amy Chew and Reuters, 'Myanmar Coup: Death Toll Passes 600 as Crackdown Continues and Security Forces Detain Celebrities', *South China Morning Post*, 8 April 2021, https://www.scmp.com/news/asia/southeast-asia/article/3128824/myanmar-coup-death-toll-passes-600-crackdown-continues-and.

2   IISS, 'Myanmar Conflict Map', https://myanmar.iiss.org/. Accessed March 2023.

3   UN Security Council, 'Resolution 2669 (2022 Adopted by the Security Council at its 9231st meeting, on 21 December 2022', S/RES/2669, 21 December 2022. See also 'UN Security Council: Historic Censure of Myanmar Junta', Human Rights Watch, 21 December 2022, https://www.hrw.org/news/2022/12/21/un-security-council-historic-censure-myanmar-junta.

4   See Noeleen Heyzer speaking at the 2022 IISS Shangri-La Dialogue: IISS, 'Special Session 2: Myanmar: Finding a Way Forward', YouTube, https://www.youtube.com/watch?v=KldI75Yzq1Y.

5   'Myanmar Coup: "Everything Will Be OK" Teenage Protester Mourned', BBC News, 4 March 2021, https://www.bbc.com/news/world-asia-56277165.

6   '500 Days of Spring: The Kalay Protesters Who Never Quit', *Frontier Myanmar*, 3 June 2022, https://www.frontiermyanmar.net/en/500-days-of-spring-the-kalay-protesters-who-never-quit/.

7   Joyce Sohyun Lee et al., 'Anatomy of a Crackdown: How Myanmar's Military Terrorized Its People with Weapons of War', *Washington Post*, 25 August 2021, https://www.washingtonpost.com/world/interactive/2021/myanmar-crackdown-military-coup/.

8   Joanne Lin and Moe Thuzar, 'The Struggle for International Recognition: Myanmar After the 2021 Coup', *Fulcrum*, 12 December 2022, https://fulcrum.sg/the-struggle-for-international-recognition-myanmar-after-the-2021-coup/.

9   Ye Myo Hein, 'Understanding the People's Defense Forces in Myanmar', United States Institute of Peace, 3 November 2022, https://www.usip.org/publications/2022/11/understanding-peoples-defense-forces-myanmar.

10 *Ibid*.

11 *Ibid*.

12 Shona Loong, 'Post-coup Myanmar in Six Warscapes', IISS Myanmar Conflict Map, 10 June 2022, https://myanmar.iiss.org/analysis/introduction.

13 Martin Smith, *Burma: Insurgency and the Politics of Ethnicity* (New York: St Martin's Press, 1999), p. 121.

14 Htet Myet Min Tun, Moe Thuzar and Michael Montesano, 'Min Aung Hlaing and His Generals: Data on the Military Members of Myanmar's State Administration Council Junta', ISEAS–Yusof Ishak Institute, *ISEAS Perspectives*, no. 97, 23 July 2021, https://www.iseas.edu.sg/articles-commentaries/iseas-perspective/2021-97-min-aung-hlaing-and-his-generals-data-on-the-military-members-of-myanmars-state-administration-council-junta-by-htet-myet-min-tun-moe-thuzar-and-michael-montesano/.

15 *Ibid*.

16 Anthony Davis, 'Prospects for a People's War in Myanmar', *Asia Times*, 6 August 2021, https://asiatimes.com/2021/08/prospects-for-a-peoples-war-in-myanmar/.

17 Anthony Davis, 'Myanmar's Junta in a Serious but Not Desperate Fight', *Asia Times*, 31 August 2022, https://asiatimes.com/2022/08/myanmars-junta-in-a-serious-but-not-desperate-fight/.

18 Special Advisory Council for Myanmar, 'Fatal Business: Supplying the Myanmar Military's Weapon Production', 16 January 2023, https://specialadvisorycouncil.org/wp-content/uploads/2023/01/SAC-M-REPORT-Fatal-Business-ENGLISH-1.pdf.

19 Davis, 'Myanmar's Junta in a Serious but Not Desperate Fight'.

20 '"Around 1,500" Soldiers Have Defected and Joined the Civil Disobedience Movement Since Coup', Myanmar Now, 17 August 2021, https://myanmar-now.org/en/news/around-1500-soldiers-have-defected-and-joined-the-civil-disobedience-movement-since-coup.

21 'Desperate Junta Recruitment Drive Leaves Delta Villagers Fearful – and in Debt', *Frontier Myanmar*, 19 August 2022, https://www.frontiermyanmar.net/en/desperate-junta-recruitment-drive-leaves-delta-villagers-fearful-and-in-debt/.

22 These new militias are separate from and additional to militias formed before the coup, which were largely splinter factions of EAOs. See John Buchanan, 'Militias in Myanmar', The Asia Foundation, July 2016, https://asiafoundation.org/wp-content/uploads/2016/07/Militias-in-Myanmar.pdf.

23 International Crisis Group, 'Resisting the Resistance: Myanmar's Pro-military Pyusawhti Militias', *Crisis Group Asia Briefing,* no. 171, 6 April 2022, https://www.crisisgroup. org/asia/south-east-asia/myanmar/ resisting-resistance-myanmars-pro-military- pyusawhti-militias.

24 'Myanmar's Anti-junta Unity Government Forms "Defence Force"', Reuters, 5 May 2021, https://www.reuters.com/world/asia-pacific/ myanmar-state-media-says-five-killed-blast- were-building-bomb-2021-05-05/.

25 Ye Myo Hein, 'Understanding the People's Defense Forces in Myanmar'.

26 *Ibid.*, pp. 3–4.

27 *Ibid.*, p. 4.

28 IISS, 'Myanmar Conflict Map'.

29 'Electricity Boycott Buckles in Yangon but Powers On in the Dry Zone', *Frontier Myanmar*, 11 November 2022, https://www.frontiermyanmar.net/en/ electricity-boycott-buckles-in-yangon-but- powers-on-in-the-dry-zone/.

30 Khin Yi Yi Zaw, 'Anti-Junta Forces Retreat After Holding Strategic River Village for Several Days', Myanmar Now, 6 February 2023, https:// myanmar-now.org/en/news/anti-junta-forces- retreat-after-holding-strategic-river- village-for-several-days; and Anthony Davis, 'Is Myanmar's Military Starting to Lose the War?', *Asia Times*, 30 May 2022, https://asiatimes.com/2022/05/ is-myanmars-military-starting-to-lose-the-war/.

31 'Myanmar Shadow Government Raises $132m to Oppose Junta', *Straits Times*, 16 January 2022, https://www.straitstimes.com/asia/se-asia/ myanmar-shadow-government-raises-131m-to- oppose-junta; and Zachary Abuza, 'The NUG's Economic War on Myanmar's Military', Stimson Centre, 27 September 2022, https://www. stimson.org/2022/the-nugs-economic-war-on- myanmars-military/.

32 International Crisis Group, 'Crowdfunding a War: The Money Behind Myanmar's Resistance', Asia Report no. 328, 20 December 2022, https:// www.crisisgroup.org/asia/south-east-asia/ myanmar/328-crowdfunding-war-money- behind-myanmars-resistance.

33 *Ibid.*

34 Ye Myo Hein, 'Understanding the People's Defense Forces in Myanmar', p. 5.

35 'Cooperation in Kayin Turns a Corner', *Frontier Myanmar*, 12 January 2023, https://www.

frontiermyanmar.net/en/cooperation-in-kayin- turns-a-corner/. The number of troops in each column is unclear, and likely to be variable.

36 Shona Loong, 'Rakhine: A Precarious Ceasefire Hangs in the Balance', IISS Myanmar Conflict Map, 26 July 2022, https://myanmar.iiss.org/ analysis/rakhine.

37 RFA Burmese, 'Despite Rakhine Cease- fire, Myanmar Military Blocks Shipments of Aid, Fuel and Goods', Radio Free Asia (RFA), 28 December 2022, https://www. rfa.org/english/news/myanmar/rakh- ine-blocked-12282022101234.html.

38 Jason Tower, 'The Limits of Beijing's Support for Myanmar's Military', US Institute of Peace, 24 February 2023, https://www.usip.org/ publications/2023/02/limits-beijings-support- myanmars-military.

39 David Scott Mathieson, 'Myanmar's "Peace Talks" a Dangerous Diversion', *Asia Times*, 7 July 2022, https://asiatimes.com/2022/07/ myanmars-peace-talks-a-dangerous-diversion/; Agence France-Presse (AFP), 'China-backed Myanmar Rebels Call on Junta to Embrace Peace Talks', *South China Morning Post*, 31 May 2022, https://www.scmp.com/news/asia/southeast- asia/article/3179904/china-backed-myanmar- rebels-call-junta-embrace-peace-talks.

40 Mathieson, 'Myanmar's "Peace Talks" a Dangerous Diversion'.

41 Shona Loong, 'Northeast Myanmar: Three Axes of Conflict', IISS Myanmar Conflict Map, 16 August 2022, https://myanmar.iiss.org/analysis/northeast.

42 Linn Htin and May Yu, 'Myanmar Junta Suffers Heavy Losses in KNLA–PDF Attacks on Bases in Karen State', Myanmar Now, 10 January 2023, https://myanmar-now.org/en/news/ myanmar-junta-suffers-heavy-losses-in-knla- pdf-attacks-on-bases-in-karen-state.

43 Shona Loong, 'Southeast Myanmar: A Shared Struggle for Federal Democracy', IISS Myanmar Conflict Map, 23 September 2022, https:// myanmar.iiss.org/analysis/southeast.

44 IISS, 'Myanmar Conflict Map'.

45 'Myanmar Emergency Overview Map', UN High Commissioner for Refugees, 16 January 2023, https://data.unhcr.org/en/documents/ details/98182.

46 See 'Thailand', UN High Commissioner for Refugees, https://www.unhcr.org/thailand.html.

47 Emily Fishbein et al., '"Our Hearts Are on Fire": Hpakant Airstrikes Fuel Kachin Revolutionary

Spirit', *Frontier Myanmar*, 2 November 2022, https://www.frontiermyanmar.net/en/our-hearts-are-on-fire-hpakant-airstrikes-fuel-kachin-revolutionary-spirit/.

48 Meg Kelly, Shibani Mahtani and Joyce Sohyun Lee, '"Burn It All Down": How Myanmar's Military Razed Villages to Crush a Growing Resistance', *Washington Post*, 23 December 2021, https://www.washingtonpost.com/world/interactive/2021/myanmar-military-burn-villages-tatmadaw/.

49 'Myanmar Emergency Overview Map', UN High Commissioner for Refugees.

50 *Ibid.*

51 Loong, 'Northeast Myanmar: Three Axes of Conflict'.

52 David Brenner, *Rebel Politics: A Political Sociology of Armed Struggle in Myanmar's Borderlands* (Ithaca, NY: Cornell University Press, 2019), pp. 75–96.

53 'KIO/A Seizes Prominent Burma Army Mountaintop Camp in Kachin State', Burma News International, 26 March 2022, https://www.bnionline.net/en/news/kioa-seizes-prominent-burma-army-mountaintop-camp-kachin-state.

54 Billy Ford and Ye Myo Hein, 'For Myanmar, the Only Path to Stability Runs Through Its Web of Resistance Forces', US Institute of Peace, 1 December 2022, https://www.usip.org/publications/2022/12/myanmar-only-path-stability-runs-through-its-web-resistance-forces.

55 Shona Loong, 'Northwest Myanmar: A Quiet Corner Transformed by Resistance', IISS Myanmar Conflict Map, 15 November 2022, https://myanmar.iiss.org/analysis/northwest.

56 Emily Fishbein, 'Chin Nationalism "Blossoms" on Northwestern Front Against Junta', *Frontier Myanmar*, 9 January 2023, https://www.frontiermyanmar.net/en/chin-nationalism-blossoms-on-northwestern-front-against-junta/.

57 Loong, 'Northwest Myanmar: A Quiet Corner Transformed by Resistance'.

58 *Ibid.*

59 'Mindat PAF Reopens Primary Schools in the Shadow of Conflict', Democratic Voice of Burma, 27 October 2021, https://burmese.dvb.no/archives/496592.

60 See, for example, 'Jewellery Store Owned by Junta Minister Bombed in Yangon', Myanmar Now, 9 July 2021, https://myanmar-now.org/en/news/jewellery-store-owned-by-junta-minister-bombed-in-yangon.

61 Shona Loong, 'The Dry Zone: An Existential Struggle in Central Myanmar', IISS Myanmar Conflict Map, 5 July 2022, https://myanmar.iiss.org/analysis/dryzone.

62 Ye Myo Hein, 'One Year On: The Momentum of Myanmar's Armed Rebellion', Wilson Centre, May 2022, pp. 60–61, https://www.wilsoncenter.org/publication/one-year-momentum-myanmars-armed-rebellion.

63 IISS, 'Myanmar Conflict Map'.

64 Ye Myo Hein, 'Understanding the People's Defense Forces in Myanmar', p. 5. For sub-machine guns, see Nora Aung, 'Myanmar Resistance Groups Get Creative to Manufacture Weapons', *Irrawaddy*, 31 May 2022, https://www.irrawaddy.com/news/burma/myanmar-resistance-groups-get-creative-to-manufacture-weapons.html.

65 Loong, 'The Dry Zone: An Existential Struggle in Central Myanmar'.

66 Loong, 'Northwest Myanmar: A Quiet Corner Transformed by Resistance'.

67 Myanmar Emergency Overview Map', UNHCR, 13 February 2023, https://data.unhcr.org/en/documents/details/98862.

68 Zubaidah Abdul Jalil, 'Myanmar: Military Executes Four Democracy Activists Including Ex-MP', BBC News, 25 July 2022, https://www.bbc.com/news/world-asia-62287815.

69 'How Myanmar's Coup Has Left Thousands in Yangon Homeless', Myanmar Now, 10 January 2023, https://myanmar-now.org/en/news/how-myanmars-coup-has-left-thousands-in-yangon-homeless.

70 Loong, 'The Dry Zone: An Existential Struggle in Central Myanmar'.

71 *Ibid.*

72 'Arakanese, Kokang Groups Pledge Support for Fellow Alliance Member TNLA on Ta'ang National Revolution Day', Burma News International, 14 January 2023, https://www.bnionline.net/en/news/arakanese-kokang-groups-pledge-support-fellow-alliance-member-tnla-taang-national-revolution.

73 Loong, 'Rakhine: A Precarious Ceasefire Hangs in the Balance'.

74 Loong, 'Northeast Myanmar: Three Axes of Conflict'.

75 Andrew Nachemson, 'China's Xi Turns to Myanmar as He Pushes for "Belt and Road" Plan', Al-Jazeera, 17 January 2020, https://www.aljazeera.com/economy/2020/1/17/chinas-xi-turns-to-myanmar-as-he-pushes-for-belt-and-road-plan.

76 Bertil Lintner, 'Why Myanmar's Wa Always Get What They Want', *Asia Times*, 18 September 2019, https://asiatimes.com/2019/09/why-myanmars-wa-always-get-what-they-want/.

77 Kyaw Hsan Hlaing, 'Arakan Army Extends Administrative Grip on Rakhine State', *Frontier Myanmar*, 6 August 2021, https://www.frontiermyanmar.net/en/arakan-army-extends-administrative-grip-on-rakhine-state/.

78 ASEAN, 'ASEAN Chairman's Statement on the Developments in the Republic of the Union of Myanmar', 1 February 2021, https://asean.org/asean-chairmans-statement-on-the-developments-in-the-republic-of-the-union-of-myanmar-2/.

79 See France, Ministry for Europe and Foreign Affairs, 'Myanmar – G7 Foreign Ministers' Statement (03 February 2021)', 3 February 2021, https://www.diplomatie.gouv.fr/en/country-files/myanmar/news/article/myanmar-g7-for-eign-ministers-statement-03-feb-2021; 'Japan, US, India, Australia Call for Return of Democracy in Myanmar', Reuters, 18 February 2021, https://www.reuters.com/article/us-usa-blinken-quad-myanmar-idUSKBN2AI20K; and UN Human Rights Council, 'Human Rights Implications of the Crisis in Myanmar', Human Rights Council Twenty-ninth special session, A/HRC/S-29/L.1, 12 February 2021, https://documents-dds-ny.un.org/doc/UNDOC/LTD/G21/031/62/PDF/G2103162.pdf?OpenElement.

80 Tan Hui Yee, 'Myanmar's Anti-coup Groups Denounce Asean Consensus', *Straits Times*, 26 April 2021, https://www.straitstimes.com/asia/se-asia/myanmars-anti-coup-groups-denounce-asean-consensus.

81 'China's Ambassador to Myanmar Says Situation "Not What China Wants to See"', Reuters, 16 February 2021, https://www.reuters.com/article/us-myanmar-politics-china-idUSKBN2AG1AA.

82 Kallol Bhattacherjee, 'India to Handover Kilo Class Attack Submarine to Myanmar', *Hindu*, 16 October 2020, https://www.thehindu.com/news/national/india-to-handover-kilo-class-attack-submarine-to-myanmar/article32866535.ece; and Dinakar Peri, 'Indian Navy's MILAN Exercise to Be Held in Visakhapatnam from February 25', *Hindu*, 23 February 2022, https://www.thehindu.com/news/national/warships-from-quad-various-other-countries-to-take-part-in-indian-navys-largest-multilateral-exercise-milan/article65077573.ece.

83 Gwen Robinson, 'Diplomatic Snubs Isolate Myanmar's Military Regime', *Nikkei Asia*, 9 May 2022, https://asia.nikkei.com/Spotlight/Myanmar-Crisis/Diplomatic-snubs-isolate-Myanmar-s-military-regime. Malaysia and the Philippines have likewise chosen not to replace outgoing ambassadors, while Brunei sent a new ambassador in 2022 then withdrew the diplomat.

84 Sebastian Strangio, 'Australia to Downgrade Diplomatic Representation in Myanmar: Report', *Diplomat*, 19 May 2022, https://thediplomat.com/2022/05/australia-to-downgrade-diplomatic-representation-in-myanmar-report/.

INDEX